3rd Workshop on Evaluating Vector Space Representations for NLP (RepEVAL 2019)

Minneapolis, Minnesota, USA
6 June 2019

ISBN: 978-1-5108-8774-9

NAACL HLT 2019

The 3rd Workshop on Evaluating Vector Space Representations for NLP

Proceedings of the Workshop

June 6, 2019
Minneapolis, USA

Preface

The RepEval series of workshops started in the midst of a boom of word embeddings with the goals of promoting new benchmarks for vector space meaning representations, highlighting the issues with existing benchmarks and improving on them. In addition to proposals for new evaluation tasks, it has played an important role by providing an outlet for critical analysis, negative results, and methodological caveats (reproducibility, parameters impact, the issue of attribution of results to the representation or the whole system, dataset structure/balance/representativeness).

Three years later, mainstream NLP is switching to contextualized representations, but we are still facing many of the same issues: reliable intrinsic metrics are scarce, which means that we rarely know what features of representations make them successful for a given downstream task. This makes development of new meaning representations and their fine-tuning a slow and expensive process with too many variables - even more so than before.

The 3rd edition of RepEval aims to foster the discussion of the following issues:

- approaches to intrinsic and extrinsic evaluation of all kinds of distributional meaning representations;

- evaluation motivated by linguistic, psycholinguistic or neurological evidence, its predictive power, and interpretability of meaning representations;

- the (in)stability of vector representations, best practices for reproducible and reliable experiments;

- evaluation of representations at subword level, especially for morphologically complex languages;

- evaluation of phrase, sentence, paragraph and document-level representations: evidence of compositionality, further diagnostic tests, and how much the preservation of abstract syntactic information actually contributes to performance;

- formal analysis of properties of embedding spaces and their impact on downstream tasks;

- the contribution of representations per se vs. other modeling choices to system performance in extrinsic evaluations;

- validation of evaluation methodology and findings in cross-lingual studies;

- specialized vs general-purpose representations, and whether the latter have inherent limits in downstream tasks;

- internal states of end-to-end systems as meaning representations, and ways to make more sense of them.

In the long run, the methodological and practical contributions of RepEval will add to the discussions on what kinds of representations work best for what tasks, how we can interpret and reliably optimize them, and to what extent it is possible to create cross-task meaning representations that would be necessary for general AI.

The third edition of RepEval received 25 submissions (2 more were withdrawn). 4 submissions presented an analysis of existing proposals, 3 contributed proposals for new evaluation tasks, and 3 dealt with scaling, improving or extending prior proposals to other languages. 8 proposals focused on interpretation/analysis of meaning representations, and 7 - on their applications. We accepted 13 submissions, with acceptance rate of 52%.

Organizers:

Anna Rogers, Univeristy of Massachusetts Lowell (USA)
Aleksandr Drozd, RIKEN (Japan)
Anna Rumshisky, University of Massachusetts Lowell (USA)
Yoav Goldbgerg, Bar-Ilan University (Israel)

Program Committee:

Omri Abend, The Hebrew University of Jerusalem (Israel)
Emily Bender, University of Washington (USA)
Sam Bowman, New York University (USA)
Jose Camacho Collados, Cardiff University (UK)
Alexis Conneau, Facebook AI Research (USA)
Barry Devereux, Queen's University Belfast (UK)
Georgiana Dinu, Amazon AWS (USA)
Allyson Ettinger, University of Chicago (USA)
Mohit Iyyer, University of Massachusetts Amherst (USA)
Hila Gonen, Bar-Ilan University (Israel)
Douwe Kiela, Facebook AI Research (USA)
Jonathan K. Kummerfeld, University of Michigan (USA)
Tal Linzen, Johns Hopkins University (USA)
Preslav Nakov, Qatar Computing Research Institute (Qatar)
Neha Nayak, University of Massachusetts Amherst (USA)
Mark Neumann, Allen Institute for Artificial Intelligence (USA)
Denis Paperno, Utrecht University (the Netherlands)
Ellie Pavlick, Brown University (USA)
Marek Rei, University of Cambridge (UK)
Roi Reichart, Technion (Israel)
Vered Shwartz, Bar-Ilan University (Israel)
Diarmuid O'Seaghdha, Apple (UK)
Gabriel Stanovsky, University of Washington (USA)
Karl Stratos, Toyota Technological Institute at Chicago (USA)
Yulia Tsvetkov, Carnegie Mellon University (USA)
Ivan Vulić, University of Cambridge (UK)
Luke Zettlemoyer, University of Washington (USA)

Invited Speakers:

Tal Linzen, Johns Hopkins University (USA)
Kristina Toutanova, Google AI (USA)

Panelists:

Sam Bowman, New York University (USA)
Ryan Cotterell, University of Cambridge (UK)
Barry Devereux, Queen's University Belfast (UK)
Allyson Ettinger, University of Chicago (USA)
Tal Linzen, Johns Hopkins University (USA)

Table of Contents

Conference Program

Thursday, June 6, 2019

9:00–9:30   *Opening Remarks. Evaluation of meaning representations for NLP: directions and milestones.*

9:30–10:30   *Invited talk: Tal Linzen (Johns Hopkins University)*

10:30–11:00   *Coffee Break*

11:00–12:00   *Invited talk: Kristina Toutanova (Google AI)*

12:00–13:30   *Lunch*

13:30–14:45   ***Oral session***

13:30–13:45   *Neural Vector Conceptualization for Word Vector Space Interpretation*
Robert Schwarzenberg, Lisa Raithel and David Harbecke

13:45–14:00   *Characterizing the Impact of Geometric Properties of Word Embeddings on Task Performance*
Brendan Whitaker, Denis Newman-Griffis, Aparajita Haldar, Hakan Ferhatosman-oglu and Eric Fosler-Lussier

14:00–14:15   *The Influence of Down-Sampling Strategies on SVD Word Embedding Stability*
Johannes Hellrich, Bernd Kampe and Udo Hahn

14:15–14:30   *How Well Do Embedding Models Capture Non-compositionality? A View from Multiword Expressions*
Navnita Nandakumar, Timothy Baldwin and Bahar Salehi

14:30–14:45   *Measuring Semantic Abstraction of Multilingual NMT with Paraphrase Recognition and Generation Tasks*
Jörg Tiedemann and Yves Scherrer

14:45–15:00   ***1-minute poster madness***

15:00–15:45 *Poster Session*

SWOW-8500: Word Association task for Intrinsic Evaluation of Word Embeddings
Avijit Thawani, Biplav Srivastava and Anil Singh

Classification of Semantic Paraphasias: Optimization of a Word Embedding Model
Katy McKinney-Bock and Steven Bedrick

CODAH: An Adversarially-Authored Question Answering Dataset for Common Sense
Michael Chen, Mike D'Arcy, Alisa Liu, Jared Fernandez and Doug Downey

Syntactic Interchangeability in Word Embedding Models
Daniel Hershcovich, Assaf Toledo, Alon Halfon and Noam Slonim

Evaluation of Morphological Embeddings for English and Russian Languages
Vitaly Romanov and Albina Khusainova

Probing Biomedical Embeddings from Language Models
Qiao Jin, Bhuwan Dhingra, William Cohen and Xinghua Lu

Dyr Bul Shchyl. Proxying Sound Symbolism With Word Embeddings
Ivan Yamshchikov, Viascheslav Shibaev and Alexey Tikhonov

Multi-Context Term Embeddings: the Use Case of Corpus-based Term Set Expansion
Jonathan Mamou, Oren Pereg, Moshe Wasserblat and Ido Dagan

15:45–16:00 *Coffee break*

16:00–17:15 *A linguist, an NLP engineer, and a psycholinguist walk into a bar... Panel discussion with Sam Bowman, Ryan Cotterell, Barry Devereux, Allyson Ettinger, and Tal Linzen.*

17:15–17:30 *Closing remarks*

Neural Vector Conceptualization for Word Vector Space Interpretation

Robert Schwarzenberg*, Lisa Raithel*, David Harbecke
German Research Center for Artificial Intelligence (DFKI), Berlin, Germany
`{firstname.lastname}@dfki.de`

Abstract

Distributed word vector spaces are considered hard to interpret which hinders the understanding of natural language processing (NLP) models. In this work, we introduce a new method to interpret arbitrary samples from a word vector space. To this end, we train a neural model to conceptualize word vectors, which means that it activates higher order concepts it recognizes in a given vector. Contrary to prior approaches, our model operates in the original vector space and is capable of learning non-linear relations between word vectors and concepts. Furthermore, we show that it produces considerably less entropic concept activation profiles than the popular cosine similarity.

1 Introduction

In the vast majority of state-of-the-art NLP models, as for instance in translation models (Bojar et al., 2018) or text classifiers (Howard and Ruder, 2018), language is represented in distributed vector spaces. Using distributed representations comes at the price of low interpretability as they are generally considered uninterpretable, without further means (Levy and Goldberg, 2014; Montavon et al., 2018). In this work, we address this lack of interpretability with *neural vector conceptualization* (NVC), a neural mapping from a word vector space to a concept space (e.g. "chair" should activate the concept "furniture").

Using concepts to interpret distributed vector representations of language is inspired by the finding that "humans understand languages through multi-step cognitive processes which involves building rich models of the world and making multi-level generalizations from the input text" (Shalaby and Zadrozny, 2019). We are not the first, however, to utilize concepts for this purpose.

Koç et al. (2018), for instance, modify the objective function of `GloVe` (Pennington et al., 2014) to align semantic concepts with word vector dimensions to create an interpretable space. Their method does not, however, offer an interpretation of vectors in the original space.

Senel et al. (2018), in contrast, do offer an interpretation of the original space: They propose a mapping of word vector dimensions to concepts. This mapping, however, is linear and consequently, their method is incapable of modeling non-linear relations.

Our method offers an interpretation of the original space and is capable of modeling non-linear relations between the word and the concept space. Furthermore, arguably, we interpret vectors similar to how a neural NLP model would, because a neural NLP model lies at the heart of our method. In addition, by design, our model is able to conceptualize random continuous samples, drawn from the word vector space.

This is particularly important as word vectors are sparse in their vector space and vectors without a word representative do not have intrinsic meaning. This hinders adapting methods from vision, such as activation maximization (Simonyan et al., 2013) or generative adversarial networks (Goodfellow et al., 2014), as in NLP these methods potentially produce vectors without word representations.

For introspection, one could map any vector onto its nearest neighbor with a word representative. However, nearest neighbor search does not necessarily find the closest semantic representative in the vector space (Schnabel et al., 2015). Moreover, we show that concept activation profiles produced with nearest neighbor search tend to be considerably more entropic than the activation profiles our method returns.

---

* Shared first authorship.

1

Proceedings of the 3rd Workshop on Evaluating Vector Space Representations for NLP, pages 1–7
Minneapolis, USA, June 6, 2019. ©2019 Association for Computational Linguistics

2 Method

For NVC, we propose to train a neural model to map word vectors onto associated concepts. More formally, the model should learn a meaningful mapping

$$f : \mathbb{R}^d \to \mathbb{R}^{|C|} \tag{1}$$

where d denotes the number of word vector dimensions and C is a set of concepts. The training objective should be a multi-label classification to account for instances that belong to more than one concept (e.g. "chair" should also activate "seat").

For the training, we need to make two basic choices:

1. We need a ground truth concept knowledge base that provides the concepts a training instance should activate and

2. we need to choose a model architecture appropriate for the task.

In the following, we motivate our choices.

2.1 Ground Truth Concept Knowledgebase

As a ground truth concept knowledge base we chose the Microsoft Concept Graph (MCG), which is built on top of Probase, for the following reasons:

1. Wu et al. (2012) convincingly argue that with Probase they built a universal taxonomy that is more comprehensive than other existing candidates, such as for example, *Freebase* (Bollacker et al., 2008).

2. Furthermore, Probase is huge. The core taxonomy contains about 5.38 million concepts, 12.5 million unique instances, and 85.1 million *isA* relations. This allows our model to illuminate the word vector space from many angles.

3. Instance-concept relations are probabilistic in the MCG: For (instance, concept) tuples a *rep* score can be retrieved. The *rep* score describes the "representativeness" of an instance for a concept, and vice versa. According to the MCG, for example, the instance "chair" is a few thousand times more representative for the concept "furniture" than is the instance "car." During training, we exploit the *rep* scores to retrieve representative target concepts for a training instance.

The scores are based on the notion of Basic Level Concepts (BLC) which were first introduced

by Rosch et al. (1976), as part of Prototype Theory. A basic level concept is a concept on which all people of the same culture consciously or unconsciously agree. For instance, according to Prototype Theory, most humans would categorize a "wood frog" simply as a "frog." "Wood frog" is a representative instance of the concept "frog."

Aiming to provide an approach to the computation of the BLC of an instance i in the MCG, Wang et al. (2015) combine pointwise mutual information (PMI) with co-occurrence counts of concept c and instance i. The authors compute the "representativeness" of an instance i for a concept c as

$$rep(i, c) = P(c|i) \cdot P(i|c). \tag{2}$$

By taking the logarithm of the rep score, we can isolate the involvement of PMI:

$$log\, rep(i, c) - log\, P(i, c) = PMI(i, c). \tag{3}$$

In doing so, the authors boost concepts in the middle of the taxonomy (the basic level concepts) while reducing extreme values leading to superor subordinate concepts. To find the BLC of a single instance, Wang et al. (2015) maximize over the rep value of all concepts associated with i.

To train our model, for a training instance i, we collect all concepts for which $rep(i, c)$[1] is above a certain threshold and use them as the target labels for i. We discard concepts that have very few instances above a threshold rep value in the graph.

2.2 Model

During training, the model repeatedly receives a word vector instance as input and a multi-hot vector retrieved from the MCG as the target concept vector. Thus, it must identify concepts encoded in the word vector.

We do not see any sequentiality or recurrence in this task which is why we discarded recurrent and Transformer candidate models. Concerning convolutional networks, we disregard small receptive fields because dimensional adjacency is semantically irrelevant in word vectors. However, any convolutional network with a receptive field over the whole input vector is equivalent to a fully-connected (FC) feed-forward network. Thus, we ultimately trained an FC feed-forward network to conceptualize vectors.

---

[1] We computed the rep values ourselves as we only acquired a count-based version of the graph.

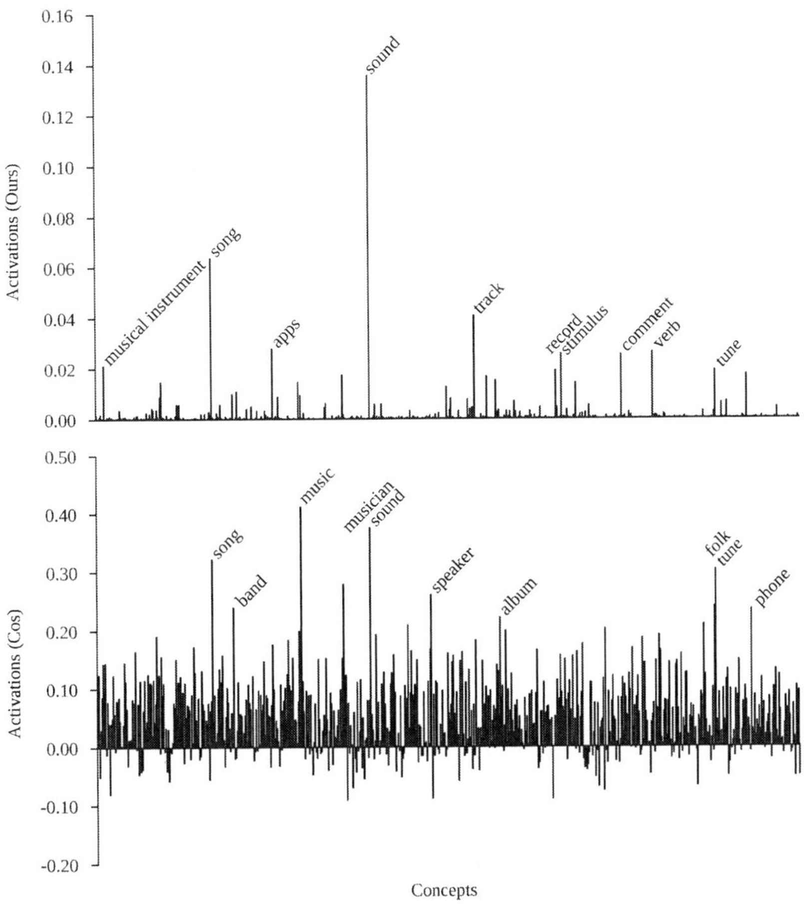

Figure 1: Vector interpretations of the word vector of "listening" with 637 concepts. Top: Neural vector conceptualization (our method, 10 highest activations labelled). Bottom: Cosine similarity (baseline, 10 highest activations labelled). Both activation profiles are unnormalized.

3 Experiments

For a proof of concept, we chose the `word2vec` embedding (Mikolov et al., 2013) as the word vector space to interpret. Recently, contextualized representations, like `ELMo` (Peters et al., 2018) and `BERT` (Devlin et al., 2019), received increased attention. Nevertheless, well-established global representations, such as `word2vec` remain highly relevant: `ELMo` still benefits from using global embeddings as additional input and `BERT` trains its own global token embedding space.

The `word2vec` model and the MCG are based on different corpora. As a consequence of using data from two different sources, we sometimes needed to modify MCG instances to match the `word2vec` vocabulary.

We filtered the MCG for concepts that have at least 100 instances with a *rep* value of at least -10. This leaves 637 concepts with an average of 184 instances per concept and gives a class imbalance of 524 negative samples for every positive sample.

With the obtained data, we trained a three-layer FC network to map word vectors onto their concepts in the MCG. The model returns independent sigmoid activations for each concept. We trained with categorical cross entropy and applied weights regularization with a factor of 10^{-7}. For all experiments, we optimized parameters with the ADAM optimizer (Kingma and Ba, 2015).[2]

To estimate task complexity, Table 1 lists the precision, recall and F_1 scores that our model achieved on a fixed, randomly sampled test set that

---

[2]Our experiments are open source and can be replicated out of the box: `https://github.com/dfki-nlp/nvc`.

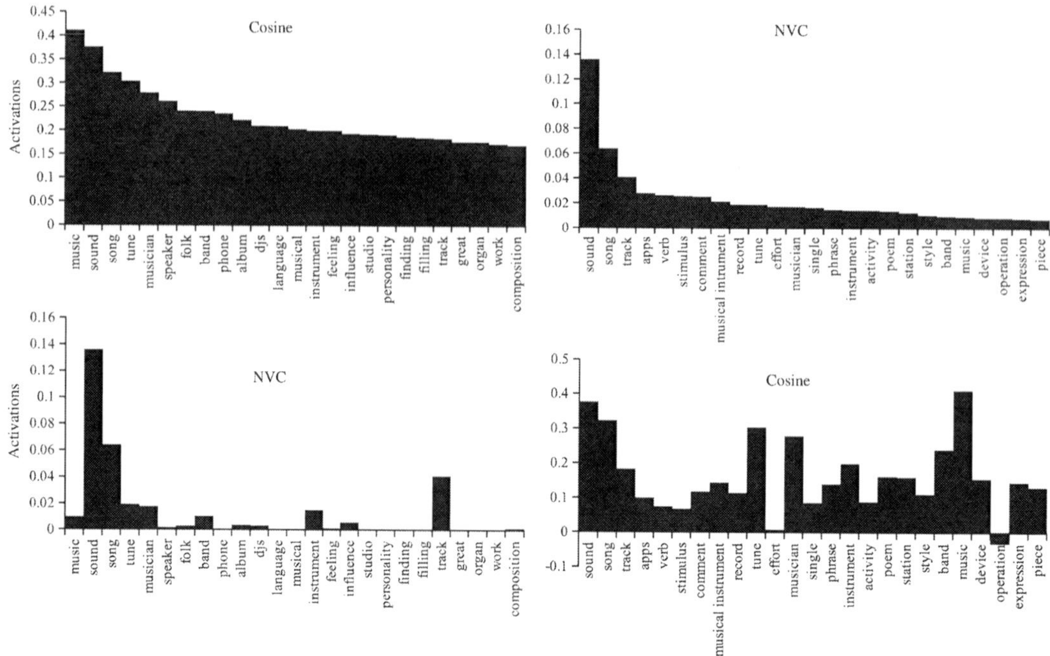

Figure 2: Concept activations for the instance "listening." Upper left: Top 25 concepts according to cosine similarity. Bottom left: NVC activations of the same cosine top 25 concepts. Upper right: Top 25 concepts according to NVC. Bottom right: Cosine activations of the same NVC top 25 concepts.

contained 10 % of the data. The table contains the weighted average scores accomplished for all concepts as well as the scores the model achieved for selected individual concepts, grouped semantically.

Fig. 1 juxtaposes the NVC and the baseline activation profile of the word vector of "listening", which was not encountered during training. Several other NVCs can be found in the appendix (see Figs. 3, 4 and 5) as well as selected concept activations of continuous samples (see Fig. 6).

While Fig. 1 shows a global perspective of the activation profiles, Fig. 2 zooms in on the top 25 concepts, activated by the baseline method (first column) and our method (second column).

4 Discussion

The weighted classification F_1 score is 0.22 which suggests that the task is complex, probably due to the highly imbalanced data set. According to Table 1, however, F_1 scores vary significantly along individual concepts. While we observe a high score for *province*, our model has difficulties classifying *location*s, for instance. The same trend can be observed for *choreographer*s and *legend*s. What we see reflected in this table is the sharpness

	P	R	F	S
all concepts	0.43	0.16	0.22	9766
province	0.81	0.81	0.81	36
district	0.79	0.62	0.69	78
island	0.96	0.38	0.54	64
locality	0.5	0.03	0.06	29
location	0	0	0	14
choreographer	0.85	0.69	0.76	16
composer	0.8	0.66	0.72	61
artist	0.57	0.36	0.44	70
legend	0	0	0	33
dish	0	0	0	34
meal	0	0	0	17
delicacy	0	0	0	11
salad	0	0	0	9

Table 1: Precision (P), recall (R), F_1 Score (F), and support (S) for all 637 concepts (F_1 Score weighted by support) and selected individual concepts. Class membership was determined by an activation threshold of 0.5.

of concept boundaries. Arguably, the definition of a *province* is sharper than that of *location*. The same is true for *choreographer* and *legend*. We assume that the more precise a concept boundary, the higher the classification performance tends to be. We cannot, however, offer an explanation for the poor classification performance on some other concepts, such as the last ones in Table 1.

Fig. 1 (top) shows the NVC of "listening" with the top ten peaks labelled. For Table 1, a class membership was determined by an activation threshold of 0.5 of the relevant output neuron. Fig. 1 (top), however, illustrates that the model activates many meaningful concepts beneath this threshold and thus 0.5 might not be appropriate to determine class membership.

Some of the peaks are also reflected in the bottom plot of Fig. 1, which depicts the activation profile of the cosine similarity baseline method. The most notable difference between our method and the baseline is that the latter produces much more entropic activation profiles. It is less selective than NVC as NVC deactivates many concepts.

Fig. 2 (first column) shows that NVC indeed deactivates unrelated concepts, such as *personality*, *finding*, *filling*, *great*, and *work* that, according to cosine similarity, are close to the instance "listening." *Speaker*, *phone*, and *organ* arguably are reasonable concepts and yet deactivated by NVC but NVC replaces them with more meaningful concepts, as can be seen in the upper right plot in Fig. 2. Note that, contrary to NVC, the baseline method is not able to deactivate concepts that have close vectors in the word vector space, nor is it able to activate concepts that have vectors that are far from the input vector. Overall, a manual analysis suggests that the top 25 NVC concepts are more fitting than the top 25 cosine concepts.

5   Related Work

Concept knowledge bases such as the MCG exist because concepts are powerful abstractions of natural language instances that have been used for many downstream tasks, such as text classification (Song et al., 2011), ad-query similarity and query similarity (Kim et al., 2013), document similarity (Song and Roth, 2015), and semantic relatedness (Bekkali and Lachkar, 2019). The approaches mentioned above all implement some form of text conceptualization (TC).

TC models the probability $P(c|I)$ of a concept c being reflected in a set of observed natural language instances I (Shalaby and Zadrozny, 2019; Song et al., 2011). This is also the objective function of the model we train and our interpretability method can thus be understood as an implementation of TC.

Furthermore, besides the methods already discussed in the introduction, there is more research into the interpretability of language representations. Adi et al. (2017), for instance, also use auxiliary prediction tasks to analyse vector representations. However, they work on sentence level, not word level. Moreover, instead of retrieving concepts, they probe sentence length, word content conservation and word order conservation in the representation.

An approach similar to ours was introduced by Sommerauer and Fokkens (2018). The authors investigate the kind of semantic information encoded in word vectors. To this end, they train a classifier that recognizes whether word vectors carry specific semantic properties, some of which can be regarded as concepts.

6   Conclusion & Future Work

We introduced neural vector conceptualization as a means of interpreting continuous samples from a word vector space. We demonstrated that our method produces considerably less entropic concept activation profiles than the cosine similarity measure. For an input word vector, NVC activated meaningful concepts and deactivated unrelated ones, even if they were close in the word vector space.

Contrary to prior methods, by design, NVC operates in the original language space and is capable of modeling non-linear relations between language instances and concepts. Furthermore, our method is flexible: At the heart of it lies a neural NLP model that we trained on an instance-concept ground truth that could be replaced by another one.

In the future, we would like to extend NVC to contextualized representations. We consider this non-trivial because it may not be possible to directly apply the current instance-concept ground truth to contextualized instances, in particular if they are represented by sub-word embeddings.

Acknowledgements

This research was partially supported by the German Federal Ministry of Education and Research through the project DEEPLEE (01IW17001). We would also like to thank the anonymous reviewers for their feedback and Leonhard Hennig for data and feedback.

References

Yossi Adi, Einat Kermany, Yonatan Belinkov, Ofer Lavi, and Yoav Goldberg. 2017. Fine-grained analysis of sentence embeddings using auxiliary prediction tasks. In *International Conference of Learning Representations (ICLR)*.

Mohammed Bekkali and Abdelmonaime Lachkar. 2019. An effective short text conceptualization based on new short text similarity. *Social Network Analysis and Mining*, 9(1):1.

Ondřej Bojar, Christian Federmann, Mark Fishel, Yvette Graham, Barry Haddow, Philipp Koehn, and Christof Monz. 2018. Findings of the 2018 Conference on Machine Translation (WMT18). In *Proceedings of the Third Conference on Machine Translation: Shared Task Papers*, pages 272–303. Association for Computational Linguistics.

Kurt Bollacker, Colin Evans, Praveen Paritosh, Tim Sturge, and Jamie Taylor. 2008. Freebase: a collaboratively created graph database for structuring human knowledge. In *Proceedings of the 2008 ACM SIGMOD international conference on Management of data*, pages 1247–1250. AcM.

Jacob Devlin, Ming-Wei Chang, Kenton Lee, and Kristina Toutanova. 2019. BERT: Pre-training of Deep Bidirectional Transformers for Language Understanding. *Proceedings of the 2019 Conference of the North American Chapter of the Association for Computational Linguistics: Human Language Technologies*.

Ian Goodfellow, Jean Pouget-Abadie, Mehdi Mirza, Bing Xu, David Warde-Farley, Sherjil Ozair, Aaron Courville, and Yoshua Bengio. 2014. Generative Adversarial Nets. In *Advances in neural information processing systems*, pages 2672–2680.

Jeremy Howard and Sebastian Ruder. 2018. Universal language model fine-tuning for text classification. In *Proceedings of the 56th Annual Meeting of the Association for Computational Linguistics (Volume 1: Long Papers)*, volume 1, pages 328–339.

Dongwoo Kim, Haixun Wang, and Alice Oh. 2013. Context-dependent conceptualization. In *Twenty-Third International Joint Conference on Artificial Intelligence*.

Diederick P. Kingma and Jimmy Ba. 2015. Adam: A Method for Stochastic Optimization. In *International Conference on Learning Representations (ICLR)*.

Aykut Koç, Lutfi Kerem Senel, İhsan Utlu, and Haldun M. Ozaktas. 2018. Imparting Interpretability to Word Embeddings while Preserving Semantic Structure. *arXiv:1807.07279*.

Omer Levy and Yoav Goldberg. 2014. Dependency-Based Word Embeddings. In *Proceedings of the 52nd Annual Meeting of the Association for Computational Linguistics (Volume 2: Short Papers)*, pages 302–308. Association for Computational Linguistics.

Tomas Mikolov, Kai Chen, Greg Corrado, and Jeffrey Dean. 2013. Efficient Estimation of Word Representations in Vector Space. *arXiv:1301.3781*.

Grégoire Montavon, Wojciech Samek, and Klaus-Robert Müller. 2018. Methods for interpreting and understanding deep neural networks. *Digital Signal Processing*, 73:1–15.

Jeffrey Pennington, Richard Socher, and Christopher Manning. 2014. Glove: Global Vectors for Word Representation. In *Proceedings of the 2014 Conference on Empirical Methods in Natural Language Processing (EMNLP)*, pages 1532–1543. Association for Computational Linguistics.

Matthew Peters, Mark Neumann, Mohit Iyyer, Matt Gardner, Christopher Clark, Kenton Lee, and Luke Zettlemoyer. 2018. Deep contextualized word representations. In *Proceedings of the 2018 Conference of the North American Chapter of the Association for Computational Linguistics: Human Language Technologies*, pages 2227–2237.

Eleanor Rosch, Carolyn B. Mervis, Wayne D. Gray, David M. Johnson, and Penny Boyes-Braem. 1976. Basic objects in natural categories. *Cognitive Psychology*, 8(3):382 – 439.

Tobias Schnabel, Igor Labutov, David Mimno, and Thorsten Joachims. 2015. Evaluation methods for unsupervised word embeddings. In *Proceedings of the 2015 Conference on Empirical Methods in Natural Language Processing*, pages 298–307. Association for Computational Linguistics.

Lutfi Kerem Senel, Ihsan Utlu, Veysel Yucesoy, Aykut Koc, and Tolga Cukur. 2018. Semantic Structure and Interpretability of Word Embeddings. *IEEE/ACM Transactions on Audio, Speech, and Language Processing*, 26(10):1769–1779.

Walid Shalaby and Wlodek Zadrozny. 2019. Learning concept embeddings for dataless classification via efficient bag-of-concepts densification. *Knowledge and Information Systems*, pages 1–24.

Karen Simonyan, Andrea Vedaldi, and Andrew Zisserman. 2013. Deep Inside Convolutional Networks: Visualising Image Classification Models and Saliency Maps. *arXiv:1312.6034*.

Pia Sommerauer and Antske Fokkens. 2018. Firearms and tigers are dangerous, kitchen knives and zebras are not: Testing whether word embeddings can tell. In *Proceedings of the 2018 EMNLP Workshop BlackboxNLP: Analyzing and Interpreting Neural Networks for NLP*, pages 276–286.

Yangqiu Song and Dan Roth. 2015. Unsupervised sparse vector densification for short text similarity. In *Proceedings of the 2015 Conference of the North American Chapter of the Association for Computational Linguistics: Human Language Technologies*, pages 1275–1280. Association for Computational Linguistics.

Yangqiu Song, Haixun Wang, Zhongyuan Wang, Hongsong Li, and Weizhu Chen. 2011. Short text conceptualization using a probabilistic knowledge-base. In *Twenty-Second International Joint Conference on Artificial Intelligence*, pages 2330–2336.

Zhongyuan Wang, Haixun Wang, Ji-Rong Wen, and Yanghua Xiao. 2015. An Inference Approach to Basic Level of Categorization. In *Proceedings of the 24th ACM International on Conference on Information and Knowledge Management - CIKM '15*, pages 653–662. ACM Press.

Wentao Wu, Hongsong Li, Haixun Wang, and Kenny Q. Zhu. 2012. Probase: A Probabilistic Taxonomy for Text Understanding. In *Proceedings of the 2012 ACM SIGMOD International Conference on Management of Data*, SIGMOD '12, pages 481–492. ACM.

A NVCs

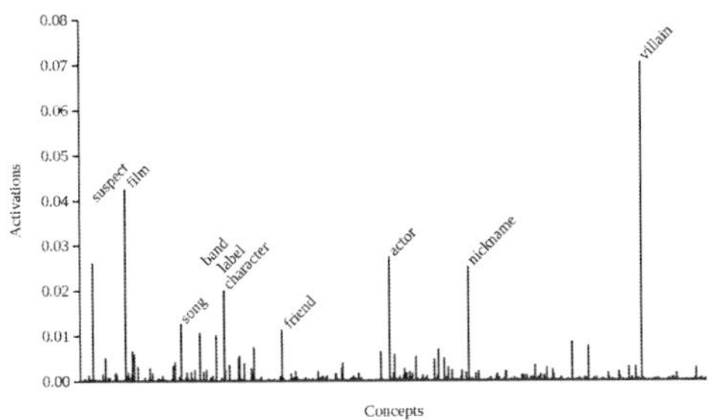

Figure 3: NVC of the word vector for "mafioso" (the instance was not encountered during training).

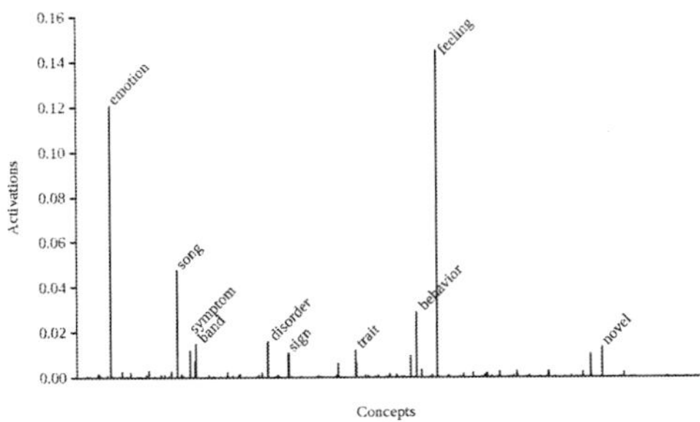

Figure 4: NVC of the word vector for "Jealousy" (the instance was not encountered during training).

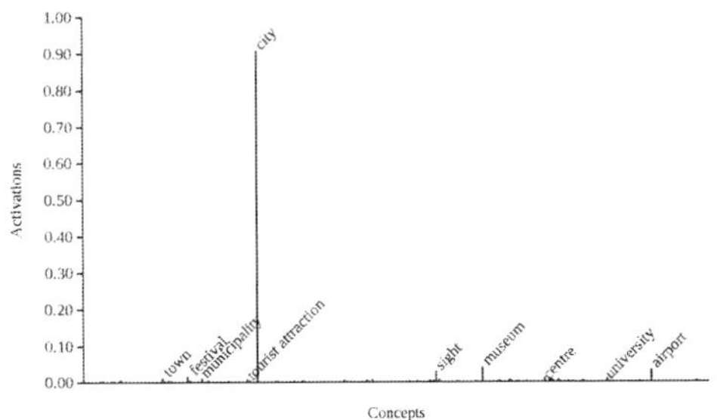

Figure 5: NVC of the word vector for "Berlin" (the instance was not encountered during training).

B Concept Activations for Continuous Samples

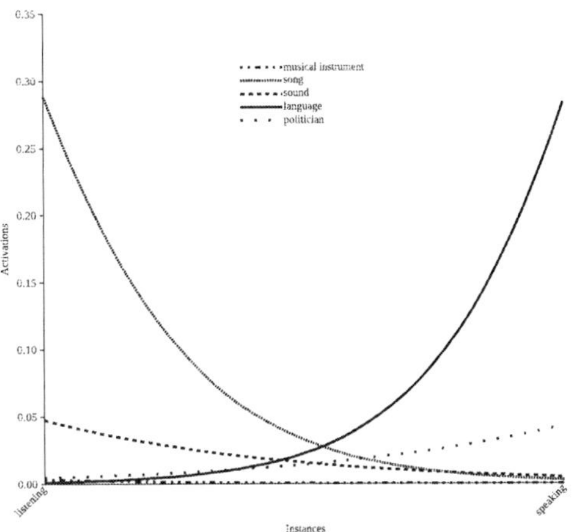

Figure 6: Concept activations of five selected concepts of word vectors sampled on the path between the instances "listening" and "speaking". Note the steady, non-oscillating paths between the instances.

Characterizing the Impact of Geometric Properties
of Word Embeddings on Task Performance

Brendan Whitaker[1][*]   **Denis Newman-Griffis**[1][*]   **Aparajita Haldar**[2][*]
Hakan Ferhatosmanoglu[2]   **Eric Fosler-Lussier**[1]
[1]The Ohio State University, Columbus, OH, USA
[2]University of Warwick, Coventry, UK
{whitaker.213, newman-griffis.1, fosler-lussier.1}@osu.edu
{aparajita.haldar, h.ferhatosmanoglu}@warwick.ac.uk

Abstract

Analysis of word embedding properties to inform their use in downstream NLP tasks has largely been studied by assessing nearest neighbors. However, geometric properties of the continuous feature space contribute directly to the use of embedding features in downstream models, and are largely unexplored. We consider four properties of word embedding geometry, namely: position relative to the origin, distribution of features in the vector space, global pairwise distances, and local pairwise distances. We define a sequence of transformations to generate new embeddings that expose subsets of these properties to downstream models and evaluate change in task performance to understand the contribution of each property to NLP models. We transform publicly available pretrained embeddings from three popular toolkits (word2vec, GloVe, and FastText) and evaluate on a variety of intrinsic tasks, which model linguistic information in the vector space, and extrinsic tasks, which use vectors as input to machine learning models. We find that intrinsic evaluations are highly sensitive to absolute position, while extrinsic tasks rely primarily on local similarity. Our findings suggest that future embedding models and post-processing techniques should focus primarily on similarity to nearby points in vector space.

1 Introduction

Learned vector representations of words, known as word embeddings, have become ubiquitous throughout natural language processing (NLP) applications. As a result, analysis of embedding spaces to understand their utility as input features has emerged as an important avenue of inquiry, in order to facilitate proper use of embeddings in downstream NLP tasks. Many analyses have focused on nearest neighborhoods, as a viable proxy for semantic information (Rogers et al.,

2018; Pierrejean and Tanguy, 2018). However, neighborhood-based analysis is limited by the unreliability of nearest neighborhoods (Wendlandt et al., 2018). Further, it is intended to evaluate the *semantic content* of embedding spaces, as opposed to characteristics of the feature space itself.

Geometric analysis offers another recent angle from which to understand the properties of word embeddings, both in terms of their distribution (Mimno and Thompson, 2017) and correlation with downstream performance (Chandrahas et al., 2018). Through such geometric investigations, neighborhood-based semantic characterizations are augmented with information about the continuous feature space of an embedding. Geometric features offer a more direct connection to the assumptions made by neural models about continuity in input spaces (Szegedy et al., 2014), as well as the use of recent contextualized representation methods using continuous language models (Peters et al., 2018; Devlin et al., 2018).

In this work, we aim to bridge the gap between neighborhood-based semantic analysis and geometric performance analysis. We consider four components of the geometry of word embeddings, and transform pretrained embeddings to expose only subsets of these components to downstream models. We transform three popular sets of embeddings, trained using word2vec (Mikolov et al., 2013),[1] GloVe (Pennington et al., 2014),[2] and FastText (Bojanowski et al., 2017),[3] and use the resulting embeddings in a battery of standard evaluations to measure changes in task performance.

We find that intrinsic evaluations, which model linguistic information directly in the vector space,

---

[*]These authors contributed equally to this work.

[1]3M 300-d GoogleNews vectors from https://code.google.com/archive/p/word2vec/

[2]2M 300-d 840B Common Crawl vectors from https://nlp.stanford.edu/projects/glove/

[3]1M 300-d WikiNews vectors with subword information from https://fasttext.cc/docs/en/english-vectors

Proceedings of the 3rd Workshop on Evaluating Vector Space Representations for NLP, pages 8–17
Minneapolis, USA, June 6, 2019. ©2019 Association for Computational Linguistics

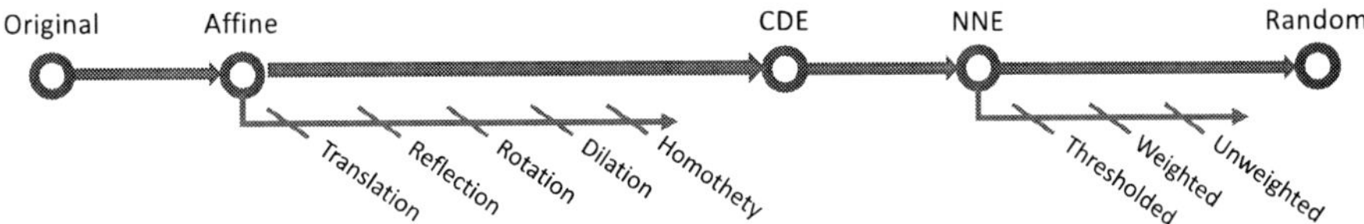

Figure 1: Sequence of transformations applied to word embeddings, including transformation variants. Note that each transformation is applied independently to source word embeddings. Transformations are presented in order of decreasing geometric information retained about the original vectors.

are highly sensitive to absolute position in pretrained embeddings; while extrinsic tasks, in which word embeddings are passed as input features to a trained model, are more robust and rely primarily on information about local similarity between word vectors. Our findings, including evidence that global organization of word vectors is often a major source of noise, suggest that further development of embedding learning and tuning methods should focus explicitly on local similarity, and help to explain the success of several recent methods.

2   Related Work

Word embedding models and outputs have been analyzed from several angles. In terms of performance, evaluating the "quality" of word embedding models has long been a thorny problem. While intrinsic evaluations such as word similarity and analogy completion are intuitive and easy to compute, they are limited by both confounding geometric factors (Linzen, 2016) and task-specific factors (Faruqui et al., 2016; Rogers et al., 2017). Chiu et al. (2016) show that these tasks, while correlated with some semantic content, do not always predict downstream performance. Thus, it is necessary to use a more comprehensive set of intrinsic and extrinsic evaluations for embeddings.

Nearest neighbors in sets of embeddings are commonly used as a proxy for qualitative semantic information. However, their instability across embedding samples (Wendlandt et al., 2018) is a limiting factor, and they do not necessarily correlate with linguistic analyses (Hellrich and Hahn, 2016). Modeling neighborhoods as a graph structure offers an alternative analysis method (Cuba Gyllensten and Sahlgren, 2015), as does 2-D or 3-D visualization (Heimerl and Gleicher, 2018). However, both of these methods provide qualitative insights only. By systematically analyzing geometric information with a wide variety of eval-

uations, we provide a quantitative counterpart to these understandings of embedding spaces.

3   Methods

In order to investigate how different geometric properties of word embeddings contribute to model performance on intrinsic and extrinsic evaluations, we consider the following attributes of word embedding geometry:

- position relative to the origin;
- distribution of feature values in $\mathbb{R}^d$;
- global pairwise distances, i.e. distances between any pair of vectors;
- local pairwise distances, i.e. distances between nearby pairs of vectors.

Using each of our sets of pretrained word embeddings, we apply a variety of transformations to induce new embeddings that only expose subsets of these attributes to downstream models. These are: affine transformation, which obfuscates the original position of the origin; cosine distance encoding, which obfuscates the original distribution of feature values in $\mathbb{R}^d$; nearest neighbor encoding, which obfuscates global pairwise distances; and random encoding. This sequence is illustrated in Figure 1, and the individual transformations are discussed in the following subsections.

General notation for defining our transformations is as follows. Let W be our vocabulary of words taken from some source corpus. We associate with each word $w \in W$ a vector $\mathbf{v} \in \mathbb{R}^d$ resulting from training via one of our embedding generation algorithms, where d is an arbitrary dimensionality for the embedding space. We define V to be the set of all pretrained word vectors $\mathbf{v}$ for a given corpus, embedding algorithm, and parameters. The matrix of embeddings M_V associated with this set then has shape $|V| \times d$. For simplicity, we restrict our analysis to transformed embeddings of the same dimensionality d as the original vectors.

3.1 Affine transformations

Affine transformations have been previously utilized for post-processing of word embeddings. For example, Artetxe et al. (2016) learn a matrix transform to align multilingual embedding spaces, and Faruqui et al. (2015) use a linear sparsification to better capture lexical semantics. In addition, the simplicity of affine functions in machine learning contexts (Hofmann et al., 2008) makes them a good starting point for our analysis.

Given a set of embeddings in $\mathbb{R}^d$, referred to as an **embedding space**, affine transformations

$$f_{\text{affine}} : \mathbb{R}^d \to \mathbb{R}^d$$

change positions of points relative to the origin.

While prior work has typically focused on linear transformations, which fix the origin, we consider the broader class of affine transformations, which do not. Thus, affine transformations such as translation cannot in general be represented as a square matrix for finite-dimensional spaces.

We use the following affine transformations:

- translations;
- reflections over a hyperplane;
- rotations about a subspace;
- homotheties.

We give brief definitions of each transformation.

Definition 1. A **translation** is a function $T_{\mathbf{x}} : \mathbb{R}^d \to \mathbb{R}^d$ given by

$$T_{\mathbf{x}}(\mathbf{v}) = \mathbf{v} + \mathbf{x} \qquad (3.1)$$

where $\mathbf{x} \in \mathbb{R}^d$.

Definition 2. For every $\mathbf{a} \in \mathbb{R}^d$, we call the map $\text{Refl}_{\mathbf{a}} : \mathbb{R}^d \to \mathbb{R}^d$ given by

$$\text{Refl}_{\mathbf{a}}(\mathbf{v}) = \mathbf{v} - 2\frac{\mathbf{v} \cdot \mathbf{a}}{\mathbf{a} \cdot \mathbf{a}}\mathbf{a} \qquad (3.2)$$

the **reflection** over the hyperplane through the origin orthogonal to $\mathbf{a}$.

Definition 3. A **rotation** through the span of vectors $\mathbf{u}, \mathbf{x}$ by angle θ is a map $\text{Rot}_{\mathbf{u},\mathbf{x}} : \mathbb{R}^d \to \mathbb{R}^d$ given by

$$\text{Rot}_{\mathbf{u},\mathbf{x}}(\mathbf{v}) = A\mathbf{v} \qquad (3.3)$$

where

$$\begin{aligned} A = I &+ \sin\theta(\mathbf{x}\mathbf{u}^T - \mathbf{u}\mathbf{x}^T) \\ &+ (\cos\theta - 1)(\mathbf{u}\mathbf{u}^T + \mathbf{x}\mathbf{x}^T) \end{aligned} \qquad (3.4)$$

and $I \in \text{Mat}_{d,d}(\mathbb{R})$ is the identity matrix.

Definition 4. For every $\mathbf{a} \in \mathbb{R}^d$ and $\lambda \in \mathbb{R} \setminus \{0\}$, we call the map $H_{\mathbf{a},\lambda} : \mathbb{R}^d \to \mathbb{R}^d$ given by

$$H_{\mathbf{a},\lambda}(\mathbf{v}) = \mathbf{a} + \lambda(\mathbf{v} - \mathbf{a}) \qquad (3.5)$$

a **homothety** of center $\mathbf{a}$ and ratio λ. A homothety centered at the origin is called a **dilation**.

Parameters used in our analysis for each of these transformations are provided in Appendix A.

3.2 Cosine distance encoding (CDE)

Our cosine distance encoding transformation

$$f_{\text{CDE}} : \mathbb{R}^d \to \mathbb{R}^{|V|}$$

obfuscates the distribution of features in $\mathbb{R}^d$ by representing a set of word vectors as a pairwise distance matrix. Such a transformation might be used to avoid the non-interpretability of embedding features (Fyshe et al., 2015) and compare embeddings based on relative organization alone.

Definition 5. Let $\mathbf{a}, \mathbf{b} \in \mathbb{R}^d$. Then their **cosine distance** $d_{\cos} : \mathbb{R}^d \times \mathbb{R}^d \to [0, 2]$ is given by

$$d_{\cos}(\mathbf{a}, \mathbf{b}) = 1 - \frac{\mathbf{a} \cdot \mathbf{b}}{||\mathbf{a}||||\mathbf{b}||} \qquad (3.6)$$

where the second term is the **cosine similarity**.

As all three sets of embeddings evaluated in this study have vocabulary size on the order of 10^6, use of the full distance matrix is impractical. We use a subset consisting of the distance from each point to the embeddings of the 10K most frequent words from each embedding set, yielding

$$f_{\text{CDE}} : \mathbb{R}^d \to \mathbb{R}^{10^4}$$

This is not dissimilar to the global frequency-based negative sampling approach of word2vec (Mikolov et al., 2013). We then use an autoencoder to map this back to $\mathbb{R}^d$ for comparability.

Definition 6. Let $\mathbf{v} \in \mathbb{R}^{|V|}$, $\mathbf{W_1}, \mathbf{W_2} \in \mathbb{R}^{|V| \times d}$. Then an **autoencoder** over $\mathbb{R}^{|V|}$ is defined as

$$\mathbf{h} = \varphi(\mathbf{v}\mathbf{W_1}) \qquad (3.7)$$

$$\hat{\mathbf{v}} = \varphi(\mathbf{W_2}^T\mathbf{h}) \qquad (3.8)$$

Vector $\mathbf{h} \in \mathbb{R}^d$ is then used as the compressed representation of $\mathbf{v}$.

In our experiments, we use ReLU as our activation function φ, and train the autoencoder for 50 epochs to minimize L^2 distance between $\mathbf{v}$ and $\hat{\mathbf{v}}$.

We recognize that low-rank compression using an autoencoder is likely to be noisy, thus potentially inducing additional loss in evaluations. However, precedent for capturing geometric structure with autoencoders (Li et al., 2017b) suggests that this is a viable model for our analysis.

3.3 Nearest neighbor encoding (NNE)

Our nearest neighbor encoding transformation

$$f_{\text{NNE}} : \mathbb{R}^d \to \mathbb{R}^{|V|}$$

discards the majority of the global pairwise distance information modeled in CDE, and retains only information about nearest neighborhoods. The output of $f_{\text{NNE}}(\mathbf{v})$ is a sparse vector.

This transformation relates to the common use of nearest neighborhoods as a proxy for semantic information (Wendlandt et al., 2018; Pierrejean and Tanguy, 2018). We take the previously proposed approach of combining the output of $f_{\text{NNE}}(\mathbf{v})$ for each $\mathbf{v} \in V$ to form a sparse adjacency matrix, which describes a directed nearest neighbor graph (Cuba Gyllensten and Sahlgren, 2015; Newman-Griffis and Fosler-Lussier, 2017), using three versions of f_{NNE} defined below.

Thresholded The set of non-zero indices in $f_{\text{NNE}}(\mathbf{v})$ correspond to word vectors $\tilde{\mathbf{v}}$ such that the cosine similarity of $\mathbf{v}$ and $\tilde{\mathbf{v}}$ is greater than or equal to an arbitrary threshold t. In order to ensure that every word has non-zero out degree in the graph, we also include the k nearest neighbors by cosine similarity for every word vector. Non-zero values in $f_{\text{NNE}}(\mathbf{v})$ are set to the cosine similarity of $\mathbf{v}$ and the relevant neighbor vector.

Weighted The set of non-zero indices in $f_{\text{NNE}}(\mathbf{v})$ corresponds to only the set of k nearest neighbors to $\mathbf{v}$ by cosine similarity. Cosine similarity values are used for edge weights.

Unweighted As in the previous case, only k nearest neighbors are included in the adjacency matrix. All edges are weighted equally, regardless of cosine similarity.

We report results using $k = 5$ and $t = 0.05$; other settings are discussed in Appendix B.

Finally, much like the CDE method, we use a second mapping function

$$\psi : \mathbb{R}^{|V|} \to \mathbb{R}^d$$

to transform the nearest neighbor graph back to d-dimensional vectors for evaluation. Following Newman-Griffis and Fosler-Lussier (2017), we

use node2vec (Grover and Leskovec, 2016) with default parameters to learn this mapping. Like the autoencoder, this is a noisy map, but the intent of node2vec to capture patterns in local graph structure makes it a good fit for our analysis.

3.4 Random encoding

Finally, as a baseline, we use a random encoding

$$f_{\text{Rand}} : \mathbb{R}^d \to \mathbb{R}^d$$

that discards original vectors entirely.

While intrinsic evaluations rely only on input embeddings, and thus lose all source information in this case, extrinsic tasks learn a model to transform input features, making even randomly-initialized vectors a common baseline (Lample et al., 2016; Kim, 2014). For fair comparison, we generate one set of random baselines for each embedding set and re-use these across all tasks.

3.5 Other transformations

Many other transformations of a word embedding space could be included in our analysis, such as arbitrary vector-valued polynomial functions, rational vector-valued functions, or common decomposition methods such as principal components analysis (PCA) or singular value decomposition (SVD). Additionally, though they cannot be effectively applied to the unordered set of word vectors in a raw embedding space, transformations for sequential data such as discrete Fourier transforms or discrete wavelet transforms could be used for word sequences in specific text corpora.

For this study, we limit our scope to the transformations listed above. These transformations align with prior work on analyzing and post-processing embeddings for specific tasks, and are highly interpretable with respect to the original embedding space. However, other complex transformations represent an intriguing area of future work.

4 Evaluation

In order to measure the contributions of each geometric aspect described in Section 3 to the utility of word embeddings as input features, we evaluate embeddings transformed using our sequence of operations on a battery of standard intrinsic evaluations, which model linguistic information directly in the vector space; and extrinsic evaluations, which use the embeddings as input to learned models for downstream applications Our intrinsic evaluations include:

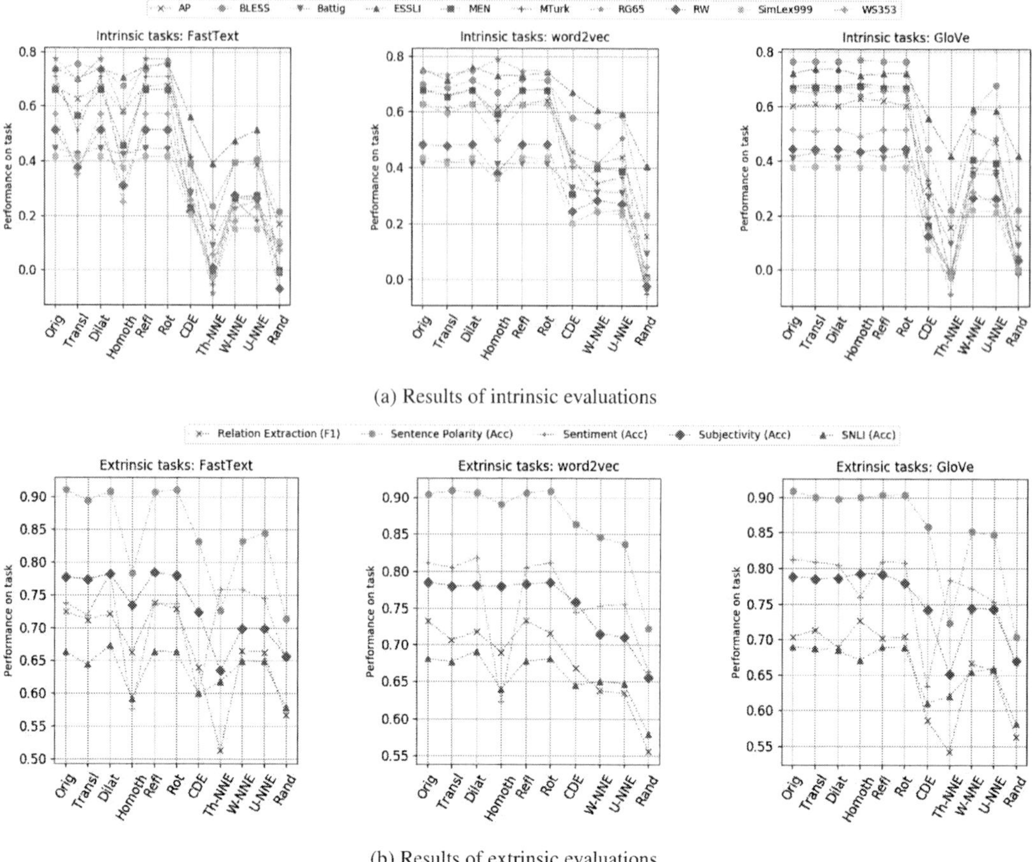

Figure 2: Performance metrics on intrinsic and extrinsic tasks, comparing across different transformations applied to each set of word embeddings. Dotted lines are for visual aid in tracking performance on individual tasks, and do not indicate continuous transformations. Transformations are presented in order of decreasing geometric information about the original vectors, and are applied independent of one another to the original source embedding.

- Word similarity and relatedness, using cosine similarity: WordSim-353 (Finkelstein et al., 2001), SimLex-999 (Hill et al., 2015), RareWords (Luong et al., 2013), RG65 (Rubenstein and Goodenough, 1965), MEN (Bruni et al., 2014), and MTURK (Radinsky et al., 2011).[4]

- Word categorization, using an oracle combination of agglomerative and k-means clustering: AP (Almuhareb and Poesio, 2005), BLESS (Baroni and Lenci, 2011), Battig (Battig and Montague, 1969), and the ESSLLI 2008 shared task (Baroni et al. (2008), performance averaged across nouns, verbs,

and concrete nouns).[5]

Given the well-documented issues with using vector arithmetic-based analogy completion as an intrinsic evaluation (Linzen, 2016; Rogers et al., 2017; Newman-Griffis et al., 2017), we do not include it in our analysis.

We follow Rogers et al. (2018) in evaluating on a set of five extrinsic tasks:[5]

- Relation classification: SemEval-2010 Task 8 (Hendrickx et al., 2010), using a CNN with word and distance embeddings (Zeng et al., 2014).

- Sentence-level sentiment polarity classification: MR movie reviews (Pang and Lee, 2005), with a simplified CNN model from (Kim, 2014).

---

[4]`https://github.com/kudkudak/`
`word-embeddings-benchmarks` using single-word datasets only. For brevity, we omit the Sim/Rel splits of WordSim-353 (Agirre et al., 2009), which showed the same trends as the full dataset.

[5]`https://github.com/drgriffis/`
`Extrinsic-Evaluation-tasks`

- Sentiment classification: IMDB movie reviews (Maas et al., 2011), with a single 100-d LSTM.
- Subjectivity/objectivity classification: Rotten Tomato snippets (Pang and Lee, 2004), using a logistic regression over summed word embeddings (Li et al., 2017a).
- Natural language inference: SNLI (Bowman et al., 2015), using separate LSTMs for premise and hypothesis, combined with a feed-forward classifier.

5   Analysis and Discussion

Figure 2 presents the results of each intrinsic and extrinsic evaluation on the transformed versions of our three sets of word embeddings.[6] The largest drops in performance across all three sets for intrinsic tasks occur when explicit embedding features are removed with the CDE transformation. While some cases of NNE-transformed embeddings recover a measure of this performance, they remain far under affine-transformed embeddings. Extrinsic tasks are similarly affected by the CDE transformation; however, NNE-transformed embeddings recover the majority of performance.

Comparing within the set of affine transformations, the innocuous effect of rotations, dilations, and reflections on both intrinsic and extrinsic tasks suggests that the models used are robust to simple linear transformations. Extrinsic evaluations are also relatively insensitive to translations, which can be modeled with bias terms, though the lack of learned models and reliance on cosine similarity for the intrinsic tasks makes them more sensitive to shifts relative to the origin. Interestingly, homothety, which effectively combines a translation and a dilation, leads to a noticeable drop in performance across all tasks. Intuitively, this result makes sense: by both shifting points relative to the origin and changing their distribution in the space, angular similarity values used for intrinsic tasks can be changed significantly, and the zero mean feature distribution preferred by neural models (Clevert et al., 2016) becomes harder to achieve. This suggests that methods for tuning embeddings should attempt to preserve the origin whenever possible.

The large drops in performance observed when using the CDE transformation is likely to relate

to the instability of nearest neighborhoods and the importance of locality in embedding learning (Wendlandt et al., 2018), although the effects of the autoencoder component also bear further investigation. By effectively increasing the size of the neighborhood considered, CDE adds additional sources of semantic noise. The similar drops from thresholded-NNE transformations, by the same token, is likely related to observations of the relationship between the frequency ranks of a word and its nearest neighbors (Faruqui et al., 2016). With thresholded-NNE, we find that the words with highest out degree in the nearest neighbor graph are rare words (e.g., "Chanterelle" and "Courtier" in FastText, "Tiegel" and "demangler" in GloVe), which link to other rare words. Thus, node2vec's random walk method is more likely to traverse these dense subgraphs of rare words, adding noise to the output embeddings.

Finally, we note that Melamud et al. (2016) showed significant variability in downstream task performance when using different embedding dimensionalities. While we fixed vector dimensionality for the purposes of this study, varying d in future work represents a valuable follow-up.

Our findings suggest that methods for training and tuning embeddings, especially for downstream tasks, should explicitly focus on local geometric structure in the vector space. One concrete example of this comes from Chen et al. (2018), who demonstrate empirical gains when changing the negative sampling approach of word2vec to choose negative samples that are currently near to the target word in vector space, instead of the original frequency-based sampling (which ignores geometric structure). Similarly, successful methods for tuning word embeddings for specific tasks have often focused on enforcing a specific neighborhood structure (Faruqui et al., 2015). We demonstrate that by doing so, they align qualitative semantic judgments with the primary geometric information that downstream models learn from.

6   Conclusion

Analysis of word embeddings has largely focused on qualitative characteristics such as nearest neighborhoods or relative distribution. In this work, we take a quantitative approach analyzing geometric attributes of embeddings in $\mathbb{R}^d$, in order to understand the impact of geometric properties on downstream task performance. We character-

---

[6]Due to their large vocabulary size, we were unable to run Thresholded-NNE experiments with word2vec embeddings.

ized word embedding geometry in terms of absolute position, vector features, global pairwise distances, and local pairwise distances, and generated new embedding matrices by removing these attributes from pretrained embeddings. By evaluating the performance of these transformed embeddings on a variety of intrinsic and extrinsic tasks, we find that while intrinsic evaluations are sensitive to absolute position, downstream models rely primarily on information about local similarity.

As embeddings are used for increasingly specialized applications, and as recent contextualized embedding methods such as ELMo (Peters et al., 2018) and BERT (Devlin et al., 2018) allow for dynamic generation of embeddings from specific contexts, our findings suggest that work on tuning and improving these embeddings should focus explicitly on local geometric structure in sampling and evaluation methods. The source code for our transformations and complete tables of our results are available online at `https://github.com/OSU-slatelab/geometric-embedding-properties`.

Acknowledgments

We gratefully acknowledge the use of Ohio Supercomputer Center (Ohio Supercomputer Center, 1987) resources for this work, and thank our anonymous reviewers for their insightful comments. Denis is supported via a Pre-Doctoral Fellowship from the National Institutes of Health, Clinical Center. Aparajita is supported via a Feuer International Scholarship in Artificial Intelligence.

References

Eneko Agirre, Oier Lopez De Lacalle, and Aitor Soroa. 2009. Knowledge-based wsd on specific domains: Performing better than generic supervised WSD. *IJ-CAI International Joint Conference on Artificial Intelligence*, pages 1501–1506.

A Almuhareb and M Poesio. 2005. Concept Learning and Categorization from the Web. *Proceedings of the Annual Meeting of the Cognitive Science Society*, 27.

Mikel Artetxe, Gorka Labaka, and Eneko Agirre. 2016. Learning principled bilingual mappings of word embeddings while preserving monolingual invariance. In *Proceedings of the 2016 Conference on Empirical Methods in Natural Language Processing*, pages 2289–2294, Austin, Texas. Association for Computational Linguistics.

Marco Baroni, Stefan Evert, and Alessandro Lenci, editors. 2008. *Proceedings of the ESSLLI Workshop on Distributional Lexical Semantics: Bridging the gap between semantic theory and computational simulations*. Hamburg, Germany.

Marco Baroni and Alessandro Lenci. 2011. How we BLESSed distributional semantic evaluation. *GEMS '11 Proceedings of the GEMS 2011 Workshop on GEometrical Models of Natural Language Semantics*, pages 1–10.

William F Battig and William E Montague. 1969. Category norms of verbal items in 56 categories A replication and extension of the Connecticut category norms. *Journal of Experimental Psychology*, 80(3, Pt.2):1–46.

Piotr Bojanowski, Edouard Grave, Armand Joulin, and Tomas Mikolov. 2017. Enriching Word Vectors with Subword Information. *Transactions of the ACL*, 5:135–146.

Samuel R Bowman, Gabor Angeli, Christopher Potts, and Christopher D Manning. 2015. A large annotated corpus for learning natural language inference. In *Proceedings of the 2015 Conference on Empirical Methods in Natural Language Processing*, pages 632–642, Lisbon, Portugal. Association for Computational Linguistics.

Elia Bruni, Nam Khanh Tran, and Marco Baroni. 2014. Multimodal Distributional Semantics. *Journal of Artificial Intelligence Research*, 49(1):1–47.

Chandrahas, Aditya Sharma, and Partha Talukdar. 2018. Towards Understanding the Geometry of Knowledge Graph Embeddings. In *Proceedings of the 56th Annual Meeting of the Association for Computational Linguistics (Volume 1: Long Papers)*, pages 122–131. Association for Computational Linguistics.

Long Chen, Fajie Yuan, Joemon M. Jose, and Weinan Zhang. 2018. Improving negative sampling for word representation using self-embedded features. In *Proceedings of the Eleventh ACM International Conference on Web Search and Data Mining*, WSDM '18, pages 99–107, New York, NY, USA. ACM.

Billy Chiu, Anna Korhonen, and Sampo Pyysalo. 2016. Intrinsic Evaluation of Word Vectors Fails to Predict Extrinsic Performance. *Proceedings of the 1st Workshop on Evaluating Vector Space Representations for NLP*, pages 1–6.

Djork-Arne Clevert, Thomas Unterthiner, and Sepp Hochreiter. 2016. Fast and Accurate Deep Network Learning by Exponential Linear Units (ELUs). In *Proceedings of the International Conference on Learning Representations (ICLR)*.

Amaru Cuba Gyllensten and Magnus Sahlgren. 2015. Navigating the Semantic Horizon using Relative Neighborhood Graphs. In *Proceedings of the 2015*

Conference on Empirical Methods in Natural Language Processing, pages 2451–2460. Association for Computational Linguistics.

Jacob Devlin, Ming-Wei Chang, Kenton Lee, and Kristina Toutanova. 2018. BERT: Pre-training of Deep Bidirectional Transformers for Language Understanding. In *arXiv preprint arXiv:1810.04805v1*.

Manaal Faruqui, Yulia Tsvetkov, Pushpendre Rastogi, and Chris Dyer. 2016. Problems With Evaluation of Word Embeddings Using Word Similarity Tasks. In *Proceedings of the 1st Workshop on Evaluating Vector-Space Representations for NLP*, pages 30–35, Berlin, Germany. Association for Computational Linguistics.

Manaal Faruqui, Yulia Tsvetkov, Dani Yogatama, Chris Dyer, and Noah A Smith. 2015. Sparse Overcomplete Word Vector Representations. In *Proceedings of the 53rd Annual Meeting of the Association for Computational Linguistics and the 7th International Joint Conference on Natural Language Processing (Volume 1: Long Papers)*, pages 1491–1500, Beijing, China. Association for Computational Linguistics.

Lev Finkelstein, Evgeniy Gabrilovich, Yossi Matias, Ehud Rivlin, Zach Solan, Gadi Wolfman, and Eytan Ruppin. 2001. Placing Search in Context: The Concept Revisited. In *Proceedings of the 10th International Conference on World Wide Web*, WWW '01, pages 406–414, Hong Kong. ACM.

Alona Fyshe, Leila Wehbe, Partha P Talukdar, Brian Murphy, and Tom M Mitchell. 2015. A Compositional and Interpretable Semantic Space. In *Proceedings of the 2015 Conference of the North American Chapter of the Association for Computational Linguistics: Human Language Technologies*, pages 32–41, Denver, Colorado. Association for Computational Linguistics.

Aditya Grover and Jure Leskovec. 2016. Node2Vec: Scalable Feature Learning for Networks. In *Proceedings of the 22Nd ACM SIGKDD International Conference on Knowledge Discovery and Data Mining*, KDD '16, pages 855–864, New York, NY, USA. ACM.

F Heimerl and M Gleicher. 2018. Interactive Analysis of Word Vector Embeddings. *Computer Graphics Forum*, 37(3):253–265.

Johannes Hellrich and Udo Hahn. 2016. Bad Company—Neighborhoods in Neural Embedding Spaces Considered Harmful. In *Proceedings of COLING 2016, the 26th International Conference on Computational Linguistics: Technical Papers*, pages 2785–2796. The COLING 2016 Organizing Committee.

Iris Hendrickx, Su Nam Kim, Zornitsa Kozareva, Preslav Nakov, Diarmuid 'O S 'eaghdha, Sebastian Pad 'o, Marco Pennacchiotti, Lorenza Romano, and Stan Szpakowicz. 2010. SemEval-2010 Task 8: Multi-Way Classification of Semantic Relations between Pairs of Nominals. In *Proceedings of the 5th International Workshop on Semantic Evaluation*, pages 33–38. Association for Computational Linguistics.

Felix Hill, Roi Reichart, and Anna Korhonen. 2015. SimLex-999: Evaluating Semantic Models with (Genuine) Similarity Estimation. *Computational Linguistics*, 41(4):665–695.

Thomas Hofmann, Bernhard Schölkopf, and Alexander J. Smola. 2008. Kernel methods in machine learning. *The Annals of Statistics*, 36(3):1171–1220.

Yoon Kim. 2014. Convolutional Neural Networks for Sentence Classification. In *Proceedings of the 2014 Conference on Empirical Methods in Natural Language Processing (EMNLP)*, pages 1746–1751. Association for Computational Linguistics.

Guillaume Lample, Miguel Ballesteros, Sandeep Subramanian, Kazuya Kawakami, and Chris Dyer. 2016. Neural architectures for named entity recognition. *arXiv preprint arXiv:1603.01360*.

Bofang Li, Tao Liu, Zhe Zhao, Buzhou Tang, Aleksandr Drozd, Anna Rogers, and Xiaoyong Du. 2017a. Investigating Different Syntactic Context Types and Context Representations for Learning Word Embeddings. In *Proceedings of the 2017 Conference on Empirical Methods in Natural Language Processing*, pages 2421–2431. Association for Computational Linguistics.

Jun Li, Kai Xu, Siddhartha Chaudhuri, Ersin Yumer, Hao Zhang, and Leonidas Guibas. 2017b. Grass: Generative recursive autoencoders for shape structures. *ACM Trans. Graph.*, 36(4):52:1–52:14.

Tal Linzen. 2016. Issues in evaluating semantic spaces using word analogies. In *Proceedings of the 1st Workshop on Evaluating Vector-Space Representations for NLP*, pages 13–18.

Thang Luong, Richard Socher, and Christopher Manning. 2013. Better Word Representations with Recursive Neural Networks for Morphology. In *Proceedings of the Seventeenth Conference on Computational Natural Language Learning*, pages 104–113, Sofia, Bulgaria. Association for Computational Linguistics.

Andrew L Maas, Raymond E Daly, Peter T Pham, Dan Huang, Andrew Y Ng, and Christopher Potts. 2011. Learning Word Vectors for Sentiment Analysis. In *Proceedings of the 49th Annual Meeting of the Association for Computational Linguistics: Human Language Technologies*, pages 142–150. Association for Computational Linguistics.

Oren Melamud, David McClosky, Siddharth Patwardhan, and Mohit Bansal. 2016. The Role of Context Types and Dimensionality in Learning Word Embeddings. In *Proceedings of the 2016 Conference of* the North American Chapter of the Association for Computational Linguistics: Human Language Technologies*, NAACL-HLT '16, pages 1030–1040, San Diego, CA. Association for Computational Linguistics.

Tomas Mikolov, Kai Chen, Greg Corrado, and Jeffrey Dean. 2013. Efficient estimation of word representations in vector space. *arXiv preprint arXiv:1301.3781*.

David Mimno and Laure Thompson. 2017. The strange geometry of skip-gram with negative sampling. In *Proceedings of the 2017 Conference on Empirical Methods in Natural Language Processing*, pages 2873–2878, Copenhagen, Denmark. Association for Computational Linguistics.

Denis Newman-Griffis and Eric Fosler-Lussier. 2017. Second-order word embeddings from nearest neighbor topological features. *arXiv preprint arXiv:1705.08488*.

Denis Newman-Griffis, Albert M Lai, and Eric Fosler-Lussier. 2017. Insights into Analogy Completion from the Biomedical Domain. In *BioNLP 2017*, pages 19–28, Vancouver, Canada. Association for Computational Linguistics.

Ohio Supercomputer Center. 1987. Ohio supercomputer center. http://osc.edu/ark: /19495/f5s1ph73.

Bo Pang and Lillian Lee. 2004. A Sentimental Education: Sentiment Analysis Using Subjectivity Summarization Based on Minimum Cuts. In *Proceedings of the 42nd Annual Meeting of the Association for Computational Linguistics (ACL-04)*.

Bo Pang and Lillian Lee. 2005. Seeing Stars: Exploiting Class Relationships for Sentiment Categorization with Respect to Rating Scales. In *Proceedings of the 43rd Annual Meeting of the Association for Computational Linguistics (ACL'05)*, pages 115–124. Association for Computational Linguistics.

Jeffrey Pennington, Richard Socher, and Christopher D. Manning. 2014. Glove: Global Vectors for Word Representation. In *Proceedings of the 2014 Conference on Empirical Methods in Natural Language Processing*, pages 1532–1543, Doha, Qatar. Association for Computational Linguistics.

Matthew E Peters, Mark Neumann, Mohit Iyyer, Matt Gardner, Christopher Clark, Kenton Lee, and Luke Zettlemoyer. 2018. Deep Contextualized Word Representations. In *Proceedings of the 2018 Conference of the North American Chapter of the Association for Computational Linguistics: Human Language Technologies, Volume 1 (Long Papers)*, pages 2227–2237, New Orleans, Louisiana. Association for Computational Linguistics.

Benedicte Pierrejean and Ludovic Tanguy. 2018. Towards Qualitative Word Embeddings Evaluation: Measuring Neighbors Variation. In *Proceedings of the 2018 Conference of the North American Chapter of the Association for Computational Linguistics: Student Research Workshop*, pages 32–39. Association for Computational Linguistics.

Kira Radinsky, Eugene Agichtein, Evgeniy Gabrilovich, and Shaul Markovitch. 2011. A Word at a Time: Computing Word Relatedness Using Temporal Semantic Analysis. In *Proceedings of the 20th International Conference on World Wide Web*, WWW '11, pages 337–346, New York, NY, USA. ACM.

Anna Rogers, Aleksandr Drozd, and Bofang Li. 2017. The (too Many) Problems of Analogical Reasoning with Word Vectors. *Proceedings of the 6th Joint Conference on Lexical and Computational Semantics (*SEM 2017)*, pages 135–148.

Anna Rogers, Shashwath Hosur Ananthakrishna, and Anna Rumshisky. 2018. What's in Your Embedding, And How It Predicts Task Performance. In *Proceedings of the 27th International Conference on Computational Linguistics*, pages 2690–2703, Santa Fe, NM, USA. Association for Computational Linguistics.

Herbert Rubenstein and John B. Goodenough. 1965. Contextual correlates of synonymy. *Communications of the ACM*, 8(10):627–633.

Christian Szegedy, Wojciech Zaremba, Ilya Sutskever, Joan Bruna, Dumitru Erhan, Ian Goodfellow, and Rob Fergus. 2014. Intriguing properties of neural networks. In *International Conference on Learning Representations*.

Laura Wendlandt, Jonathan K Kummerfeld, and Rada Mihalcea. 2018. Factors Influencing the Surprising Instability of Word Embeddings. In *Proceedings of the 2018 Conference of the North American Chapter of the Association for Computational Linguistics: Human Language Technologies, Volume 1 (Long Papers)*, pages 2092–2102. Association for Computational Linguistics.

Daojian Zeng, Kang Liu, Siwei Lai, Guangyou Zhou, and Jun Zhao. 2014. Relation Classification via Convolutional Deep Neural Network. In *Proceedings of COLING 2014, the 25th International Conference on Computational Linguistics: Technical Papers*, pages 2335–2344. Dublin City University and Association for Computational Linguistics.

Appendix A   Parameters

We give the following library of vectors in $\mathbb{R}^d$ used as parameter values:

$$\mathbf{v}_{\text{diag}} = \begin{bmatrix} \frac{1}{\sqrt{d}} \\ \vdots \\ \frac{1}{\sqrt{d}} \end{bmatrix} ; \qquad \mathbf{v}_{\text{diagNeg}} = \begin{bmatrix} -\frac{1}{\sqrt{d}} \\ \frac{1}{\sqrt{d}} \\ \vdots \\ \frac{1}{\sqrt{d}} \end{bmatrix} . \tag{A.1}$$

Transform	Parameter	Value
Translation	Direction:	0
	Magnitude:	1
Dilation	Magnitude:	2
Homothety	Center:	$\mathbf{v}_{\text{diag}}$
	Magnitude:	0.25
Reflection	Hyperplane Vector:	$\mathbf{v}_{\text{diag}}$
2-D Rotation	Basis Vector 1:	$\mathbf{v}_{\text{diag}}$
	Basis Vector 2:	$\mathbf{v}_{\text{diagNeg}}$
	Angle:	$\pi/4$

Table 1: Transform parameters.

Appendix B   NNE settings

We experimented with $k \in \{5, 10, 15\}$ for our weighted and unweighted NNE transformations. For thresholded NNE, in order to best evaluate the impact of thresholding over uniform k, we used the minimum $k = 5$ and experimented with $t \in \{0.01, 0.05, 0.075\}$; higher values of t increased graph size sufficiently to be impractical. We report using $k = 5$ for weighted and unweighted settings in our main results for fairer comparison with the thresholded setting.

The effect of thresholding on nearest neighbor graphs was a strongly right-tailed increase in out degree for a small portion of nodes. Our reported value of $t = 0.05$ increased the out degree of 20,229 nodes for FastText (out of 1M total nodes), with the maximum increase being 819 ("Chanterelle"), and 1,354 nodes increasing out degree by only 1. For GloVe, 7,533 nodes increased in out degree (out of 2M total), with maximum increase 240 ("Tiegel"), and 372 nodes increasing out degree by only 1.

Table 2 compares averaged performance values across all intrinsic tasks for these settings, and Table 3 compares average extrinsic task performance.

NNE params	FastText	word2vec	GloVe
Thresholded			
$k = 5, t = 0.01$	0.160	–	0.106
$k = 5, t = 0.05$	0.129	–	0.130
$k = 5, t = 0.075$	0.150	–	0.132
Weighted			
$k = 5$	0.320	0.419	0.426
$k = 10$	0.342	0.363	0.460
$k = 15$	0.346	0.376	0.448
Unweighted			
$k = 5$	0.330	0.428	0.435
$k = 10$	0.351	0.396	0.463
$k = 15$	0.341	0.365	0.432

Table 2: Mean performance on intrinsic tasks under different NNE settings.

NNE params	FastText	word2vec	GloVe
Thresholded			
$k = 5, t = 0.01$	0.642	–	0.666
$k = 5, t = 0.05$	0.650	–	0.664
$k = 5, t = 0.075$	0.649	–	0.663
Weighted			
$k = 5$	0.721	0.720	0.738
$k = 10$	0.728	0.713	0.740
$k = 15$	0.725	0.713	0.739
Unweighted			
$k = 5$	0.720	0.717	0.732
$k = 10$	0.724	0.712	0.738
$k = 15$	0.729	0.708	0.725

Table 3: Mean performance on extrinsic tasks under different NNE settings.

The Influence of Down-Sampling Strategies on SVD Word Embedding Stability

Johannes Hellrich   **Bernd Kampe**   **Udo Hahn**

{firstname.lastname}@uni-jena.de

Jena University Language & Information Engineering (JULIE) Lab
Friedrich-Schiller-Universität Jena, Jena, Germany
julielab.de

Abstract

The stability of word embedding algorithms, i.e., the consistency of the word representations they reveal when trained repeatedly on the same data set, has recently raised concerns. We here compare word embedding algorithms on three corpora of different sizes, and evaluate both their stability and accuracy. We find strong evidence that down-sampling strategies (used as part of their training procedures) are particularly influential for the stability of SVD_{PPMI}-type embeddings. This finding seems to explain diverging reports on their stability and lead us to a simple modification which provides superior stability as well as accuracy on par with skip-gram embeddings.

1 Introduction

Word embedding algorithms implement the latest form of distributional semantics originating from the seminal work of Harris (1954) or Rubenstein and Goodenough (1965). They generate dense vector space representations for words based on co-occurrences within a context window. They sample word-context pairs, i.e., typically two co-occurring tokens, from a corpus and use these to generate vector representations of words and their context. Changes to the algorithm's sampling mechanism can lead to new capabilities, e.g., processing dependency information instead of linear co-occurrences (Levy and Goldberg, 2014a), or increased performance, e.g., using word association values instead of raw co-occurrence counts (Bullinaria and Levy, 2007).

Word embedding algorithms commonly down-sample contexts to lessen the impact of high-frequency words (termed 'subsampling' in Levy et al. (2015)) or increase the relative importance of words closer to the center of a context window (called 'dynamic context window' in Levy et al. (2015)). The effect of using such down-sampling

strategies on accuracy in word similarity and analogy tasks was explored in several papers (e.g., Levy et al. (2015)).

However, down-sampling and details of its implementation also have major effects on the stability of word embeddings (also known as 'reliability'), i.e., the degree to which models trained independently on the same data agree on the structure of the resulting embedding space. This problem has lately raised severe concerns in the word embedding community (e.g., Hellrich and Hahn (2016b); Antoniak and Mimno (2018); Wendlandt et al. (2018)) and is also of interest to the wider machine learning community due to the influence of probabilistic—and thus unstable—methods on experimental results (Reimers and Gurevych, 2017; Henderson et al., 2018), as well as replicability and reproducibility (Ivie and Thain, 2018, pp. 63:3–4).

Stability is critical for studies examining the underlying semantic space as a more advanced form of corpus linguistics, e.g., tracking lexical change (Kim et al., 2014; Kulkarni et al., 2015; Hellrich et al., 2018). Unstable word embeddings can lead to serious problems in such applications, as interpretations will depend on the luck of the draw. This might also affect high-stake fields like medical informatics where patients could be harmed as a consequence of misleading results (Coiera et al., 2018).

In the light of these concerns, we here evaluate down-sampling strategies by modifying the SVD_{PPMI} (Singular Value Decomposition of a Positive Pointwise Mutual Information matrix; Levy et al. (2015)) algorithm and comparing its results with those of two other embedding algorithms, namely, GLoVe (Pennington et al., 2014) and SGNS (Mikolov et al., 2013a,c). Our analysis is based on three corpora of different sizes and investigates effects on both accuracy and stability.

18

Proceedings of the 3rd Workshop on Evaluating Vector Space Representations for NLP, pages 18–26
Minneapolis, USA, June 6, 2019. ©2019 Association for Computational Linguistics

The inclusion of accuracy measurements and the larger size of our training corpora exceed prior work. We show how the choice of down-sampling strategies, a seemingly minor detail, leads to major differences in the characterization of SVD_{PPMI} in recent studies (Hellrich and Hahn, 2017; Antoniak and Mimno, 2018). We also present SVD_{WPPMI}, a simple modification of SVD_{PPMI} that replaces probabilistic down-sampling with weighting. What, at first sight, appears to be a small change leads, nevertheless, to an unrivaled combination of stability and accuracy, making it particularly well-suited for the above-mentioned corpus linguistic applications.

2 Computational Methodology

2.1 Measuring Stability

Measuring word embedding stability can be linked to older research comparing distributional thesauri (Salton and Lesk, 1971) by the most similar words they contain for particular anchor words (Weeds et al., 2004; Padró et al., 2014). Most stability experiments focused on repeatedly training the *same* algorithm on one corpus (Hellrich and Hahn, 2016a,b, 2017; Antoniak and Mimno, 2018; Pierrejean and Tanguy, 2018; Chugh et al., 2018), whereas Wendlandt et al. (2018) quantified stability by comparing word similarity for models trained with *different* algorithms. We follow the former approach, since we deem it more relevant for ensuring that study results can be **replicated or reproduced**.

Stability can be quantified by calculating the overlap between sets of words considered most similar in relation to pre-selected anchor words. Reasonable metrical choices are, e.g., the Jaccard coefficient (Jaccard, 1912) between these sets (Antoniak and Mimno, 2018; Chugh et al., 2018), or a percentage based coefficient (Hellrich and Hahn, 2016a,b; Wendlandt et al., 2018; Pierrejean and Tanguy, 2018). We here use $j@n$, i.e., the Jaccard coefficient for the n most similar words. It depends on a set M of word embedding models, m, for which the n most similar words (by cosine) from a set A of anchor words, a, as provided by the 'most similar words' function $\mathrm{msw}(a, n, m)$, are compared:

$$j@n := \frac{1}{|A|} \sum_{a \in A} \frac{|\bigcap_{m \in M} \mathrm{msw}(a, n, m)|}{|\bigcup_{m \in M} \mathrm{msw}(a, n, m)|} \quad (1)$$

2.2 SVD_{PPMI} Word Embeddings

The SVD_{PPMI} algorithm from Levy et al. (2015) generates word embeddings in a three-step process. First, a corpus is transformed to a word-context matrix listing co-occurrence frequencies. Next, the frequency-based word-context matrix is transformed into a word-context matrix that contains word association values. Finally, singular value decomposition (SVD; Berry (1992); Saad (2003)) is applied to the latter matrix to reduce its dimensionality and generate word embeddings.

Each token from the corpus is successively processed in the first step by recording co-occurrences with other tokens within a symmetric window of a certain size. For example, in a token sequence $\ldots, w_{i-2}, w_{i-1}, w_i, w_{i+1}, w_{i+2}, \ldots$, with w_i as the currently modeled token, a window of size 1 would be concerned with w_{i-1} and w_{i+1} only. Down-sampling as described by Levy et al. (2015) increases accuracy by ignoring certain co-occurrences while populating the word-context matrix (further details are described below). A word-context matrix is also used in GLoVe, whereas SGNS directly operates on sampled co-occurrences in a streaming manner.

Positive pointwise mutual information (PPMI) is a variant of pointwise mutual information (Fano, 1961; Church and Hanks, 1990), independently developed by Niwa and Nitta (1994) and Bullinaria and Levy (2007). PPMI measures the ratio between observed co-occurrences (normalized and treated as a joint probability) and the expected co-occurrences (based on normalized frequencies treated as individual probabilities) for two words i and j while ignoring all cases in which the observed co-occurrences are fewer than the expected ones:

$$PPMI(i, j) := \begin{cases} 0 & \text{if } \frac{P(i,j)}{P(i)P(j)} < 1 \\ log(\frac{P(i,j)}{P(i)P(j)}) & \text{otherwise} \end{cases}$$

$$(2)$$

Truncated SVD reduces the dimensionality of the vector space described by the PPMI word-context matrix M. SVD factorizes M in three special[1] matrices, so that $M = U\Sigma V^T$. Entries of Σ are ordered by their size, allowing to infer the relative importance of vectors in U and V. This can be used to discard all but the highest d values

---

[1] U and V are orthogonal matrices containing so called singular vectors. Σ is a diagonal matrix containing singular values.

and corresponding vectors during truncated SVD, so that $M_d = U_d \Sigma_d V_d^T \approx M$. Both GLOVE and SGNS start with randomly initialized vectors of the desired dimensionality d and have thus no comparable step in their processing pipeline. However, Levy and Goldberg (2014c) showed SGNS to perform as an approximation of SVD applied to a PPMI matrix.

2.3 Down-sampling

Down-sampling by some factor requires both a formal expression to define the factor, as well as a strategy to perform down-sampling according to this factor—data can either be sampled probabilistically or weighted (see below). The following set of formulae is shared by SGNS and SVD$_{PPMI}$, whereas GLOVE uses a distinct one.

Distance-based down-sampling depends on the distance between the currently modeled token w_i and a second token w_j in a token sequence (such as the above example). The distance d between w_i and w_j is given as:

$$d(w_i, w_j) := |j - i| \qquad (3)$$

To increase the effect of the nearest—and thus assumedly most salient—tokens both SVD$_{PPMI}$ and SGNS down-sample words based on this distance with a distance factor, df (s being the size of the window used for sampling):

$$df(w_i, w_j) := \frac{s + 1 - d(w_i, w_j)}{s} \qquad (4)$$

To limit the effect of high-frequency words— likely to be function words—both algorithms also down-sample words according to a frequency factor (ff), which compares each token's relative frequency $r(w)$ with a threshold t:

$$ff(w) := \begin{cases} \sqrt{t/r(w)} & \text{if } r(w) > t \\ 1 & \text{otherwise} \end{cases} \qquad (5)$$

The frequency down-sampling factor for the co-occurrence of two tokens w_i and w_j is then given by the product of their down-sampling factors, i.e., the probabilities are treated as being independent:

$$ff(w_i, w_j) := ff(w_i) \cdot ff(w_j) \qquad (6)$$

The strategy used to apply these down-sampling factors can affect accuracy and, especially, stability, as can the decision not to apply them at all. These down-sampling processes can either be probabilistic, i.e., each word-context pair is processed with a probability given by $df(w_i, w_j) \cdot$

$ff(w_i, w_j)$, or operate by weighting, i.e., for each observed co-occurrence only a fraction of a count according to the product of df and ff is added to the word-context matrix. SGNS uses probabilistic down-sampling, GLOVE uses weighting and SVD$_{PPMI}$ by Levy et al. (2015) allows for probabilistic down-sampling or no down-sampling at all. As SVD itself is non-probabilistic[2] (Saad, 2003, chs. 6.3 & 7.1) any instability observed for SVD$_{PPMI}$ must be caused by its probabilistic down-sampling. We thus suggest SVD$_{wPPMI}$, i.e., SVD of a PPMI matrix with weighted entries, a simple modification which uses fractional counts according to $df(w_i, w_j) \cdot ff(w_i, w_j)$. As shown in Section 5, this modification is beneficial for both accuracy and stability.

3 Corpora

The corpora used in most stability studies are relatively small. For instance, the largest corpus in Antoniak and Mimno (2018) contains 15M tokens, whereas the corpus used by Hellrich and Hahn (2017) and the largest corpus from Wendlandt et al. (2018) each contain about 60M tokens. Pierrejean and Tanguy (2018) used three corpora of about 100M words each. Two exceptions are Hellrich and Hahn (2016a,b) using relatively large Google Books Ngram corpus subsets (Michel et al., 2011) with 135M to 4.7G n-grams, as well as Chugh et al. (2018) who investigated the influence of embedding dimensionality on stability based on three corpora with only 1.2– 2.6M tokens.[3]

We used three different English corpora as training material: the 2000s decade of the Corpus of Historical American English (COHA; Davies (2012)), the English News Crawl Corpus (NEWS) collected for the 2018 WMT Shared Task[4] and a Wikipedia corpus (WIKI).[5] COHA contains 14k texts and 28M tokens, NEWS 27M texts and 550M tokens, and WIKI 4.5M texts and 1.7G tokens, respectively. COHA was selected as it is commonly used in corpus linguistic studies, whereas NEWS and WIKI serve to gauge the performance of all algorithms in general applica-

---

[2] Assuming that a non-stochastic SVD algorithm (Halko et al., 2011) is used, as in Levy et al. (2015).

[3] Size information from personal communication.

[4] `statmt.org/wmt18/translation-task.html`

[5] To ease replication, we used a pre-compiled 2014 Wikipedia corpus: `linguatools.org/tools/corpora/wikipedia-monolingual-corpora/`

tions. The latter two corpora are far larger than common in stability studies, making our study the largest-scale evaluation of embedding stability we are aware of.

All three corpora were tokenized, transformed to lower case and cleaned from punctuation. We used both the corpora as-is, as well as independently drawn random subsamples (see also Hellrich and Hahn (2016a); Antoniak and Mimno (2018)) to simulate the arbitrary content selection in most corpora—texts could be removed or replaced with similar ones without changing the overall nature of a corpus, e.g., Wikipedia articles are continuously edited. Subsampling allows us to quantify the effect of this arbitrariness on the stability of embeddings, i.e., how consistently word embeddings are trained on variations of a corpus. Subsampling was performed on the level of the constituent texts of each corpus, e.g., individual news articles. For a corpus with n texts we drew n samples with replacement. Texts could be drawn multiple times, but only one copy was kept, reducing corpora to $1 - 1/e \approx 2/3$ of their original size.

4 Experimental Set-up

We compared five algorithm variants: GLOVE, SGNS, SVD_{PPMI} without down-sampling, SVD_{PPMI} with probabilistic down-sampling, and SVD_{wPPMI}. While we could use SGNS[6] and GLOVE[7] implementations directly, we had to modify SVD_{PPMI}[8] to support the weighted sampling used in SVD_{wPPMI}. As proposed by Antoniak and Mimno (2018), we further modified our SVD_{PPMI} implementation to use random numbers generated with a non-fixed seed for probabilistic down-sampling. A fixed seed would benefit reliability, but also act as a bias during all analyses—seed choice has been shown to cause significant differences in experimental results (Henderson et al., 2018).

Down-sampling strategies for df and ff can be chosen independently of each other, e.g., using probabilistic down-sampling for df together with weighted down-sampling for ff. However, we decided to use the same down-sampling strategies, e.g., weighting, for both factors, taking into ac-

count computational limitations as well as results from pre-tests that revealed little benefit of mixed strategies.[9]

We trained ten models for each algorithm variant and corpus.[10] In the case of subsampling, each model was trained on one of the independently drawn samples. Stability was evaluated by selecting the 1k most frequent words in each non-bootstrap subsampled corpus as anchor words and calculating $j@10$ (see Equation 1).[11]

Following Hellrich and Hahn (2016a,b), we did not only investigate stability, but also the accuracy of our models to gauge potential trade-offs. We measured the Spearman rank correlation between cosine-based word similarity judgments and human ones with four psycholinguistic test sets, i.e., the two crowdsourced test sets MEN (Bruni et al., 2012) and MTurk (Radinsky et al., 2011), the especially strict SimLex-999 (Hill et al., 2014) and the widely used WordSim-353 (WS-353; Finkelstein et al. (2002)). We also measured the percentage of correctly solved analogies (using the multiplicative formula from Levy and Goldberg (2014b)) with two test sets developed at Google (Mikolov et al., 2013a) and Microsoft Research (MSR; Mikolov et al. (2013b)).

5 Experimental Results

Table 1 shows the accuracy and stability for all tested combinations of algorithm and corpus variants. Accuracy differences between test sets are in line with prior observations and general

---

[9] The strongest counterexample is a combination of probabilistic down-sampling for df and weighting for ff which lead to small, yet significant improvements in the MEN (0.703 ± 0.001) and MTurk (0.568 ± 0.015) similarity tasks (cf. Table 1). However, other accuracy tasks showed no improvements and the stability of this approach (0.475 ± 0.001) was far closer to SVD_{PPMI} with fully probabilistic down-sampling than to the perfect stability of SVD_{wPPMI}.

[10] Hyperparameters roughly follow Levy et al. (2015). We used symmetric 5 word context windows for all models as well as frequent word down-sampling thresholds of 100 (GLOVE) and 10^{-4} (others). Default learning rates and numbers of iterations were used for all models. Eigenvalues as well as context vectors were ignored for SVD_{PPMI} embeddings. 5 negative samples were used for SGNS. The minimum frequency threshold was 50 for COHA, 100 for NEWS and 750 for WIKI—increased thresholds were necessary due to SVD_{PPMI}'s memory consumption scaling quadratically with vocabulary size.

[11] Stability calculation was not performed directly between all 10 models, as this would result in a single value and preclude significance tests. Instead, we generated ten $j@10$ values by calculating the stability of all subsets formed by leaving out each model once in a jackknife procedure.

---

[6] github.com/tmikolov/word2vec
[7] github.com/stanfordnlp/GloVe
[8] github.com/hellrich/hyperwords – See also further experimental code: github.com/hellrich/embedding_downsampling_comparison

Corpus	Algorithm	Down-sampling	MEN	MTurk	SimLex	WS-353	Google	MSR	Stability
COHA	SVD_{PPMI}	none	0.697	**0.582**	0.318	0.591	0.248	0.226	**1.000**
		prob.	0.689	**0.571**	0.333	0.577	0.224	0.257	0.324
		weight	**0.702**	0.551	0.351	**0.594**	**0.262**	0.277	**1.000**
	SGNS	prob.	0.642	0.560	**0.394**	0.551	0.248	**0.311**	0.288
	GLoVe	weight	0.590	0.522	0.222	0.405	0.167	0.214	0.808
COHA Subs.	SVD_{PPMI}	none	0.645	**0.537**	0.267	**0.569**	0.192	0.184	0.310
		prob.	0.632	**0.519**	0.287	0.542	0.169	0.203	0.198
		weight	**0.651**	**0.534**	0.305	**0.568**	**0.206**	0.235	0.329
	SGNS	prob.	0.551	0.486	**0.363**	0.479	0.192	**0.243**	0.091
	GLoVe	weight	0.518	0.470	0.182	0.383	0.120	0.165	**0.330**
NEWS	SVD_{PPMI}	none	0.775	0.559	0.406	0.643	0.469	0.357	**1.000**
		prob.	0.784	0.561	0.431	0.666	0.492	0.445	0.654
		weight	**0.786**	0.568	**0.435**	0.667	0.502	0.444	**1.000**
	SGNS	prob.	0.739	**0.675**	0.430	**0.672**	**0.643**	**0.553**	0.652
	GLoVe	weight	0.698	0.576	0.309	0.536	0.548	0.444	0.679
NEWS Subs.	SVD_{PPMI}	none	0.771	0.558	0.401	0.623	0.445	0.335	0.584
		prob.	0.776	0.564	0.423	0.642	0.463	0.420	0.571
		weight	**0.781**	0.567	**0.430**	**0.649**	0.476	0.421	**0.635**
	SGNS	prob.	0.734	**0.673**	0.417	**0.647**	**0.601**	**0.513**	0.452
	GLoVe	weight	0.687	0.572	0.301	0.508	0.505	0.408	0.461
WIKI	SVD_{PPMI}	none	0.731	0.510	0.353	0.715	0.432	0.246	**1.000**
		prob.	**0.747**	0.571	0.392	**0.718**	0.482	0.311	0.714
		weight	0.743	0.560	**0.393**	**0.717**	0.482	0.305	**1.000**
	SGNS	prob.	0.735	**0.659**	0.372	**0.717**	**0.669**	**0.421**	0.488
	GLoVe	weight	0.744	0.651	0.354	0.667	0.653	0.397	0.666
WIKI Subs.	SVD_{PPMI}	none	0.726	0.526	0.355	0.699	0.410	0.244	0.635
		prob.	**0.742**	0.568	**0.391**	**0.706**	0.448	0.304	0.604
		weight	0.740	0.555	**0.389**	0.704	0.451	0.300	**0.651**
	SGNS	prob.	0.723	**0.657**	0.364	0.686	**0.629**	**0.407**	0.501
	GLoVe	weight	0.735	0.642	0.345	0.655	0.599	0.382	0.486

Table 1: Performance of different algorithms and down-sampling strategies with models trained on corpora with and without subsampling. **Bold** values are best or not significantly different by independent t-tests (with $p < 0.05$).

performance on WIKI is roughly in-line with the data reported in Levy et al. (2015).

In general, corpus size does seem to have a positive effect on accuracy. However, for MEN, MTurk and MSR the highest values are achieved with NEWS and not with WIKI. SVD_{PPMI} variants seem to be less hampered by small training corpora, matching observations by Sahlgren and Lenci (2016). Stability is clearly positively influenced by corpus size for all probabilistic algorithm variants except GLoVe, which, in contrast, benefits from small training corpora. Also, randomly subsampling corpora has a negative effect on both accuracy and stability—this can be explained by the smaller corpus size for accuracy and the differences in training material (as subsampling was performed independently for each model) for stability.

Figure 1 illustrates the stability of all tested algorithm variants. SVD_{wPPMI} and SVD_{PPMI} without down-sampling are the only systems which achieve perfect stability when trained on non-subsampled corpora. GLoVe is the third most reliable algorithm in this scenario, except for the large WIKI corpus. Corpus subsampling decreases the stability of all algorithms, with SVD_{wPPMI} still performing better than all other alternatives. The only exception is subsampled COHA where the otherwise suboptimal GLoVe narrowly (0.330 instead of 0.329; difference significant with $p < .05$ by two-sided t-test) outperforms SVD_{wPPMI}. SVD_{wPPMI} can achieve stability values on subsampled corpora that are competitive with those for SGNS and GLoVe trained on **non**-subsampled corpora. We found standard deviations for stability to be very low, the highest being 0.01 for GLoVe trained on non-subsampled WIKI, probably due to the overlap in our jackknife procedure.

Finally, we tested[12] the overall performance of each algorithm variant by first performing a Quade test (Quade, 1979) as a safeguard against type I

---

[12] All tests were conducted on the averaged accuracy values of the ten individual models per corpus (both subsampled and as-is) and algorithm variant (as listed in Table 1). Using the models directly would have been ill-advised because of their overlapping training data (see Demšar (2006, p. 15)). Analyses on individual corpora would have resulted in insufficient samples given the pre-conditions of our tests.

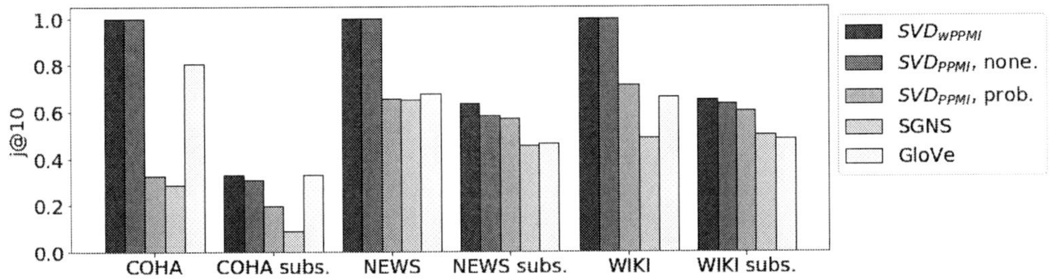

Figure 1: Stability for each combination of algorithm variant and corpus. Measured with j@10 metric (higher is better). Same data as in Table 1, standard deviations too small to display.

errors, thus confirming the existence of significant differences between algorithms ($p = 1.3 \cdot 10^{-7}$). We then used a pairwise Wilcoxon rank-sum test with Holm-Šidák correction (see Demšar (2006)) in order to compare other algorithms with SVD_{wPPMI}.[13] We found it to be not significantly different in accuracy from SGNS ($p = 0.101$), but significantly better than SVD_{PPMI} without down-sampling (corrected $p = 5.4 \cdot 10^{-6}$) or probabilistic down-sampling (corrected $p = 0.015$), as well as GLOVE (corrected $p = 0.027$).

Our results show SVD_{wPPMI} to be both highly reliable and accurate, especially on COHA, which has a size common in both stability studies and corpus linguistic applications. Diverging reports on SVD_{PPMI} stability—described as perfectly reliable in Hellrich and Hahn (2017), yet not in Antoniak and Mimno (2018)—can thus be explained by their difference in down-sampling options, i.e., no down-sampling or probabilistic down-sampling. GLOVE's high stability in other studies (Antoniak and Mimno, 2018; Wendlandt et al., 2018) seems to be counterbalanced by its low accuracy and also appears to be limited to training on small corpora.

6 Discussion

We investigated the effect of down-sampling strategies on word embedding stability by comparing five algorithm variants on three corpora, two of which were larger than those typically used in stability studies. We proposed a simple modification to the down-sampling strategy used for the SVD_{PPMI} algorithm, SVD_{wPPMI}, which uses weighting, to achieve an otherwise unmatched combination of accuracy and stability. We also gathered evidence that GLOVE lacks accuracy and is only stable when trained on small corpora.

We thus recommend using SVD_{wPPMI}, especially for studies targeting (qualitative) interpretations of semantic spaces (e.g., Kim et al. (2014)). Overall, SGNS provided no benefit in accuracy over SVD_{wPPMI} and the latter seemed especially well-suited for small training corpora. The only downside of SVD_{wPPMI} we are aware of is its relatively large memory consumption during training shared by all SVD_{PPMI} variants.

Further research could investigate the performance of SVD_{wPPMI} with other sets of hyperparameters or scrutinize the effect of down-sampling strategies on the ill-understood geometry of embedding spaces (Mimno and Thompson, 2017). It would also be interesting to investigate the effect of down-sampling and stability on downstream tasks in a follow-up to Wendlandt et al. (2018).

Finally, the increasingly popular contextualized embedding algorithms, e.g., BERT (Devlin et al., 2018) or ELMo (Peters et al., 2018), are also probabilistic in nature and should thus be affected by stability problems. A direct transfer of our type specific evaluation strategy is impossible. However, an indirect one could be achieved by averaging token-specific contextualized embeddings to generate type representations.

Acknowledgments

This work was supported by the German Federal Ministry of Education and Research (BMBF) within the *SMITH* project (grant 01ZZ1803G), Deutsche Forschungsgemeinschaft (DFG) within the *STAKI²B²* project (grant HA 2097/8-1), the SFB *AquaDiva* (CRC 1076) and the Graduate School *The Romantic Model* (GRK 2041/1).

---

[13] This test is a non-parametric alternative to the t-test; corrections prevent false results due to multiple comparisons.

References

Maria Antoniak and David Mimno. 2018. Evaluating the stability of embedding-based word similarities. *Transactions of the Association for Computational Linguistics*, 6:107–120.

M. W. Berry. 1992. Large-scale sparse singular value computations. *The International Journal of Supercomputer Applications*, 6(1):13–49.

Elia Bruni, Gemma Boleda, Marco Baroni, and Nam Khanh Tran. 2012. Distributional semantics in technicolor. In *ACL 2012 — Proceedings of the 50th Annual Meeting of the Association for Computational Linguistics: Long Papers. Jeju Island, Republic of Korea, July 8–14, 2012*, pages 136–145.

John A. Bullinaria and Joseph P. Levy. 2007. Extracting semantic representations from word co-occurrence statistics: a computational study. *Behavior Research Methods*, 39(3):510–526.

Mansi Chugh, Peter A. Whigham, and Grant Dick. 2018. Stability of word embeddings using word2vec. In *Advances in Artificial Intelligence. AI 2018 — Proceedings of the 31st Australasian Joint Conference on Artificial Intelligence. Wellington, New Zealand. December 11-14, 2018*, pages 812–818.

Kenneth Ward Church and Patrick Hanks. 1990. Word association norms, mutual information, and lexicography. *Computational Linguistics*, 16(1):22–29.

Enrico Coiera, Elske Ammenwerth, Andrew Georgiou, and Farah Magrabi. 2018. Does health informatics have a replication crisis? *Journal of the American Medical Informatics Association*, 25(8):963–968.

Mark Davies. 2012. Expanding horizons in historical linguistics with the 400-million word Corpus of Historical American English. *Corpora*, 7:121–157.

Janez Demšar. 2006. Statistical comparisons of classifiers over multiple data sets. *Journal of Machine Learning Research*, 7:1–30.

Jacob Devlin, Ming-Wei Chang, Kenton Lee, and Kristina Toutanova. 2018. BERT: pre-training of deep bidirectional transformers for language understanding. http://arxiv.org/abs/1810.04805.

Robert M. Fano. 1961. *Transmission of Information. A Statistical Theory of Communications*. MIT Press. 3rd printing, 1966.

Lev Finkelstein, Evgeniy Gabrilovich, Yossi Matias, Ehud Rivlin, Zach Solan, Gadi Wolfman, and Eytan Ruppin. 2002. Placing search in context: the concept revisited. *ACM Transactions on Information Systems*, 20(1):116–131.

Nathan Halko, Per-Gunnar Martinsson, and Joel A. Tropp. 2011. Finding structure with randomness: probabilistic algorithms for constructing approximate matrix decompositions. *SIAM Review*, 53(2):217–288.

Zellig S. Harris. 1954. Distributional structure. *Word*, 10(2-3):146–162.

Johannes Hellrich, Sven Buechel, and Udo Hahn. 2018. JeSeme: a website for exploring diachronic changes in word meaning and emotion. In *COLING 2018 — Proceedings of the 27th International Conference on Computational Linguistics: System Demonstrations. Santa Fe, NM, USA, August 20–26, 2018*, pages 10–14.

Johannes Hellrich and Udo Hahn. 2016a. An assessment of experimental protocols for tracing changes in word semantics relative to accuracy and reliability. In *LaTeCH 2016 — Proceedings of the 10th SIGHUM Workshop on Language Technology for Cultural Heritage, Social Sciences, and Humanities @ ACL 2016, Berlin, Germany, August 11, 2016*, pages 111–117.

Johannes Hellrich and Udo Hahn. 2016b. Bad company: neighborhoods in neural embedding spaces considered harmful. In *COLING 2016 — Proceedings of the 26th International Conference on Computational Linguistics: Technical Papers. Osaka, Japan, December 11–16, 2016*, pages 2785–2796.

Johannes Hellrich and Udo Hahn. 2017. Don't get fooled by word embeddings: better watch their neighborhood. In *Digital Humanities 2017 — Conference Abstracts of the 2017 Conference of the Alliance of Digital Humanities Organizations (ADHO). Montréal, Quebec, Canada, August 8–11, 2017*, pages 250–252.

Peter Henderson, Riashat Islam, Philip Bachman, Joelle Pineau, Doina Precup, and David Meger. 2018. Deep reinforcement learning that matters. In *AAAI-IAAI-EAAI '18 — Proceedings of the 32nd AAAI Conference on Artificial Intelligence & 30th Conference on Innovative Applications of Artificial Intelligence & 8th Symposium on Educational Advances in Artificial Intelligence. New Orleans, Louisiana, USA, February 2-7, 2018*, pages 3207–3214.

Felix Hill, Roi Reichart, and Anna Korhonen. 2014. SimLex-999: Evaluating semantic models with (genuine) similarity estimation. *Computational Linguistics*, 41(4):665–695.

Peter Ivie and Douglas Thain. 2018. Reproducibility in scientific computing. *ACM Computing Surveys*, 51(3):63:1–63:36.

Paul Jaccard. 1912. The distribution of the flora in the alpine zone. *New Phytologist*, XI(2):37–50. [Translation of 1901 article].

Yoon Kim, Yi-I Chiu, Kentaro Hanaki, Darshan Hegde, and Slav Petrov. 2014. Temporal analysis of language through neural language models. In *Proceedings of the Workshop on Language Technologies and Computational Social Science @ ACL 2014. Baltimore, Maryland, USA, June 26, 2014*, pages 61–65.

Vivek Kulkarni, Rami Al-Rfou, Bryan Perozzi, and Steven Skiena. 2015. Statistically significant detection of linguistic change. In *WWW 2015 — Proceedings of the 24th International Conference on World Wide Web: Technical Papers. Florence, Italy, May 18–22, 2015*, pages 625–635.

Omer Levy and Yoav Goldberg. 2014a. Dependency-based word embeddings. In *ACL 2014 — Proceedings of the 52nd Annual Meeting of the Association for Computational Linguistics: Short Papers. Baltimore, Maryland, USA, June 22–27, 2014*, pages 302–308.

Omer Levy and Yoav Goldberg. 2014b. Linguistic regularities in sparse and explicit word representations. In *CoNLL 2014 — Proceedings of the 18th Conference on Computational Natural Language Learning @ ACL 2014. Baltimore, Maryland, USA, June 26-27, 2014*, pages 171–180.

Omer Levy and Yoav Goldberg. 2014c. Neural word embedding as implicit matrix factorization. In *Advances in Neural Information Processing Systems 27 — NIPS 2014. Proceedings of the 28th Annual Conference on Neural Information Processing Systems 2014. Montréal, Québec, Canada, December 8-13, 2014*, pages 2177–2185.

Omer Levy, Yoav Goldberg, and Ido Dagan. 2015. Improving distributional similarity with lessons learned from word embeddings. *Transactions of the Association for Computational Linguistics*, 3:211–225.

Jean-Baptiste Michel, Yuan Kui Shen, Aviva Presser Aiden, Adrian Veres, Matthew K. Gray, The Google Books Team, Joseph P. Pickett, Dale Hoiberg, Dan Clancy, Peter Norvig, Jon Orwant, Steven Pinker, Martin A. Nowak, and Erez Lieberman Aiden. 2011. Quantitative analysis of culture using millions of digitized books. *Science*, 331(6014):176–182.

Tomas Mikolov, Kai Chen, Gregory S. Corrado, and Jeffrey Dean. 2013a. Efficient estimation of word representations in vector space. In *ICLR 2013 — Workshop Proceedings of the International Conference on Learning Representations. Scottsdale, Arizona, USA, May 2–4, 2013*. https://arxiv.org/abs/1301.3781.

Tomas Mikolov, Wen-tau Yih, and Geoffrey Zweig. 2013b. Linguistic regularities in continuous space word representations. In *NAACL-HLT 2013 — Proceedings of the 2013 Conference of the North American Chapter of the Association for Computational Linguistics: Human Language Technologies. Atlanta, GA, USA, 9–14 June 2013*, pages 746–751.

Tomáš Mikolov, Ilya Sutskever, Kai Chen, Gregory S. Corrado, and Jeffrey Dean. 2013c. Distributed representations of words and phrases and their compositionality. In *Advances in Neural Information Processing Systems 26 — NIPS 2013. Proceedings of the 27th Annual Conference on Neural Information Processing Systems. Lake Tahoe, Nevada, USA, December 5-10, 2013*, pages 3111–3119.

David Mimno and Laure Thompson. 2017. The strange geometry of skip-gram with negative sampling. In *EMNLP 2017 — Proceedings of the 2017 Conference on Empirical Methods in Natural Language Processing. Copenhagen, Denmark, September 7–11, 2017*, pages 2863–2868.

Yoshiki Niwa and Yoshihiko Nitta. 1994. Co-occurrence vectors from corpora vs. distance vectors from dictionaries. In *COLING 1994 — Proceedings of the 15th Conference on Computational Linguistics: Volume 1. Kyoto, Japan, August 5–9, 1994*, pages 304–309.

Muntsa Padró, Marco Idiart, Aline Villavicencio, and Carlos Ramisch. 2014. Comparing similarity measures for distributional thesauri. In *LREC 2014 — Proceedings of the 9th International Conference on Language Resources and Evaluation. Reykjavik, Iceland, May 26-31, 2014*, pages 2694–2971.

Jeffrey Pennington, Richard Socher, and Christopher D. Manning. 2014. GloVe: Global vectors for word representation. In *EMNLP 2014 — Proceedings of the 2014 Conference on Empirical Methods in Natural Language Processing. Doha, Qatar, October 25–29, 2014*, pages 1532–1543.

Matthew E. Peters, Mark Neumann, Mohit Iyyer, Matt Gardner, Christopher T. Clark, Kenton Lee, and Luke S. Zettlemoyer. 2018. Deep contextualized word representations. In *NAACL-HLT 2018 — Proceedings of the 2018 Conference of the North American Chapter of the Association for Computational Linguistics: Human Language Technologies. New Orleans, Louisiana, USA, June 1-6, 2018*, volume 1: Long Papers, pages 2227–2237.

Bénédicte Pierrejean and Ludovic Tanguy. 2018. Étude de la reproductibilité des word embeddings: repérage des zones stables et instables dans le lexique. In *TALN 2018 — Actes de la 25ème conférence sur le Traitement Automatique des Langues Naturelles. Rennes, France, 14-18 Mai, 2018.*, volume 1: Articles longs, articles courts de TALN, pages 33–46.

Dana Quade. 1979. Using weighted rankings in the analysis of complete blocks with additive block effects. *Journal of the American Statistical Association*, 74(367):680–683.

Kira Radinsky, Eugene Agichtein, Evgeniy Gabrilovich, and Shaul Markovitch. 2011. A word at a time: computing word relatedness using temporal semantic analysis. In *WWW 2011 —*

Proceedings of the 20th International Conference on World Wide Web. Hyderabad, India, March 28 - April 1, 2011, pages 337–346.

Nils Reimers and Iryna Gurevych. 2017. Reporting score distributions makes a difference: performance study of LSTM-networks for sequence tagging. In *EMNLP 2017 — Proceedings of the 2017 Conference on Empirical Methods in Natural Language Processing. Copenhagen, Denmark, September 9-11, 2017*, pages 338–348.

Herbert Rubenstein and John B. Goodenough. 1965. Contextual correlates of synonymy. *Communications of the ACM*, 8(10):627–633.

Yousef Saad. 2003. *Iterative Methods for Sparse Linear Systems*, 2nd edition. Society for Industrial and Applied Mathematics, Philadelphia/PA.

Magnus Sahlgren and Alessandro Lenci. 2016. The effects of data size and frequency range on distributional semantic models. In *EMNLP 2016 — Proceedings of the 2016 Conference on Empirical Methods in Natural Language Processing. Austin, Texas, USA, November 1–5, 2016*, pages 975–980.

Gerald Salton and Michael E. Lesk. 1971. Information analysis and dictionary construction. In Gerald Salton, editor, *The* SMART *Retrieval System: Experiments in Automatic Document Processing*, chapter 6, pages 115–142. Prentice-Hall, Englewood Cliffs/NJ.

Julie Weeds, David Weir, and Diana McCarthy. 2004. Characterising measures of lexical distributional similarity. In *COLING 2004 — Proceedings of the 20th International Conference on Computational Linguistics. Geneva, Switzerland, Aug 23–27, 2004*, pages 1015–1021.

Laura Wendlandt, Jonathan K. Kummerfeld, and Rada Mihalcea. 2018. Factors influencing the surprising instability of word embeddings. In *NAACL-HLT 2018 — Proceedings of the 2018 Conference of the North American Chapter of the Association for Computational Linguistics: Human Language Technologies: Long Papers. New Orleans, LA, USA, June 2–4, 2018*, pages 2092–2102.

How Well Do Embedding Models Capture Non-compositionality? A View from Multiword Expressions

Navnita Nandakumar   **Timothy Baldwin**   **Bahar Salehi**

School of Computing and Information Systems

The University of Melbourne

Victoria 3010, Australia

nnandakumar@student.unimelb.edu.au   {tbaldwin|salehi.b}@unimelb.edu.au

Abstract

In this paper, we apply various embedding methods to multiword expressions to study how well they capture the nuances of non-compositional data. Our results from a range of word-, character-, and document-level embbedings suggest that word2vec performs the best, followed by fastText and infersent. Moreover, we find that recently-proposed contextualised embedding models such as BERT and ELMo are not adept at handling non-compositionality in multiword expressions.

1 Introduction

Modern embedding models, including contextual embeddings, have been shown to work impressively well across a range of tasks (Peters et al., 2018; Devlin et al., 2018). However, study of their performance on data with a mix of compositionality levels, whose meaning is often not easily predicted from that of its constituent words, has been limited (Salehi et al., 2015; Hakimi Parizi and Cook, 2018; Nandakumar et al., 2018).

At present, there exists no definitive metric to measure the modelling capabilities of an embedding technique across a spectrum of non-compositionality, especially in the case of newer, contextualised representations, such as ELMo and BERT.

In this study, we apply various embedding methods to the task of determining the compositionality of English multiword expressions ("MWEs"), specifically noun–noun and adjective–noun pairs, to test their performance on data representing a range of compositionality (Sag et al., 2002). Compositionality prediction can be modeled as a regression task (Baldwin and Kim, 2010) that involves mapping an MWE onto a continuous scale, representing its compositionality as a whole or with respect to each of its components. For example, *application form* can be considered

to be quite compositional, while *sitting duck*[1] is considered to be idiomatic or non-compositional. *Close shave*[2] could be seen as partially compositional, heavily compositional with regards to the first word and less compositional with regards to the second. In this study, we focus on predicting the compositionality of the MWE as a whole. Although we conduct our experiments on English datasets, they can be applied to other languages with ease as we do not perform any kind of language-specific manipulation of the data.

The main contributions of this paper are:

(i) we compare embeddings over 3 different MWE datasets, focusing on noun–noun and adjective–noun pairs;

(ii) we experiment with 7 character-, word-, and document-level embedding models, including contextualised models;

(iii) we show that, despite their success on a range of other tasks, recent embedding learning methods lag behind simple word2vec in capturing MWE non-compositionality.

2 Related Work

Although vector space models have been popular since the 1990s, it was only after Collobert and Weston (2008) proposed a unified neural network architecture to learning distributed word representations and demonstrated its performance on downstream tasks, that embedding learning established a footing in NLP, with word2vec (Mikolov et al., 2013a) being the catalyst to the "embedding revolution".

Language embeddings are an example of an unsupervised representation learning application done well. They are preferred primarily because they can be learned from unannotated corpora and,

---

[1]A *sitting duck* means "a person or thing with no protection against an attack or other source of danger."

[2]A *close shave* is "a narrow escape from danger or disaster."

27

Proceedings of the 3rd Workshop on Evaluating Vector Space Representations for NLP, pages 27–34

Minneapolis, USA, June 6, 2019. ©2019 Association for Computational Linguistics

therefore, eliminate the need for manual annotation (which is expensive and time-consuming).

Salehi et al. (2015) were the first to apply word embeddings to the task of predicting the compositionality of MWEs. The assumption is that the compositionality of an MWE is proportional to the relative similarity between each of the components and the overall MWE, represented by their respective embeddings. This method was recently tuned variously by Cordeiro et al. (2019) and remains state-of-the-art for the task of MWE compositionality prediction, but has the downside that it requires automatic token-level pre-identification of each MWE in the training corpus in order to train a model (i.e. all occurrences of *sitting duck* need to be pre-tokenised to a single token, such as *sitting_duck*). This is not ideal, as it means the model will need to be retrained for a new set of MWEs (as the tokenisation will necessarily change). It also requires "complete" knowledge of the MWEs before the training step, which is impractical in most cases.

Character-level embedding models (Hakimi Parizi and Cook, 2018) are one possible solution to the fixed-vocabulary problem, in being able to handle an unbounded vocabulary, including MWEs. Document embeddings (Le and Mikolov, 2014; Conneau et al., 2017a) are also highly relevant to dynamically generating embeddings for MWEs, as they generate representations of arbitrary spans of text, which are potentially able to capture the context of use of the MWE.

3 Methodology

Following Salehi et al. (2015) and Nandakumar et al. (2018), we compute the overall compositionality of an MWE with three broad metrics: direct composition, paraphrase similarity, and a combined metric. In all experiments, the similarity of a pair of vectors is measured using cosine similarity.

3.1 Direct Composition

Intuitively, an MWE appearing in similar contexts to its components is likely to be compositional. We directly compare the vector embedding of the MWE (described in Section 4.2) with that of its component words, in one of two ways: (1) performing an element-wise sum to obtain a 'combined' vector, which is then compared with the vector of the MWE ($\text{Direct}_{\text{pre}}$); and (2) a post-hoc combination of the scores obtained by individually comparing the component vectors with that of the MWE via a weighted sum ($\text{Direct}_{\text{post}}$). Formally:

$$\text{Direct}_{\text{pre}} = \cos(\mathbf{mwe}, \mathbf{w_1} + \mathbf{w_2})$$
$$\text{Direct}_{\text{post}} = \alpha \cos(\mathbf{mwe}, \mathbf{w_1}) +$$
$$(1 - \alpha) \cos(\mathbf{mwe}, \mathbf{w_2}),$$

where: $\mathbf{mwe}$, $\mathbf{w_1}$, and $\mathbf{w_2}$ are the embeddings for the combined MWE, first component and second component, respectively;[3] $\mathbf{w_1} + \mathbf{w_2}$ is the element-wise sum of the vectors of each of the component words of the MWE; and $\alpha \in [0, 1]$ is a scalar which allows us to vary the weight of the respective components in predicting the compositionality of the compound. This helps us effectively capture the compositionality of the MWE with regards to each of its individual constituents.

We do not perform any tuning of α over held-out data and are, as such, overfitting as we select the best-performing α post hoc. We do, however, present analysis of hyper-parameter sensitivity in Section 5.

3.2 Paraphrase Similarity

Assuming access to paraphrases of an MWE, another intuition is that if the MWE appears in similar contexts to the component words of its paraphrases, it is likely to be compositional (Shwartz and Waterson, 2018). Each paraphrase provides an interpretation of the semantics of the MWE, e.g. *ancient history* is "in the past", "old news" or "forever ago" (note how each paraphrase brings out a slightly different interpretation). The RAMISCH MWE dataset (described in Section 4.1) provides one or more paraphrases for each MWE contained in it. We calculate the similarity of the embeddings of the MWE and its paraphrases using the following three formulae:

$$\text{Para\_first} = \cos(\mathbf{mwe}, \mathbf{para_1})$$
$$\text{Para\_all}_{\text{pre}} = \cos(\mathbf{mwe}, \sum_i \mathbf{para_i})$$
$$\text{Para\_all}_{\text{post}} = \frac{1}{N} \sum_{i=1}^{N} \cos(\mathbf{mwe}, \mathbf{para_i}),$$

where $\mathbf{para_1}$ and $\mathbf{para_i}$ denote the embedding for the first (most popular) and i-th paraphrases, respectively.

---

[3] All methods are presented and evaluated in terms of two-element MWEs in this work, but are trivially generalisable to multi-element MWEs.

In the case of Para_all$_{\text{post}}$, we considered computing the maximum instead of the average (as we report here) of the similarity scores between each paraphrase and its MWE, following the intuition that an MWE would be similar to at least one reported paraphrase, rather than all of them. However, the results for the average similarity were empirically higher across models.

3.3 Combined Metric

Finally, we present the combined results from the two metrics stated above:

$$\begin{aligned} \text{Combined} = &\beta \max\left(\text{Direct}_{\text{pre}}, \text{Direct}_{\text{post}}\right) + \\ &(1-\beta) \max\left(\text{Para\_first}, \text{Para\_all}_{\text{pre}}, \right. \\ &\left. \text{Para\_all}_{\text{post}}\right), \end{aligned}$$

where $\beta \in [0, 1]$ is a scalar weighting factor used to balance the effects of the two methods, in order to measure the extent to which the compositionality is determined by each of the methods. The choice of the max operator here to combine the sub-methods for each of the direct composition and paraphrase methods is that all methods tend to underestimate the compositionality (and empirically, it was found to be superior to taking the mean).

4 Experiments

4.1 Datasets

We used three datasets for our experiments, evaluating each model's performance using Pearson's correlation coefficient (r) to compare the similarity scores obtained with the annotated compositionality scores provided in the dataset.

REDDY The dataset of Reddy et al. (2011) contains 90 binary English noun compounds ("NCs"), along with human-annotated scores of their overall compositionality and component-specific compositionality, both ranging from 0 to 5. For our experiments, we consider the overall compositionality scores only.

RAMISCH Similar to REDDY, the English dataset of Ramisch et al. (2016) contains 90 binary noun compounds with annotated scores of compositionality ranging from 0 to 5, both overall and component-specific (of which we use only the former). It also contains a list of paraphrases for each NC, presented in decreasing order of popularity among the annotators.

Dataset	μ	σ
REDDY	53.2	30.0
RAMISCH	52.6	35.0
DISCO	68.1	21.7
Overall	59.7	29.0

Table 1: Mean (μ) and standard deviation (σ) of the compositionality scores for the three datasets used in this research, over a normalised range $[0, 100]$.

DISCO$_{\text{ADJ}}$ The English dataset from the DiSCo shared task (Biemann and Giesbrecht, 2011) containing a total of 348 binary phrases, comprising adjective–noun, verb–noun$_{\text{subj}}$, and verb–noun$_{\text{obj}}$ pairs, along with their overall compositionality rating ranging from 0 to 100. The phrases were extracted semi-automatically and their relations were assigned by patterns and checked manually. The compositionality scores were collected from Amazon Mechanical Turk, where workers were presented 4–5 randomly sampled sentences from the UK English WACKy corpora. We focus on the 144 adjective–noun pairs in this study.

The breakdown of compositionality scores across the three datasets in Table 1 indicates there is a reasonable distribution of data in terms of compositionality, with REDDY and RAMISCH being roughly comparable and covering a broad (and somewhat balanced) spectrum of compositionalities, while DISCO is more skewed towards compositional usages, with lower standard deviation.

4.2 Embeddings

We made use of various embeddings, ranging from character- to document-level, in our study. Below is a description of each model along with how they are trained. Where available, we made use of pre-trained models as is standard practice in NLP. As the different models were trained on different corpora, we are not attempting to perform a controlled comparative evaluation of the different models, so much as a comparison of the standard pre-trained versions of each. If we were to retrain our own models over a standard dataset such as English Wikipedia, we would expect the results for the document-level embedding methods in particular to drop.

4.2.1 Word-level

A word embedding captures the context of a word in a document (in relation to other words) in the form of a vector representation. It tokenises text at the word level.

word2vec We trained word2vec (Mikolov et al., 2013b) on a recent English Wikipedia dump,[4] after pre-processing (removing the formatting and punctuation) and concatenating each occurrence of the multiword expressions in our datasets (e.g. every occurrence of *close shave* in the corpus becomes *closeshave*). We make the greedy assumption that every occurence of the component words in sequence is an occurrence of the expression. We perform this token-level identification and manipulation of the corpus in order to obtain a single embedding for the expression, instead of a separate embeddings for the individual component words. In cases where the model still fails to generate an embedding (2 for REDDY, 8 for RAMISCH and 25 for DISCO) for the expression (due to low token frequency), we assign a default compositionality score of 0.5 (neutral; based on a range of $[0, 1]$). For paraphrases, we compute an element-wise sum of the embeddings for each of the component words to serve as the embedding of the phrase. We do this because token-level identification of each paraphrase in the training corpus is not practical.

4.2.2 Character-level

Character-level embeddings can generate vectors for words based on n-gram character aggregations. This means they can generate embeddings for out-of-vocabulary (OOV) words, as well new words or misspelled words. It tokenises text at the character level.

fastText We used the 300-dimensional fastText model pre-trained on Common Crawl and Wikipedia using CBOW ($fastText_{pre}$), as well as one trained over the same Wikipedia corpus[4] using skip-gram (fastText). Again, since fastText (Bojanowski et al., 2017) assumes all words to be whitespace delimited, we preprocess our MWE and paraphrases the same way as above (removing the space between them so that *armchair critic* becomes *armchaircritic*, say).

Contextualised Embeddings Unlike classical embedding techniques, contextualised embeddings capture the semantics of a word or phrase in a manner which is sensitised to the context of usage.

We used the pretrained implementations of ELMo (Peters et al., 2018) and BERT (Devlin et al., 2018) found in the Flair framework.[5] The framework also has a contextualised string embedding model of its own, also named Flair (Akbik et al., 2018).

We supplied sentences extracted from the Brown corpus where available in order to derive a contextualised interpretation. We extracted 25 sentences at random per MWE, except where there were fewer sentences in the corpus.

However, we also included a naive context-independent implementation in our study, consistent with the other models, following the intuition that the relative compositionality of even a novel compound can often be predicted from its component words alone (e.g. *giraffe potato* having the plausible compositional interpretation of a potato shaped like a giraffe vs. *couch intelligence* having no natural interpretation).

4.2.3 Document-level

Document embeddings aggregate from words to documents, generating vector representations for entire documents. Since document and sentence embeddings are capable of generating a single embedding for a span of text, we are able to generate representations of the MWEs and paraphrases without preprocessing them (to remove space). We treat each constituent word as a single word document to generate embeddings.

infersent We used two versions of infersent (Conneau et al., 2017b): $infersent_{GloVe}$ and $infersent_{fastText}$. Each generates a representation of 300 dimensions, trained over the 1,000,000 most popular English words using GloVe (Pennington et al., 2014) and fastText, respectively.

doc2vec We used the gensim implementation of doc2vec (Le and Mikolov, 2014; Lau and Baldwin, 2016) pretrained on Wikipedia data using the word2vec skip-gram models pretrained on Wikipedia and AP News.[6]

---

[4] Dated 07-Jan-2019

Emb. method	$\text{Direct}_{\text{pre}}$	$\text{Direct}_{\text{post}}$	Para_first	$\text{Para\_all}_{\text{pre}}$	$\text{Para\_all}_{\text{post}}$	Combined
Flair	0.165	$0.295\,(\alpha = 0.1)$	0.334	0.399	0.492	$0.492\,(\beta = 0.0)$
$\text{Flair}_{\text{context}}$	0.181	$0.314\,(\alpha = 0.1)$	0.357	0.411	0.522	$0.522\,(\beta = 0.0)$
$\text{fastText}_{\text{pre}}$	0.395	$0.446\,(\alpha = 0.7)$	0.242	0.531	0.703	$0.703\,(\beta = 0.0)$
fastText	0.464	$0.532\,(\alpha = 0.7)$	0.548	0.613	0.673	$0.673\,(\beta = 0.0)$
BERT	0.071	$0.086\,(\alpha = 1.0)$	0.242	0.531	0.583	$0.583\,(\beta = 0.0)$
$\text{BERT}_{\text{context}}$	0.089	$0.111\,(\alpha = 1.0)$	0.267	0.546	0.601	$0.601\,(\beta = 0.0)$
ELMo	0.420	$0.459\,(\alpha = 0.6)$	0.361	0.488	0.546	$0.546\,(\beta = 0.2)$
$\text{ELMo}_{\text{context}}$	0.461	$0.489\,(\alpha = 0.6)$	0.373	0.492	0.552	$0.627\,(\beta = 0.2)$
word2vec	**0.581**	$\mathbf{0.571}\,(\alpha = 0.6)$	0.443	0.510	0.504	$0.677\,(\beta = 0.9)$
$\text{infersent}_{\text{GloVe}}$	0.321	$0.427\,(\alpha = 0.7)$	**0.636**	0.700	**0.741**	$\mathbf{0.783}\,(\beta = 0.5)$
$\text{infersent}_{\text{fastText}}$	0.169	$0.221\,(\alpha = 0.6)$	0.488	**0.712**	0.636	$0.774\,(\beta = 0.0)$
doc2vec	-0.157	$0.039\,(\alpha = 1.0)$	0.388	0.334	0.373	$0.419\,(\beta = 0.3)$

Table 2: Pearson correlation coefficient for compositionality prediction results on the RAMISCH dataset.

Emb. method	$\text{Direct}_{\text{pre}}$	$\text{Direct}_{\text{post}}$
Flair	-0.127	$0.024\,(\alpha = 0.0)$
$\text{Flair}_{\text{context}}$	0.012	$0.172\,(\alpha = 0.0)$
$\text{fastText}_{\text{pre}}$	0.223	$0.285\,(\alpha = 0.3, 0.4)$
fastText	0.217	$0.287\,(\alpha = 0.3, 0.4)$
BERT	0.304	$0.352\,(\alpha = 0.2)$
$\text{BERT}_{\text{context}}$	0.313	$0.377\,(\alpha = 0.2)$
ELMo	0.339	$0.406\,(\alpha = 0.5)$
$\text{ELMo}_{\text{context}}$	0.387	$0.416\,(\alpha = 0.5)$
word2vec	**0.634**	$\mathbf{0.622}\,(\alpha = 0.6)$
$\text{infersent}_{\text{GloVe}}$	0.413	$0.500\,(\alpha = 0.5)$
$\text{infersent}_{\text{fastText}}$	0.401	$0.527\,(\alpha = 0.6)$
doc2vec	-0.049	$0.025\,(\alpha = 0.0)$

Table 3: Pearson correlation coefficient for compositionality prediction results on the REDDY dataset.

Emb. method	$\text{Direct}_{\text{pre}}$	$\text{Direct}_{\text{post}}$
Flair	0.261	$0.291\,(\alpha = 0.4)$
$\text{Flair}_{\text{context}}$	0.280	$0.315\,(\alpha = 0.4)$
$\text{fastText}_{\text{pre}}$	0.339	$0.353\,(\alpha = 0.6, 0.7)$
fastText	0.374	$0.419\,(\alpha = 0.4)$
BERT	0.154	$0.177\,(\alpha = 0.3, 0.4)$
$\text{BERT}_{\text{context}}$	0.163	$0.189\,(\alpha = 0.3)$
ELMo	0.253	$0.287\,(\alpha = 0.5)$
$\text{ELMo}_{\text{context}}$	0.301	$0.319\,(\alpha = 0.5)$
word2vec	**0.427**	$\mathbf{0.419}\,(\alpha = 0.4)$
$\text{infersent}_{\text{GloVe}}$	0.321	$0.315\,(\alpha = 0.4)$
$\text{infersent}_{\text{fastText}}$	0.001	$0.202\,(\alpha = 1.0)$
doc2vec	-0.023	$0.003\,(\alpha = 0.0)$

Table 4: Pearson correlation coefficient for compositionality prediction results on the $\text{DISCO}_{\text{ADJ}}$ dataset.

5 Results and Discussion

The results from our experiments on the RAMISCH, REDDY and DISCO datasets can be found in Tables 2, 3 and 4, respectively, with the best performing αs and βs for each embedding method.

We observe that the αs in Table 2 are high, implying the compound nouns in RAMISCH are more compositional in terms of their head (second) nouns. Similarly, the lower α scores in Table 3 suggest REDDY's compound nouns are more dependent on their modifiers, or first nouns. Table 4, on the other hand, shows the αs embracing the entire range of $[0, 1]$. This suggests the adjective–noun pairs in DISCO are spread in terms of their dependency on their constituents, which also depends on the embedding method used. Overall, the methods are sensitive to the choice of the α hyperparameter, with ELMo and infersent being particularly sensitive and showing substantial change in output with change in α (Figures 1,2 and 3).

We see that for RAMISCH (Table 2), word2vec achieves the highest scores among the direct combination metrics, while infersent outperforms the other methods among the paraphrase metrics, and word2vec falls behind character embedding models like fastText, ELMo and BERT (even when the latter two were performed without context). The lower β scores also show the other models favouring the paraphrase metrics, while the high β score for word2vec shows its preference for di-

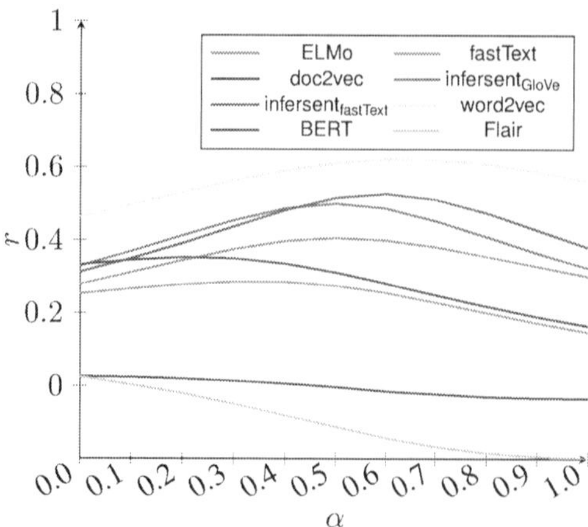

Figure 1: Sensitivity analysis of α (REDDY)

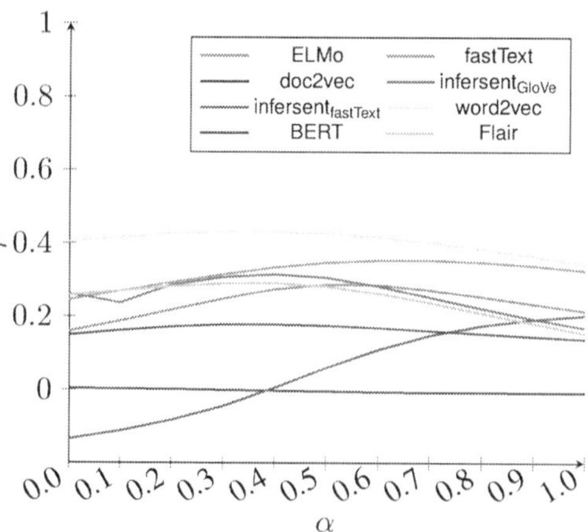

Figure 3: Sensitivity analysis of α (DISCO)

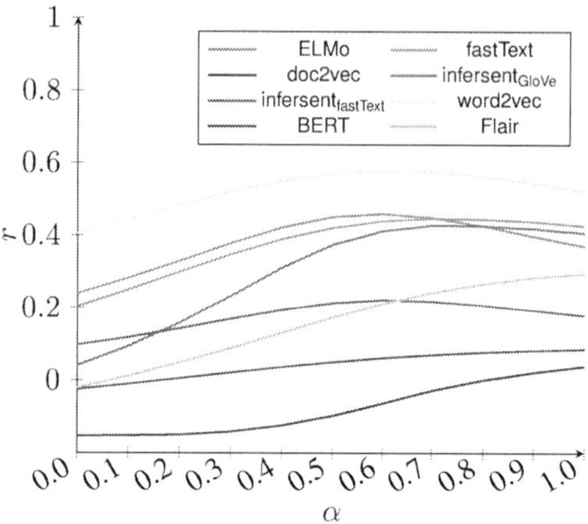

Figure 2: Sensitivity analysis of α (RAMISCH)

rect combination.

We observe that, consistent with its performance on RAMISCH, word2vec performs the best of all models for the direct combination methods.

Overall, we observe that word2vec is consistent in providing the best results based on the methods outlined in Section 3.1, while fastText and infersent come a close second and third, respectively. It is noteworthy, however, that word2vec required explicit modelling of the MWEs during the training procedure, while the other models did not.

It is not surprising that infersent, being a document-level embedding model, works better with paraphrase data than the other models. However, doc2vec has really poor scores overall across the three datasets. It does, however, redeem itself with the paraphrases, with substan-

tially higher scores than the direct metric but still quite a way behind the top-scoring methods.

We also see that the paraphrase metric seems to achieve much greater results across all models, suggesting this could be a direction for future study (noting the requirement for paraphrase data for the MWE in order to apply this method, which has inherent scalability limitations). The combined metric seems to favour the paraphrase results as well, based on the relative β values.

One of the reasons word2vec did not work as well with the paraphrases could be the naive assumption that the $\text{Direct}_{\text{pre}}$ is a representation of the paraphrase itself. As we see from the results across the datasets and methods, $\text{Direct}_{\text{pre}}$ does not entirely capture the compositionality of the MWE, so it is reasonable to assume that a paraphrase would not be accurately represented by $\text{Direct}_{\text{pre}}$ either.

We see that fastText provides us with impressive scores throughout, and we notice a slight improvement when trained on the same corpus as word2vec. However, there is a huge gap in the performance between word2vec and fastText, especially in the case of REDDY (which could be an issue of a heavier representation of a particular level of compositionality, say).

We also notice that, unlike the noun compounds in REDDY and RAMISCH, there is less variance in the relative scores of each method in the case of $\text{DISCO}_{\text{ADJ}}$, with overall results dropping appreciably, and the best-performing word2vec dropping back in raw r value compared to noun–noun pairs.

In terms of the contextualised embeddings, we

notice that across the three models, there is only a slight increase in correlation when contextualised embeddings are used. This suggests that even with context, these modern embedding techniques are unable to capture non-compositionality as well as their simpler counterparts.

Further analysis reveals that most models struggle to accurately predict the compositionality of idiomatic noun compounds, as well as semi-compositional terms wherein one of the constituent words are used in a metaphoric sense. In REDDY, we observe this for *silver bullet* and *snail mail*. Interestingly, while BERT struggles to effectively model compositionality throughout, it is surprisingly the only model able to perfectly predict the compositionality of *snail mail* (which appears as an extreme outlier). This suggests that BERT might be more successful using a different metric. In the case of the adjective–noun phrases in DISCO, we see that the models are still unable to accurately predict the compositionality of non-compositional phrases (like *big fish*, *heavy metal* and *red tape*). This time, however, they are also unable to capture *mobile phone* and *floppy disk*, perhaps because of their relatively archaic use.

6   Conclusion

In this paper, we investigated the modelling capabilities of various embedding techniques applied to the specific task of predicting the MWE compositionality, to see how well they model a mixture of compositionalities in the dataset. Our results indicate that modern character- and document-level embedding methods are inferior to the simple word2vec approach. However, the promising results of fastText and infersent across the datasets indicate that, among the more modern methods, they are better equiped to handle non-compositionality as they did not require much manipulation of the corpus or knowledge of the MWEs beforehand. We also found that the paraphrase metric results in greater correlation scores across the models.

In future work, we intend to tune our hyperparameters over held-out data, and experiment with other languages and language-independent techniques, including other models.

Acknowledgments

We would like to thank the curators and annotators of the datasets used in this study, and the anonymous reviewers for their insightful comments. We would also like to thank Chris Biemann from the University of Hamburg for making the dataset from the DiSCo shared task available to us.

References

Alan Akbik, Duncan Blythe, and Roland Vollgraf. 2018. Contextual string embeddings for sequence labeling. In *COLING 2018, 27th International Conference on Computational Linguistics*, pages 1638–1649, Santa Fe, USA.

Timothy Baldwin and Su Nam Kim. 2010. Multiword expressions. In *Nitin Indurkhya and Fred J. Damerau (eds.) Handbook of Natural Language Processing, Second Edition, CRC Press*, pages 267–292, Boca Raton, USA.

Chris Biemann and Eugenie Giesbrecht. 2011. Distributional semantics and compositionality 2011: Shared task description and results. In *Proceedings of the Workshop on Distributional Semantics and Compositionality*, pages 21–28, Portland, USA.

Piotr Bojanowski, Edouard Grave, Armand Joulin, and Tomas Mikolov. 2017. Enriching word vectors with subword information. *Transactions of the Association for Computational Linguistics*, 5:135–146.

Ronan Collobert and Jason Weston. 2008. A unified architecture for natural language processing: Deep neural networks with multitask learning. In *Proceedings of the 25th International Conference on Machine Learning*, pages 160–167.

Alexis Conneau, Douwe Kiela, Holger Schwenk, Loïc Barrault, and Antoine Bordes. 2017a. Supervised learning of universal sentence representations from natural language inference data. In *Proceedings of the 2017 Conference on Empirical Methods in Natural Language Processing*, pages 670–680, Copenhagen, Denmark.

Alexis Conneau, Douwe Kiela, Holger Schwenk, Loïc Barrault, and Antoine Bordes. 2017b. Supervised learning of universal sentence representations from natural language inference data. In *Proceedings of the 2017 Conference on Empirical Methods in Natural Language Processing*, pages 670–680, Copenhagen, Denmark. Association for Computational Linguistics.

Silvio Cordeiro, Aline Villavicencio, Marco Idiart, and Carlos Ramisch. 2019. Unsupervised compositionality prediction of nominal compounds. *Computational Linguistics*, 45(1).

Jacob Devlin, Ming-Wei Chang, Kenton Lee, and Kristina Toutanova. 2018. BERT: Pre-training of deep bidirectional transformers for language understanding. *arXiv preprint arXiv:1810.04805*.

Ali Hakimi Parizi and Paul Cook. 2018. Do character-level neural network language models capture knowledge of multiword expression compositionality? In *Proceedings of the Joint Workshop on Linguistic Annotation, Multiword Expressions and Constructions (LAW-MWE-CxG-2018)*, pages 185–192, Santa Fe, USA.

Jey Han Lau and Timothy Baldwin. 2016. An empirical evaluation of doc2vec with practical insights into document embedding generation. In *Proceedings of the 1st Workshop on Representation Learning for NLP*, pages 78–86, Berlin, Germany.

Quoc Le and Tomas Mikolov. 2014. Distributed representations of sentences and documents. In *Proceedings of the 31st International Conference on Machine Learning (ICML 2014)*, pages 1188–1196, Beijing, China.

Tomas Mikolov, G.s Corrado, Kai Chen, and Jeffrey Dean. 2013a. Efficient estimation of word representations in vector space. In *Proceddings of Workshop at the International Conference on Learning Representations*, pages 1–12.

Tomas Mikolov, Ilya Sutskever, Kai Chen, Greg S Corrado, and Jeff Dean. 2013b. Distributed representations of words and phrases and their compositionality. In *Advances in Neural Information Processing Systems 26*, pages 3111–3119.

Navnita Nandakumar, Bahar Salehi, and Timothy Baldwin. 2018. A comparative study of embedding models in predicting the compositionality of multiword expressions. In *Proceedings of the Australasian Language Technology Association Workshop 2018*, pages 71–76, Dunedin, New Zealand.

Jeffrey Pennington, Richard Socher, and Christopher D. Manning. 2014. GloVe: Global vectors for word representation. In *Empirical Methods in Natural Language Processing (EMNLP)*, pages 1532–1543.

Matthew Peters, Mark Neumann, Mohit Iyyer, Matt Gardner, Christopher Clark, Kenton Lee, and Luke Zettlemoyer. 2018. Deep contextualized word representations. In *Proceedings of the 2018 Conference of the North American Chapter of the Association for Computational Linguistics: Human Language Technologies, Volume 1 (Long Papers)*, pages 2227–2237, New Orleans, USA.

Carlos Ramisch, Silvio Cordeiro, Leonardo Zilio, Marco Idiart, and Aline Villavicencio. 2016. How naked is the naked truth? a multilingual lexicon of nominal compound compositionality. In *Proceedings of the 54th Annual Meeting of the Association for Computational Linguistics (Volume 2: Short Papers)*, pages 156–161, Berlin, Germany.

Siva Reddy, Diana McCarthy, and Suresh Manandhar. 2011. An empirical study on compositionality in compound nouns. In *Proceedings of 5th International Joint Conference on Natural Language Processing*, pages 210–218, Chiang Mai, Thailand.

Ivan A. Sag, Timothy Baldwin, Francis Bond, Ann Copestake, and Dan Flickinger. 2002. Multiword expressions: A pain in the neck for NLP. In *Proceedings of the 3rd International Conference on Intelligent Text Processing and Computational Linguistics (CICLing-2002)*, pages 1–15, Mexico City, Mexico.

Bahar Salehi, Paul Cook, and Timothy Baldwin. 2015. A word embedding approach to predicting the compositionality of multiword expressions. In *Proceedings of the 2015 Conference of the North American Chapter of the Association for Computational Linguistics: Human Language Technologies*, pages 977–983, Denver, USA.

Vered Shwartz and Chris Waterson. 2018. Olive oil is made of olives, baby oil is made for babies: Interpreting noun compounds using paraphrases in a neural model. In *Proceedings of the 2018 Conference of the North American Chapter of the Association for Computational Linguistics: Human Language Technologies, Volume 2 (Short Papers)*, pages 218–224, New Orleans, USA.

Measuring Semantic Abstraction of Multilingual NMT
with Paraphrase Recognition and Generation Tasks

Jörg Tiedemann and **Yves Scherrer**
Department of Digital Humanities / HELDIG
University of Helsinki

Abstract

In this paper, we investigate whether multilingual neural translation models learn stronger semantic abstractions of sentences than bilingual ones. We test this hypotheses by measuring the perplexity of such models when applied to paraphrases of the source language. The intuition is that an encoder produces better representations if a decoder is capable of recognizing synonymous sentences in the same language even though the model is never trained for that task. In our setup, we add 16 different auxiliary languages to a bidirectional bilingual baseline model (English-French) and test it with in-domain and out-of-domain paraphrases in English. The results show that the perplexity is significantly reduced in each of the cases, indicating that meaning can be grounded in translation. This is further supported by a study on paraphrase generation that we also include at the end of the paper.

1 Introduction

An appealing property of encoder-decoder models for machine translation is the effect of compressing information into dense vector-based representations to map source language input onto adequate translations in the target language. However, it is not clear to what extent the model actually needs to model meaning to perform that task; especially for related languages, it is often not necessary to acquire a deep understanding of the input to translate in an adequate way. The intuition that we would like to explore in this paper is based on the assumption that an increasingly difficult training objective will enforce stronger abstractions. In particular, we would like to see whether multilingual machine translation models learn representations that are closer to language-independent meaning representations than bilingual models do. Hence, our hypothesis is that

representations learned from multilingual data sets covering a larger linguistic diversity better reflect semantics than representations learned from less diverse material. This hypothesis is supported by the findings of related work focusing on universal sentence representation learning from multilingual data (Artetxe and Schwenk, 2018; Artetxe and Schwenk, 2018; Schwenk and Douze, 2017) to be used in natural language inference or other downstream tasks. In contrast to related work, we are not interested in fixed-size sentence representations that can be fed into external classifiers or regression models. Instead, we would like to fully explore the use of the encoded information in the attentive recurrent layers as they are produced by the seq2seq model.

Our basic framework consists of a standard attentional sequence-to-sequence model as commonly used for neural machine translation (Sennrich et al., 2017), with the multilingual extension proposed by Johnson et al. (2016). This extension allows a single system to learn machine translation for several language pairs, and crucially also for language pairs that have not been seen during training. We use Bible translations for training, in order to keep the genre and content of training data constant across languages, and to enable further studies on increasing levels of linguistic diversity. We propose different setups, all of which share the characteristics of having some source data in English and some target data in English. We can then evaluate these models on their capacity of recognizing and generating English paraphrases, i.e. translating English to English without explicitly learning that task. Starting with a base model using French–English and English–French training data, we select 16 additional languages as auxiliary information that are added to the base model, each of them separately.

There is a large body of related work on

Proceedings of the 3rd Workshop on Evaluating Vector Space Representations for NLP, pages 35–42
Minneapolis, USA, June 6, 2019. ©2019 Association for Computational Linguistics

paraphrase generation using machine translation (Quirk et al., 2004; Finch et al., 2004; Prakash et al., 2016) based on parallel monolingual corpora (Lin et al., 2014; Fader et al., 2013), pivot-based translation (Bannard and Callison-Burch, 2005; Mallinson et al., 2017) and paraphrase databased extracted from parallel corpora (Ganitkevitch et al., 2013). Related work on multilingual sentence representation (Artetxe and Schwenk, 2018; Schwenk and Douze, 2017; Lample and Conneau, 2019) has focused on fixed-size vector representations that can be used in natural language inference (Conneau et al., 2018; Eriguchi et al., 2018) or other downstream tasks such as bitext mining (Artetxe and Schwenk, 2018) or (cross-lingual) document classification (Schwenk and Li, 2018).

2 Experimental Setup

For our experiments, we apply a standard attentional sequence-to-sequence model with BPE-based segmentation. We use the Nematus-style models (Sennrich et al., 2017) as implemented in MarianNMT (Junczys-Dowmunt et al., 2018). These models apply gated recurrent units (GRUs) in the encoder and decoder with a bi-directional RNN on the encoder side. The word embeddings have a dimensionality of 512 and the RNN dimensionality is set to 1,024. We enable layer normalization and we use one RNN layer in both, encoder and decoder.

In training we use dynamic mini-batches to automatically fit the allocated memory (3GB in our case) based on sentence length in the selected sample of data. The optimization procedure applies Adam (Kingma and Ba, 2015) with mean cross-entropy as the optimization criterion. We also enable length normalization, exponential smoothing, scaling dropout for the RNN layers with ratio 0.2 and also apply source and target word dropout with ratio 0.1. All of these values are recommended settings that have empirically been found in the related literature. For testing convergence, we use independent development data of roughly 1,000 test examples and BLEU scores to determine the stopping criterion, which is set to five subsequent failures of improving the validation score. The translations are done with a beam search decoder of size 12. The validation frequency is set to run each 2,500 mini-batches.

For the multilingual setup, we follow Johnson

Language	Transl.	Verses	Tokens
English	19	234,173	6,750,869
French	14	369,910	10,529,929
Afrikaans	5	75,974	2,329,773
Albanian	2	58,192	1,648,242
Breton	1	1,781	44,316
German	24	499,844	13,712,459
Greek	7	87,218	2,357,095
Frisian	1	29,173	852,582
Hindi	4	93,242	2,829,274
Italian	5	122,363	3,429,182
Dutch	3	87,460	2,596,298
Ossetian	2	37,807	936,533
Polish	5	52,668	1,248,108
Russian	5	75,904	1,727,536
Slovene	1	29,088	748,367
Spanish	8	236,830	6,607,932
Serbian	2	35,019	844,299
Swedish	1	29,088	833,983

Table 1: Statistics about the Bible data in our collection: number of individual Bible translations, number of verses and number of tokens per language in the training data sets.

et al. (2016) by adding target language flags to the source text placing them as pseudo tokens in the beginning of each input sentence. We always train models in both directions enabling the model to read and generate the same language without explicitly training that task (i.e. paraphrasing is modeled as zero-shot translation). BPE (Sennrich et al., 2016) is used to avoid unknown words and to improve generalisations. Note that in our setup we need to ensure that subword-level segmentations are consistent for each language involved in several translation tasks. We opted for language-dependent BPE models with 10,000 merge operations for each code table. The total vocabulary size then depends on the combination of languages that we use in training but the vocabulary stays exactly the same for each language involved in all experiments.

2.1 Training data and configurations

The main data we use for our experiments comes from a collection of Bible translations (Mayer and Cysouw, 2014) that includes over a thousand languages. For high-density languages like English and French, various alternatives are available (see Table 1). Using the Bible makes it possible to easily extend our work with additional languages representing a wide range of linguistic variation, while at the same time keeping genre and content constant across languages.

For the sake of discussion, we selected English

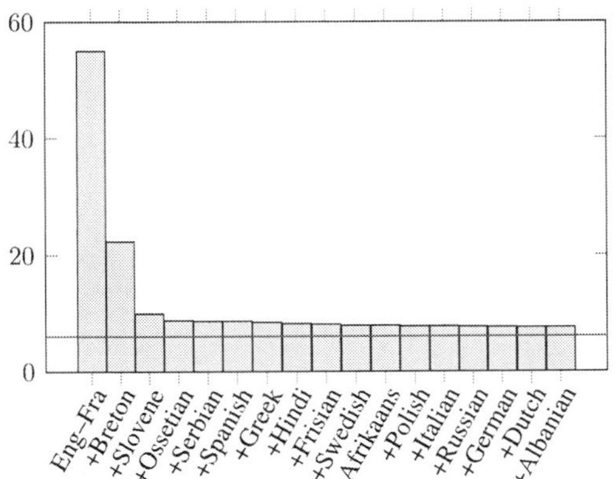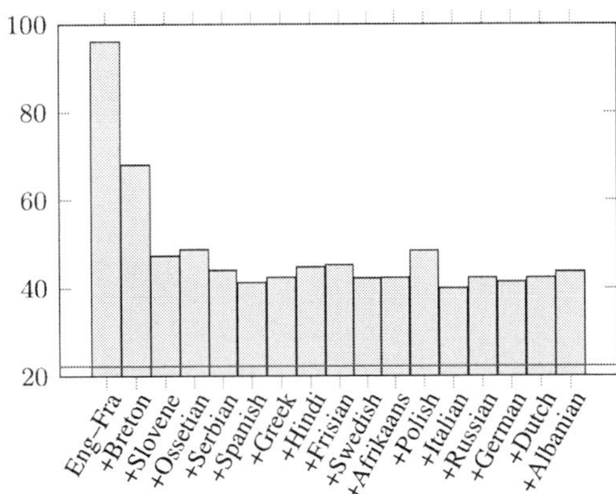

Figure 1: Paraphrase perplexity measured on Bible (left) and Tatoeba (right) test sentences (lower values are better). The figures show the effect of one auxiliary language added to the bilingual French-English model (leftmost bars). The lower red line represents the supervised model trained on English paraphrases. Languages are sorted by decreasing perplexity on the Bible data.

as our pivot language that we will use for evaluating the ability of the model to act as a paraphrase model. Furthermore, we took French as a second language to create a bilingual baseline model that can translate in both directions. As additional auxiliary languages, we then apply the ones listed in Table 1 together with some basic statistics of the training data. The idea behind the language selection is to create a somewhat diverse set of languages representing different amounts of coverage and typological relationships. The set is easy to extend but training requires extensive resources, which necessarily limits our selection at this point.

In the general setup, we do not include any pairs of English Bible translations as we do not want to evaluate a model that is specifically trained for a paraphrasing task. However, for comparison we also create a model comprising all pairs of English translation variants, which will serve as an upper bound (or rather, a lower bound in terms of perplexity) for models that are trained without explicit paraphrase data.

Exhaustively looking at all possible subsets of languages is not possible even with our small selection of 18 languages. Therefore, we restricted our study to the following test cases:

Bilingual model: A model trained on all combinations of English and French Bible translations. Each pair of aligned Bible verses represents two training instances, one for English-to-French and one for French-to-English. We also include French-to-French training instances using identical sentences in the input and output, in order to guide the model to correctly learn the semantics of the language flags.[1]

Trilingual models: Translation models trained on all bilingual combinations of Bibles in three languages – English, French and another auxiliary language (in both directions) + identical French verse pairs.

Multilingual model: One model that includes all languages in our test set with training data in both directions (translating from and to English or French) + identical French verse pairs.

Paraphrase model: A model trained on combinations of English Bible translations (the supervised upper bound).

Note that all models (including the bilingual one) cover the same English data including all Bible variants. We use exactly the same vocabulary for the English portion of each setup and no new English data is added at any point and any change that we observe when testing with English paraphrase tasks is due to the auxiliary languages that we add to the model as a translational training objective.

2.2 Test data

For our experiments, we apply test sets from two domains. One of them represents in-domain data from the Bible collection that covers 998 verses

---

[1] During our initial experiments, we realized that the language labels did not always pick up the information about the target language they are supposed to indicate. Especially in the bilingual case this makes sense as the model always sees the same language pair and identifying the source language is enough to determine what kind of output language it needs to generate. The label is not necessary and, therefore, ignored.

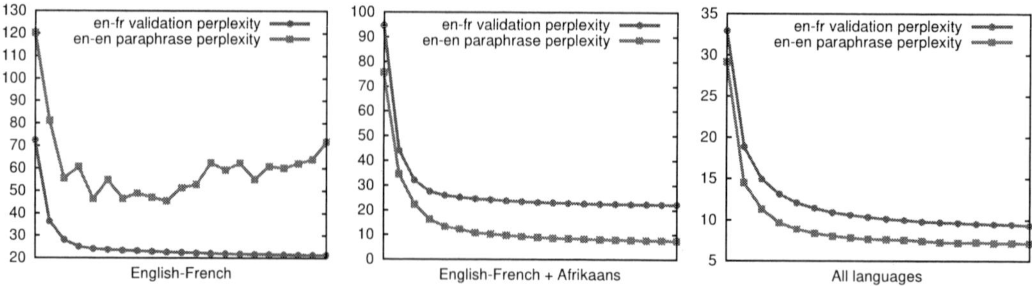

Figure 2: Learning curves from three models (the bilingual English-French model, a trilingual model and a multi-lingual one): Perplexity on Bible data, English-French in validation (blue) and English paraphrases in testing (red). Note the different scales.

from the New Testament that we held out of training and development sets. Our second test set comes from a very different source, namely data collected from user-contributed translations that are on-line in the Tatoeba database.[2] They include everyday expressions with translations in a large number of languages. As the collection includes translation alternatives, we can treat them as paraphrases of each other. We extracted altogether 3,873 pairs of synonymous sentences in English.

From both test data sources, we create a single-reference test set for paraphrase recognition and a multi-reference test set for paraphrase generation. The single-reference Bible test set uses the *Standard* English Bible as the source, and the *Common* English Bible[3] as the reference. The multi-reference Bible test set uses the *Amplified* Bible as the source (the first one on our list), and all 18 other English Bibles as the references.

The Tatoeba single-reference test set contains all 3,873 synonymous sentence pairs. For the multi-reference test set, we filtered the data to exclude near-identical sentence pairs by expanding contractions (like "I'm" to "I am") that are quite common in the data and removed all pairs that differ only in punctuation after that procedure. Furthermore, we merged alternatives of the same sentence into synonym sets and created, thus, a multi-reference corpus for testing containing a total of 2,444 sentences with their references.

3 Results

We evaluate the models on two tasks: (1) paraphrase recognition and (2) paraphrase generation.

The following sections summarize our main findings in relation to these two tasks. We also evaluated the actual translation performance to ensure that the models are properly trained. The results of that test are listed in the supplementary material.

3.1 Paraphrase Recognition

First of all, we would like to know how well our translation models are capable of handling paraphrased sentences. For this, we compute perplexity scores of the various models when observing English output sentences for given English input coming from the two paraphrase test sets. The intuition is that models with a higher level of semantic abstraction in the encoder should be less surprised by seeing paraphrased sentences on the decoder side, which will result in a lower perplexity.

Let us first look at the in-domain data from our Bible test set. Figure 1 (left half) illustrates the reduction in perplexity when adding languages to our bilingual model. The figure is sorted by decreasing perplexities. While the picture does not reveal any clear pattern about the languages that help the most, we can see that they all contribute to an improved perplexity in comparison to the bidirectional English-French model. Breton is clearly the least useful language, without doubt due to the size of that language in our collection. Note that a further 5% perplexity reduction over the best trilingual model is achieved by the model that combines all languages (perplexity of 7.23, which is very close to the lower bound of 6.05).

The picture is similar but with a slightly different pattern on out-of-domain data. Figure 1 (right half) shows the same plot for the Tatoeba test set with languages sorted in the same order as in the previous figure. Adding languages helps again,

---

[2]https://tatoeba.org/eng/

[3]CEB is an ambitious new translation rather than a revision of other translations (https://www.biblegateway.com).

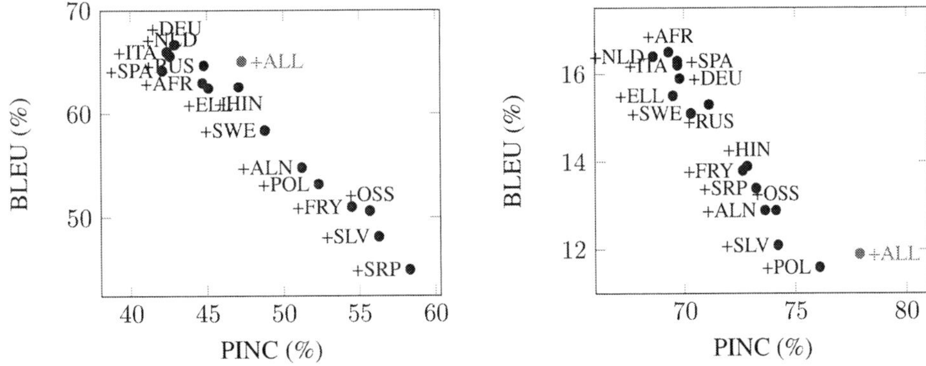

Figure 3: Paraphrase BLEU vs. PINC scores for the Bible test set (left) and the Tatoeba test set (right).

which is re-assuring, but the amount is less pronounced and further away from the lower bound (which is, however, to be expected in this setup). Again, Breton is not helping as much. Furthermore, in the out-of-domain case, the model combining all languages actually does not improve the perplexity any further (the value of 42.63 is similar to other trilingual models), which is most probably due to the strong domain mismatch that influences the scores significantly.

To further demonstrate the problems of the bilingual model to learn proper semantic representations that can be used for paraphrase detection, we can also have a look at the learning curves in Figure 2. The first plot nicely shows that the perplexity scores on paraphrase data do not follow the smooth line of the validation data in English and French whereas the models that include auxiliary languages have the capability to improve the model with respect to paraphrase recognition throughout the training procedure in a similar way as the main objective (translation) is optimized. The model that combines all languages achieves by far the lowest paraphrase perplexity. Learning curves of other trilingual models look very similar to the one included here.

3.2 Paraphrase Generation

This second experiment aims at testing the capacity of the NMT models to generate paraphrases of the input instead of translations. The hypothesis is that the generated sentences will preserve the meaning of the input, but not necessarily the same form, such that the generated sentences can be viewed as genuine paraphrases of the input sentences.

Good paraphrase models should produce sentences that are as close as possible to one of the references, yet as different as possible from the source. The first part can be measured by common machine translation metrics such as BLEU (Papineni et al., 2002), which supports multiple references. The second part can be measured by specific paraphrase quality metrics such as PINC (Chen and Dolan, 2011), which computes the proportion of non-overlapping n-grams between the source and the generated paraphrase. Good paraphrases should thus obtain high BLEU as well as high PINC scores on some paraphrase test set.

Figure 3 plots BLEU scores against PINC scores for the two test sets (lowercased and ignoring punctuations), the alternative English translations in the heldout data from the Bible and the Tatoeba paraphrase set. We exclude the bilingual model and the Breton model from the graphs, as they have BLEU scores close to 0 and PINC scores close to 100% due to the output being generated in the wrong language.

The figures show a more or less linear correlation between BLEU and PINC. This is expected to a certain extent, as there is a clear trade-off between producing varied sentences (higher PINC) and preserving the meaning of the source sentence (higher BLEU). However, we find that the model containing all languages shows the overall best performance (e.g., according to the arithmetic mean of PINC and BLEU). This suggests that a highly multilingual model provides indeed more abstract internal representations that eventually lead to higher-quality paraphrases. We also conclude that additional languages with large and diverse (i.e., many different Bibles) datasets are better at preserving the meaning of the source sentence. However, there is no obvious language fam-

Source	But even as he was on the road going down, his servants met him and reported, saying, Your son lives!
+NLD	And as he was on the road, his servants went down with him, and reported, saying, Thy son lives!
+SPA	But as it was on the road, his servants came to him and told him, "Your own Son lives!"
+ALL	And while he was on the way, his servants came to him, saying, "Your son lives!"

Source	Give attention to this! Behold, a sower went out to sow.
+AFR	Pay attention to this! Behold, the sower went out to sow.
+ALL	Take care of this. Behold, a sower went out to sow.
+BRE	Give attention to this! For, look! un semeur sortit pour semer.
+DEU	Listen to this! Behold, a sower went out to sow.

Source	He slept soundly.
Eng-Fra	Et il se prosterna devant soi.
+BRE	And, behold, he rose up quickly.
+DEU	And he began to sleep.
+ELL	He was sleeping.
+ALL	And when he had died, he was asleep.

Source	She has no brothers.
Eng-Fra	Elle n'a point de frères.
+BRE	Or, elle n'a pas de frères.
+DEU	For she has no brothers.
+OSS	No, brothers.
+ALL	You have no brothers.

Table 2: Examples of generated Bible (left) and Tatoeba (right) paraphrases.

ily or similarity effect.

The Tatoeba test set yields much lower BLEU scores than the Bible test set, due to the large number of unseen words and constructions, and also because the Tatoeba test set has only an average of 1.1 reference paraphrases per sentence, whereas the Bible test set has 18 references for each verse. This is most probably also the reason why the multilingual model including all languages (*ALL*) performs worse than most other models in terms of BLEU scores for the Tatoeba paraphrase test. It is highly likely that plausible paraphrases are not part of the test set if it only includes one or very few references like it is the case with Tatoeba, which is obviously a short-coming of BLEU as a metric for paraphrase evaluation.

Table 2 shows some examples of paraphrases generated from the Bible and Tatoeba test set. One can see that different models tend to produce different paraphrases while preserving the general meaning of the source sentence at least in the case of the Bible data. Tatoeba is more problematic due to the domain mismatch and we will come back to that issue in the discussions further down.

One caveat is that paraphrase generation could trivially be achieved by copying the input to the output especially when evaluating the results using BLEU. Therefore, we also measured the percentage of identical copies that each model produces leaving out punctuations and lowercasing the data. The results show that copying is a rare case for the multilingual models and the input is only matched in at most 1.4% of the cases (for Bible data) and at most 5.1% of the cases in the Tatoeba test set. However, adding English-English training data changes this behaviour dramatically, increasing the copying effect to over 70% of the cases in both test sets, which breaks the use of

Source	Have you never eaten a kiwi?
+AFR	Have you not eaten sour grapes?

Source	Do you have a cellphone?
+HIN	Do you have a scorpion?

Source	Do your children speak French?
+SPA	Do your children speak Greek?

Source	Could I park my car here?
+ITA	Do I get up here with my cavalry?

Source	Birds fly.
+DEU	The flying creatures shall fly away .

Figure 4: Examples of generated Tatoeba paraphrases.

such models as a paraphrase generator. This happens even though we train on pairs of different Bible translations into English, effectively training a paraphrase model with supervised learning. Details of this evaluation are given in the supplementary material.

Finally, we can also observe the effect of domain mismatch between the training data and the Tatoeba test set. A considerable proportion of the test vocabulary refers to contemporary objects which obviously do not appear in the Bible training corpus, and it will, thus, be difficult for the model to generate adequate paraphrases. A few examples of sentences containing out-of-vocabulary words are shown in Figure 4. They indicate that the models are able to partially grasp the semantics of concepts and sentences often trying to replace unknown expressions with creative but reasonable alternatives coming from the context of the Bible. However, this observation calls for a more systematic evaluation of the semantic similarity of paraphrases than it is done by n-gram overlap with reference paraphrases, which is, unfortunately, out of the scope of this paper.

4   Conclusions

We have presented a study on the meaning representations that can be learned from multilingual data sets. We show that additional linguistic diversity lead to stronger abstractions and we verify our intuitions with a paraphrase scoring task that measures perplexity of multilingual sequence-to-sequence models. We also investigate the ability of translation models to generate paraphrases and conclude that this is indeed possible with promising results even without diversified decoders. In the future, we will try to push the model further to approach truly language-independent meaning representation based on massively parallel data sets as additional translational grounding. We will also study the model with bigger and less homogenous data sets and compare it to other approaches to paraphrase generation including pivot-based back-translation models. Furthermore, we will test sentence representations obtained by multilingual NMT models with additional downstream tasks to further support the main claims of the paper.

Acknowledgments

The work in this paper is supported by the Academy of Finland through project 314062 from the ICT 2023 call on Computation, Machine Learning and Artificial Intelligence and the European Research Council (ERC) under the European Union's Horizon 2020 research and innovation programme (grant agreement No 771113). We would also like to acknowledge NVIDIA and their GPU grant.

References

Mikel Artetxe and Holger Schwenk. 2018. Margin-based parallel corpus mining with multilingual sentence embeddings. *CoRR*, abs/1811.01136.

Mikel Artetxe and Holger Schwenk. 2018. Massively Multilingual Sentence Embeddings for Zero-Shot Cross-Lingual Transfer and Beyond. *arXiv e-prints*, page arXiv:1812.10464.

Colin Bannard and Chris Callison-Burch. 2005. Paraphrasing with bilingual parallel corpora. In *Proceedings of the ACL 2005*, pages 597–604, Ann Arbor, Michigan.

David Chen and William Dolan. 2011. Collecting highly parallel data for paraphrase evaluation. In *Proceedings of ACL 2011*, pages 190–200, Portland, Oregon, USA.

Alexis Conneau, Guillaume Lample, Ruty Rinott, Adina Williams, Samuel R. Bowman, Holger Schwenk, and Veselin Stoyanov. 2018. XNLI: evaluating cross-lingual sentence representations. *CoRR*, abs/1809.05053.

Akiko Eriguchi, Melvin Johnson, Orhan Firat, Hideto Kazawa, and Wolfgang Macherey. 2018. Zero-shot cross-lingual classification using multilingual neural machine translation. *CoRR*, abs/1809.04686.

Anthony Fader, Luke Zettlemoyer, and Oren Etzioni. 2013. Paraphrase-driven learning for open question answering. In *Proceedings of ACL 2013*, pages 1608–1618, Sofia, Bulgaria.

Andrew Finch, Taro Watanabe, Yasuhiro Akiba, and Eiichiro Sumita. 2004. Paraphrasing as machine translation. 11:87–111.

Juri Ganitkevitch, Benjamin Van Durme, and Chris Callison-Burch. 2013. PPDB: The paraphrase database. In *Proceedings of NAACL 2013*, pages 758–764, Atlanta, Georgia.

Melvin Johnson, Mike Schuster, Quoc V. Le, Maxim Krikun, Yonghui Wu, Zhifeng Chen, Nikhil Thorat, Fernanda B. Viégas, Martin Wattenberg, Greg Corrado, Macduff Hughes, and Jeffrey Dean. 2016. Google's multilingual neural machine translation system: Enabling zero-shot translation. *CoRR*, abs/1611.04558.

Marcin Junczys-Dowmunt, Roman Grundkiewicz, Tomasz Dwojak, Hieu Hoang, Kenneth Heafield, Tom Neckermann, Frank Seide, Ulrich Germann, Alham Fikri Aji, Nikolay Bogoychev, André F. T. Martins, and Alexandra Birch. 2018. Marian: Fast neural machine translation in C++. *arXiv preprint arXiv:1804.00344*.

Diederik P. Kingma and Jimmy Ba. 2015. Adam: A method for stochastic optimization. In *The International Conference on Learning Representations*.

Guillaume Lample and Alexis Conneau. 2019. Cross-lingual language model pretraining. *CoRR*, abs/1901.07291.

Tsung-Yi Lin, Michael Maire, Serge Belongie, James Hays, Pietro Perona, Deva Ramanan, Piotr Dollár, and C. Lawrence Zitnick. 2014. Microsoft COCO: Common objects in context. In *Computer Vision – ECCV 2014*, pages 740–755. Springer International Publishing.

Jonathan Mallinson, Rico Sennrich, and Mirella Lapata. 2017. Paraphrasing revisited with neural machine translation. In *Proceedings of EACL 2017*, pages 881–893, Valencia, Spain.

Thomas Mayer and Michael Cysouw. 2014. Creating a massively parallel Bible corpus. In *Proc. of LREC*, pages 3158–3163, Reykjavik, Iceland. European Language Resources Association (ELRA).

Kishore Papineni, Salim Roukos, Todd Ward, and Wei-Jing Zhu. 2002. Bleu: a method for automatic evaluation of machine translation. In *Proceedings of ACL 2002*, pages 311–318, Philadelphia, Pennsylvania, USA.

Aaditya Prakash, Sadid A. Hasan, Kathy Lee, Vivek Datla, Ashequl Qadir, Joey Liu, and Oladimeji Farri. 2016. Neural paraphrase generation with stacked residual LSTM networks. In *Proceedings of COLING 2016*, pages 2923–2934.

Chris Quirk, Chris Brockett, and William Dolan. 2004. Monolingual machine translation for paraphrase generation. In *Proceedings of EMNLP 2004*, pages 142–149, Barcelona, Spain.

Holger Schwenk and Matthijs Douze. 2017. Learning joint multilingual sentence representations with neural machine translation. In *ACL workshop on Representation Learning for NLP*.

Holger Schwenk and Xian Li. 2018. A corpus for multilingual document classification in eight languages. In *LREC*, pages 3548–3551.

Rico Sennrich, Orhan Firat, Kyunghyun Cho, Alexandra Birch, Barry Haddow, Julian Hitschler, Marcin Junczys-Dowmunt, Samuel Läubli, Antonio Valerio Miceli Barone, Jozef Mokry, and Maria Nadejde. 2017. Nematus: a toolkit for neural machine translation. *CoRR*, abs/1703.04357.

Rico Sennrich, Barry Haddow, and Alexandra Birch. 2016. Neural machine translation of rare words with subword units. In *Proceedings of ACL 2016*, pages 1715–1725, Berlin, Germany. Association for Computational Linguistics.

SWOW-8500: Word Association Task for Intrinsic Evaluation of Word Embeddings

Avijit Thawani
IIT BHU / Varanasi
thawani@usc.edu

Biplav Srivastava
IBM / New York
biplav.srivastava
@gmail.com

Anil Kumar Singh
IIT BHU / Varanasi
aksingh.cse
@iitbhu.ac.in

Abstract

Downstream evaluation of pretrained word embeddings is expensive, more so for tasks where current state of the art models are very large architectures. Intrinsic evaluation using word similarity or analogy datasets, on the other hand, suffers from several disadvantages. We propose a novel intrinsic evaluation task employing large word association datasets (particularly the Small World of Words dataset). We observe correlations not just between performances on SWOW-8500 and previously proposed intrinsic tasks of word similarity prediction, but also with downstream tasks (eg. Text Classification and Natural Language Inference). Most importantly, we report better confidence intervals for scores on our word association task, with no fall in correlation with downstream performance.

1 Introduction

With the recent rise in popularity of distributional semantics, word embeddings have become the basic building block of several state-of-the-art models spanning multiple problems across Natural Language Processing and Information Retrieval. Word embeddings are essentially non-sparse representations of words in the form of one (relatively) small dimensional vector of real numbers for every word, and all of these vectors lie in the same continuous space.

Despite the clear benefits of these distributed representations, it is not obvious how to come up with apt word embeddings for a given NLP task. Approaches such as word2vec (Mikolov et al., 2013b), GloVe (Pennington et al., 2014), etc. have been shown to perform well on downstream tasks such as text classification, sequence labelling, question answering, text summarization, and machine translation.

Typically, word vectors are used in NLP models in two ways: fixed pretrained embeddings, and

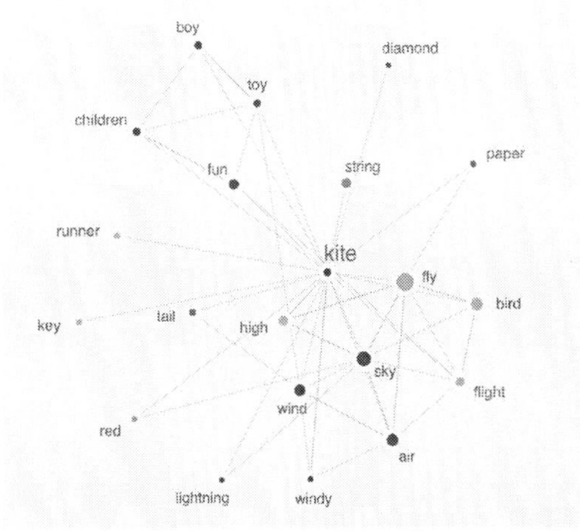

Figure 1: Visualization of the cue *Kite* and its associated words according to the SWOW dataset. Source: https://smallworldofwords.org/en/project/explore

finetuning. In the first way, word vectors have already been trained on some large dataset (e.g. Wikipedia, Twitter, Blog corpus, etc.) using one of the aforementioned techniques. These vectors are taken as fixed weights and the model merely uses them as they are rather than learning them during the training phase. On the other hand, finetuning allows for these vectors to be modified too, using backpropagation. Here the word embeddings are taken only as initialized weights for the model's first layer.

It is of natural interest to the NLP community to identify evaluation metrics for word embeddings. Besides direct performance measurement on downstream tasks, there have also been proposed several intrinsic evaluation measures such as MEN, WordSim, SimLex, etc. These are small proxy tasks which word vectors are expected to perform well on, given the assumption that they capture semantics of words. While Extrinsic evaluations use word embeddings as input features to

43

Proceedings of the 3rd Workshop on Evaluating Vector Space Representations for NLP, pages 43–51
Minneapolis, USA, June 6, 2019. ©2019 Association for Computational Linguistics

a downstream task and measure changes in performance metrics specific to that task, Intrinsic evaluations directly test for syntactic or semantic relationships between words (Schnabel et al., 2015). For example, the word similarity task asks word embeddings to predict how similar are the meanings of two prompt words. The closer this estimate is to human judgements, higher is the score allotted to the (pretrained) word embedding.

Through this paper, we propose the Word Association task for evaluating non-contextualized pretrained word embeddings, with the help of word asssociation datasets originally collected for psychological research. The datasets were formed by asking participants to respond to certain cue words. For example, given the cue *tiger*, one could respond with the words *lion, panther, wild,* etc. Large datasets of this sort are now available online, and it can be argued that they capture a notion of which words are in close association with others (as perceived by human participants).

According to cognitive theories of the mind, people form associations between concepts based on similarity, contiguity, or contrast. Our task proposal stems from the following argument: Any model that claims to understand the semantics of words should be able to mimic human beings in recognizing the associations between pairs of words. For example, a distributed representation of words, i.e., word embeddings, should be able to tell that the word *tiger* is in some way associated with *lion* but not with, say, *kettle*, assuming such a statistic is observed in the word association dataset too.

Given the scale of these datasets, they seem like a lucrative way to evaluate pretrained word embeddings. We see them as a manually annotated corpus of word associations, though not originally meant for word embedding evaluation. Therefore, we must devise a convenient way to compare the semantics captured in a given set of pretrained word vectors with that captured in such word association datasets.

We make our scripts, along with several other resources, available at `https://github.com/avi-jit/SWOW-eval`

2 Related Work

2.1 Word Embedding Evaluation

There exist several intrinsic evaluation tasks for word embeddings. One way to tell apart intrinsic from extrinsic evaluations is the lack of any trainable parameters in the former. Schnabel et al. (2015) discuss word relatedness, analogy, selective preference, and categorization as types of intrinsic tasks.

Our proposed task is most similar to the word relatedness/similarity tasks, several of which have already been proposed in literature: WS-3533 (Finkelstein et al., 2002), WS-SIM and WS-REL (Agirre et al., 2009), RG-65 (Rubenstein and Goodenough, 1965), MC-30 (Miller and Charles, 1991), MTurk-2875 (Radinsky et al., 2011), MTurk-771 (Halawi et al., 2012), MEN7 (Bruni et al., 2012), YP-130 (Yang and Powers, 2006), Rare Words (Luong et al., 2013), etc. We list the ones above specifically since those are the ones we compare our proposed task to, using the online resource wordvectors.org (Faruqui and Dyer, 2014), whose code remains available on GitHub [1]. Association of Computational Linguistics[2] and Vecto AI[3] also maintain benchmark pages for word similarity.

Likewise, VecEval (Nayak et al., 2016) and Multilingual-embeddings-eval-portal (Ammar et al., 2016) are GitHub repositories for Extrinsic Evaluation of word embeddings. [4,5].

Another direction of work has been towards critiquing intrinsic evaluation, in a bid to understand its shortcomings and potential workarounds (Schnabel et al., 2015; Zhai et al., 2016). One of the key shortcomings is **the Absence of Statistical Significance** (Faruqui et al., 2016), which we aim to tackle through this proposal. We believe that a massive dataset of word associations can be used to circumvent issues related to confidence intervals of scores reported. We put this belief to test in later sections of this paper.

2.2 Word Association

Our prime motivation behind this work was Marvin Minsky's Society of Mind (1988) which theorizes that humans learn by linking concepts together, using what Minsky calls K-Lines. If we assign meanings to concepts by associating them

---

[1] `http://github.com/mfaruqui/eval-word-vectors`

[2] `http://aclweb.org/aclwiki/Similarity_(State_of_the_art)`

[3] `http://github.com/vecto-ai/word-benchmarks`

[4] `http://github.com/NehaNayak/veceval`

[5] `http://github.com/wammar/multilingual-embeddings-eval-portal`

with each other, artificial models of semantics should also be able to do the same.

Word Association games are those wherein a participant is asked to utter the first (or first few) words that occur to him/her when given a trigger/cue/stimulus word. For example, given *king*, one could respond with *rule*, *queen*, *kingdom*, or even *kong* (from the movie King Kong). Word associations have long intrigued psychologists including Carl Jung (1918) and hence large studies have been conducted in this direction. Some prominent datasets which collect user responses to word association games are:

1. University of Southern Florida: Free Association (USF-FA) (Nelson et al., 2004) has single-word association responses from an average of 149 participants per cue for a set of 5,019 cue words.

2. Edinburgh Association Thesaurus (EAT) (Kiss et al., 1973) collects 100 responses per cue for a total of 8,400 cues.

3. JeuxDeMots: over 5 million french words (Lafourcade, 2007).

4. **Small World of Words** (SWOW) (De Deyne et al., 2018): Word association and participant data for 100 primary, secondary and tertiary responses to 12,292 cues, collected from over 90,000 participants[6].

5. Birkbeck norms (Moss et al., 1996) contain 40 to 50 responses for over 2,600 cues in British English.

Among non-English word association norms, the largest resources available include 16000 cues in Dutch (De Deyne et al., 2013), 3900 cues in Korean (Jung et al., 2010), and 2100 cues in Japanese (Joyce, 2005).

The authors of SWOW and Jeux De Mots have even attempted to employ their word association datasets for learning word embeddings (De Deyne et al., 2016; Plu et al.) . They use both count-based and random walk based strategies to learn vector representations of words. Note that we differ in using the SWOW dataset not as a corpus to learn word vectors, but as a human annotated dataset for evaluating other pretrained word vectors.

cue	response	R123	N	R123.Str
would	should	63	288	0.220
would	could	63	288	0.220
would	will	24	288	0.083
would	can	11	288	0.038
...	...	...	...	...
stumble	fall	76	290	0.262
stumble	trip	68	290	0.234
stumble	upon	16	290	0.055

Table 1: A few example cue-response tuples from the SWOW dataset, along with their associated R123.Strength scores

Summary Statistic	Value
Sample Minimum (the smallest observation)	115
Lower Quartile (the first quartile)	270
Median (the middle value)	282
Upper Quartile (the third quartile)	289
Sample Maximum (the largest observation)	300

Table 2: The five number summary for N, i.e. the number of responses per cue

3 Dataset

Here onwards, we restrict ourselves to only the Small World of Words dataset (SWOW), a part of which can be seen in Table 1. For each cue-response pair C-R, the value $R123$ is the number of participants who responded with R when given the cue C. Note that out of at most three responses collected per cue per respondent, it does not matter to the $R123$ score whether R occurred in the first response or the third. N is the number of total responses given the cue C in the processed version of released SWOW dataset. The value $R123.Strength$ is simply equal to $\frac{R123}{N}$.

There are $978,908$ cue-response pairs in the latest release of SWOW dataset. The statistics for the number of responses per cue is shown in Table 2. For our own SWOW evaluations, we got rid of anything that was not a single word, e.g. *New York* or *get-together*. We further selected only the most

6http://smallworldofwords.org/en/project

frequently co-occurring word associations. In particular, we kept only those cue-response pairs that have $R123.strength$ (i.e., number of people who cited this response for this cue within any of the three responses they gave, divided by the total number of responses for this cue word) is greater than 0.2 which corresponds to saying that at least one fifth of all respondents believe this response is one of the three top associated words for the given cue. We were now left with 8500 cues and a few of their corresponding top responses each. While we restrict ourselves to experimenting only on the SWOW-8500 dataset, we make available the code and resources to create even larger datasets (with fewer restrictions on, say, minimum strength of association, needed). [7]

Note that word association datasets are asymmetric in that they treat the pairs C-R and R-C separately, i.e., for the cue *coffee*, the response *tea* might be the most frequent one but for the cue *tea*, the most frequent response could be *black*. We need to bear this in mind when using this dataset to evaluate word embeddings intrinsically, since usually intrinsic datasets give out a single value for a word pair. This also does not fit well with the traditional measure of similarity/relatedness between two words, i.e., cosine distance, which is a symmetric metric.

4 Methodology

Supplemental Table 4 in the original SWOW dataset paper (De Deyne et al., 2018) shows high correlations with a few of the word similarity datasets mentioned above. In this aspect, our work can be seen as their direct successor, since we build upon these correlations to propose a new (and larger) task for intrinsic evaluation of word vectors.

We wish to compare performances of any pre-trained word embedding on (1) Our proposed task, (2) other Intrinsic evaluation tasks, and (3) Downstream Tasks. To that end, we first settle upon some candidate word embeddings. All embeddings had 300 dimensions, thereby avoiding different numbers of parameters to be learnt for downstream models. They were reduced to a very small common vocabulary of 7779 words. This helped in conveniently expressing results, without accounting for Out-of-Vocabulary words differently. We attempt to have a representative set

of embeddings, including the best and most popular ones:

1. Word2Vec Skip Gram (Mikolov et al., 2013b,a) trained on Google News.[8]

2. GloVe (Pennington et al., 2014) trained on Wikipedia 2014 and Gigaword 5.[9]

3. FastText (Bojanowski et al., 2017) trained with subword information on Common Crawl (600B tokens).[10]

4. ConceptNet Numberbatch (Speer et al., 2017) trained on a big knowledge graph and some text corpora.[11]

5. Baroni and Lenci's (2014) count-based embeddings, which are the result of dimensionality reduction on a large count matrix.[12]

6. Random Baseline: a baseline developed by randomly allotting 300 floating numbers to each word in the common vocabulary of the above five embeddings.

We used intrinsic evaluations in the form of 13 word similarity tasks, provided by wordvectors.org (Faruqui and Dyer, 2014). For our proposed task SWOW-8500, and for a given pre-trained embedding E, we ask E to predict top k responses for each of the 6481 cues (the ones in common between the 7779 sized vocabulary of our word vectors, and the 8500 cues in our proposed task). This corresponds to listing the top-k most similar words to the cue (which we have found from decreasing order of cosine similarity). We tried with several fixed values of k but finally report results keeping k variable, and always equal to the number of responses for that particular cue (in the SWOW-8500 dataset). Here k can be thought of as the number of guesses allotted to an image classifier. We then report how many of the correct responses (according to SWOW dataset) also occurred in the guesses made by E.

The True Positives are those words that occur both in SWOW-8500 as well as E's guesses. False

---

[7] https://github.com/avi-jit/SWOW-eval

[8] http://code.google.com/archive/p/word2vec/

[9] http://nlp.stanford.edu/projects/glove/

[10] http://fasttext.cc/docs/en/english-vectors.html

[11] http://github.com/commonsense/conceptnet-numberbatch

[12] http://clic.cimec.unitn.it/dm/

cue	Correct Guesses (TP)	Incorrect Guesses (FP)	Couldn't Guess (FN)
ConceptNet Numberbatch			
assassination	murder	assassin, killing	president, kill
sect	religion, cult	religious	group
newt	salamander	democrat, republican	lizard, amphibian
Baroni and Lenci (Count-based)			
assassination	-	killing, kidnapping, massacre	president, murder, kill
sect	cult	fraternity, republic	group, religion
newt	salamander	ladybird, alligator	lizard, amphibian

Table 3: Responses to Cues by two of the compared pretrained embeddings, along with ground truth responses

Positives are those words that were correct responses (according to SWOW-8500) but could not be guessed by E (not present in SWOW-8500). False Negatives correspond to wrong guesses by E. Note that since no ground truth responses are labelled as negative (i.e., we only have words that *should* be present in the response set for a given cue), the number of True Negatives is always 0. From a confusion matrix, we can report accuracy, error, precision, recall, F1 score, and also a confidence interval for the error score.

Lastly, we also conduct downstream evaluation of embeddings on five tasks (Sentiment Analysis, Chunking, Natural Language Inference, Named Entity Recognition, and POS Tagging) using the VecEval framework (Nayak et al., 2016). The original framework uses, on top of the embedding layers, LSTMs for some of the tasks. This brings up the question of which other architectures should then be tried out. Since bidirectional language modelling has been shown to outperform a simple left-to-right traversal (Devlin et al., 2018), should biLSTMs be used instead? What about Transformers, or self-attention layers (Vaswani et al., 2017)? To avoid a very large number of model parameters, and to conveniently report results only about the word embeddings like we intend to, we instead chose to go ahead with simple feed forward neural networks (one or two hidden layers) and no LSTM layers. Based on several experiments, we chose our hyperparameters as: 50 neurons per hidden layer, a dropout of 0.5, and 50 epochs with a batch size of 128. For details of the tasks and data involved, please refer to their paper or webpage. [13]

---

[13] http://veceval.com

5   Results

Table 3 is a sample from the cues and responses in the SWOW-8500 task. For each cue, the ground truth extracted from SWOW is the union of the words shown under columns *Correct Guesses (True Positives)* and *Couldn't Guess (False Negatives)*. It is noteworthy how (qualitatively) close-to-correct are the responses by ConceptNet as opposed to those by the Count-Based embedding, and as we shall see, the same holds in the quantitative scores assigned to the two, by SWOW-8500 task.

Table 4 shows performance of the selected pretrained embeddings on intrinsic evaluation: the upper half covering existing word similarity datasets and the lower half covers SWOW-8500. ConceptNet Numberbatch seems to outperform all the others, which could be attributed to it being based on a knowledge graph that links words based on what concepts people think are associated. Table 5 shows performances on Downstream tasks.

From Table 5 and the upper half of Table 4, one can see a good correlation between intrinsic and extrinsic evaluations, contrary to past reports (Faruqui et al., 2016), at least for Fixed versions of the tasks. However for model runs where Finetuning was allowed, and with a large enough training set, even Random Baseline embeddings quickly came at par with the others. This goes to show that, for the mostly classification-type tasks that we considered, requiring little linguistic knowledge and relying on topical semantics, our proposed task acts as a great proxy.

Within Table 4, we notice how the Precision, Recall, and F1 scores (from our proposed SWOW-8500 task) correlate well with all intrinsic evalua-

	CN	FT	GloVe	w2v	Count	Base	Pairs	OOV
EN-MEN-TR-3k	0.855	0.806	0.744	0.771	0.254	0.014	3000	423
CI width:	**0.027**	**0.036**	**0.046**	**0.041**	**0.095**	**0.102**		
EN-MC-30	0.932	0.940	0.902	0.916	0.658	0.264	30	10
CI width:	0.190	0.177	0.276	0.240	0.725	1.054		
EN-MTurk-771	0.839	0.740	0.659	0.685	0.228	0.034	771	192
CI width:	0.064	0.098	0.122	0.114	0.203	0.213		
EN-SIMLEX-999	0.638	0.426	0.359	0.435	0.179	0.030	999	113
CI width:	0.103	0.141	0.151	0.141	0.170	0.173		
EN-VERB-143	0.569	0.324	0.454	0.538	0.360	0.072	144	124
CI width:	0.833	1.026	0.940	0.864	1.005	1.105		
EN-YP-130	0.727	0.542	0.524	0.463	0.178	-0.077	130	48
CI width:	0.274	0.403	0.413	0.445	0.541	0.554		
EN-RW-STANFORD	0.815	0.666	0.552	0.648	0.401	-0.113	2034	1952
CI width:	0.200	0.325	0.402	0.338	0.480	0.558		
EN-RG-65	0.939	0.943	0.862	0.819	0.492	-0.084	65	20
CI width:	0.202	0.196	0.217	0.275	0.593	0.751		
EN-WS-353-ALL	0.814	0.738	0.615	0.707	0.287	-0.051	353	88
CI width:	0.108	0.145	0.198	0.160	0.295	0.315		
EN-WS-353-SIM	0.842	0.826	0.683	0.776	0.448	0.002	203	43
CI width:	0.121	0.132	0.221	0.166	0.327	0.406		
EN-WS-353-REL	0.771	0.709	0.608	0.659	0.090	-0.163	252	68
CI width:	0.157	0.192	0.242	0.217	0.375	0.369		
EN-MTurk-287	0.863	0.816	0.764	0.779	0.261	-0.253	287	187
CI width:	0.137	0.179	0.221	0.210	0.478	0.481		
EN-SimVerb-3500	0.580	0.337	0.208	0.341	0.088	-0.022	3500	694
CI width:	0.064	0.086	0.093	0.086	0.096	0.098		
Precision	0.254	0.223	0.171	0.169	0.059	0.000		
Recall	0.280	0.246	0.189	0.186	0.065	0.000		
F1 Score	0.266	0.233	0.180	0.177	0.061	0.000	8500	2019
Error	0.746	0.777	0.829	0.831	0.941	1.000		
(Error CI width)	**0.008**	**0.008**	**0.007**	**0.007**	**0.005**	**0.000**		

Table 4: Intrinsic tasks performance. CN: ConceptNet Numberbatch; FT: FastText; Count: Baroni and Lenci. Pairs: Number of word pairs in the dataset; OOV: Number of word pairs of which at least one word was missing (for upper half of table) or Number of cues missing (for lower half of table) in the common vocabulary shared by the six pre-trained embeddings. All Confidence Intervals (CI) reported at 99% confidence level.

tions. Thus SWOW task captures more or less the same properties already captured by existing word similarity datasets. So far the only added advantage is that it has already been built (along with others like USF and EAT), and therefore did not require additional expensive annotation efforts.

The large scale of SWOW also offers a solu-tion to the underlying shortcomings in intrinsic evaluations: reporting statistical signficance. As evident from Table 4, SWOW-8500 offers up to three times narrower confidence intervals for error rate, as opposed to the best amongst word similarity datasets, i.e. EN-MEN-TR-3k. The table cites all values at Confidence Intervals 99%. Even at

	CN	FT	GloVe	w2v	Count	Random
Ques Fixed	0.6245	0.5055	0.6099	0.6264	0.5000	0.2234
Ques Finetuned	0.7015	0.7143	0.6978	0.7033	0.4506	0.7033
Senti Fixed	0.6984	0.6663	0.5436	0.6766	0.4874	0.5092
Senti Finetuned	0.6318	0.6445	0.6468	0.6480	0.5344	0.6640
Chunk Fixed	0.6598	0.6605	0.5980	0.6352	0.4168	0.3138
Chunk Finetuned	0.5824	0.5682	0.5925	0.6002	0.3863	0.3138
NLI Fixed	0.4142	0.4222	0.3234	0.3234	0.3345	0.3233
NLI Finetuned	0.4312	0.4303	0.4334	0.4280	0.3398	0.4245
NER Fixed	0.9264	0.9297	0.9226	0.9245	0.8332	0.8332
NER Finetuned	0.9145	0.9124	0.9190	0.9197	0.8332	0.8332
POS Fixed	0.6625	0.6695	0.6285	0.6547	0.3609	0.3244
POS Finetuned	0.5323	0.5305	0.5491	0.5456	0.3535	0.3244

Table 5: Downstream tasks performance. CN: ConceptNet Numberbatch; FT: FastText; Count: Baroni and Lenci

a more modest confidence level of 90%, for the largest intrinsic dataset, i.e. SimVerb with 3500 word pairs, the accuracy of Numberbatch embeddings at 90% confidence could be reported within a span of 0.039. The smallest dataset MC had 30 data points, leading to a 90% confidence span of 0.114. For SWOW with 6481 data points, the error rate can be reported with a 90% confidence span of 0.003. Thus, we have greater confidence in reporting SWOW evaluations than with previous intrinsic datasets, yet have little difference in actual (relative) scores reported.

The Confidence Intervals for correlation scores reported are based on the Fischer Transformation (Fisher, 1915). The transformation is defined as $z_r = \frac{\ln\left(\frac{1+r}{1-r}\right)}{2}$, where r is the correlation coefficient. Thereafter, the confidence interval (lower and upper limits) can be computed as: $\hat{z} = z_r \pm \frac{z_{1-\frac{\alpha}{2}}}{\sqrt{N-3}}$, where N is the number of pairs of observations, (in our case the number of pairs shared with vocabulary).

Confidence Interval for the SWOW-8500, which is a classification task, is reported as the Wilson Score Interval (Wilson, 1927). The error interval (lower and upper limits) are defined as: $e = \hat{e} \pm z\sqrt{\frac{e(1-e)}{n}}$, where e is the error value, z is the constant (equal 2.58 for 99% CI), and n is the number of observations evaluated upon (equal to the total number of responses for all cues in SWOW-8500).

6 Conclusions and Future Work

In this paper, we've suggested a new breed of intrinsic evaluation tasks, that rely not on word similarity but on word association. More concretely, we use the Small World of Words dataset to create SWOW-8500, an intrinsic evaluation task We describe the task, and compare performance for six word embeddings, on (1) our proposed task, on (2) *thirteen* word similarity tasks, and on (3) *five* downstream tasks.

We find that the same sets of properties as captured by word similarity datasets, which have been shown to correlate with downstream tasks as well, are also captured by the Word Association task SWOW-8500. To add to that, we report higher confidence scores which shall help in reporting significance of results on intrinsic evaluation better. Thus we hope to dispel the suspicion over results reported using the (relatively) small word similarity datasets, since they are now corroborated with much larger human studies as well.

There remain several interesting directions to be explored, primarily the use of even more Word Association datasets (mentioned in Section 2.2). While in this paper, we've cited only the Response Prediction task, we tried out several others, including a Word Similarity task, and a Response Ordering task. With further experimentation, it would be interesting to see what properties of embeddings do these variations capture. Lastly, more downstream tasks could be tested for correlation, e.g. morphological analysis.

References

Eneko Agirre, Enrique Alfonseca, Keith Hall, Jana Kravalova, Marius Pasca, and Aitor Soroa. 2009. A study on similarity and relatedness using distributional and wordnet-based approaches. In *Proceedings of Human Language Technologies: The 2009 Annual Conference of the North American Chapter of the Association for Computational Linguistics*, pages 19–27, Boulder, Colorado. Association for Computational Linguistics.

Waleed Ammar, George Mulcaire, Yulia Tsvetkov, Guillaume Lample, Chris Dyer, and Noah A. Smith. 2016. Massively multilingual word embeddings. *CoRR*, abs/1602.01925.

Marco Baroni, Georgiana Dinu, and Germán Kruszewski. 2014. Don't count, predict! a systematic comparison of context-counting vs. context-predicting semantic vectors. In *Proceedings of the 52nd Annual Meeting of the Association for Computational Linguistics (Volume 1: Long Papers)*, pages 238–247, Baltimore, Maryland. Association for Computational Linguistics.

Piotr Bojanowski, Edouard Grave, Armand Joulin, and Tomas Mikolov. 2017. Enriching word vectors with subword information. *Transactions of the Association for Computational Linguistics*, 5(1):135–146.

Elia Bruni, Gemma Boleda, Marco Baroni, and Nam Khanh Tran. 2012. Distributional semantics in technicolor. In *Proceedings of the 50th Annual Meeting of the Association for Computational Linguistics (Volume 1: Long Papers)*, pages 136–145, Jeju Island, Korea. Association for Computational Linguistics.

Simon De Deyne, Daniel J Navarro, and Gert Storms. 2013. Associative strength and semantic activation in the mental lexicon: evidence from continued word associations. Cognitive Science Society.

Simon De Deyne, Danielle J Navarro, Amy Perfors, Marc Brysbaert, and Gert Storms. 2018. The small world of words english word association norms for over 12,000 cue words. *Behavior research methods*, pages 1–20.

Simon De Deyne, Amy Perfors, and Daniel J. Navarro. 2016. Predicting human similarity judgments with distributional models: The value of word associations. In *Proceedings of COLING 2016, the 26th International Conference on Computational Linguistics: Technical Papers*, pages 1861–1870, Osaka, Japan. The COLING 2016 Organizing Committee.

Jacob Devlin, Ming-Wei Chang, Kenton Lee, and Kristina Toutanova. 2018. Bert: Pre-training of deep bidirectional transformers for language understanding. *arXiv preprint arXiv:1810.04805*.

Manaal Faruqui and Chris Dyer. 2014. Community evaluation and exchange of word vectors at word-vectors.org. In *Proceedings of 52nd Annual Meeting of the Association for Computational Linguistics: System Demonstrations*, pages 19–24, Baltimore, Maryland. Association for Computational Linguistics.

Manaal Faruqui, Yulia Tsvetkov, Pushpendre Rastogi, and Chris Dyer. 2016. Problems with evaluation of word embeddings using word similarity tasks. In *Proceedings of the 1st Workshop on Evaluating Vector-Space Representations for NLP*, pages 30–35, Berlin, Germany. Association for Computational Linguistics.

Lev Finkelstein, Evgeniy Gabrilovich, Yossi Matias, Ehud Rivlin, Zach Solan, Gadi Wolfman, and Eytan Ruppin. 2002. Placing search in context: the concept revisited. *ACM Trans. Inf. Syst.*, 20(1):116–131.

R. A. Fisher. 1915. Frequency distribution of the values of the correlation coefficient in samples from an indefinitely large population. *Biometrika*, 10(4):507–521.

Guy Halawi, Gideon Dror, Evgeniy Gabrilovich, and Yehuda Koren. 2012. Large-scale learning of word relatedness with constraints. In *The 18th ACM SIGKDD International Conference on Knowledge Discovery and Data Mining, KDD '12, Beijing, China, August 12-16, 2012*, pages 1406–1414.

Terry Joyce. 2005. Constructing a large-scale database of japanese word associations. *Glottometrics*, 10:82–99.

Carl Gustav Jung. 1918. *Studies in word-association.* W. Heinemann, Limited.

Jaeyoung Jung, Li Na, and Hiroyuki Akama. 2010. Network analysis of korean word associations. In *Proceedings of the NAACL HLT 2010 First Workshop on Computational Neurolinguistics*, pages 27–35. Association for Computational Linguistics.

George R Kiss, Christine Armstrong, Robert Milroy, and James Piper. 1973. An associative thesaurus of english and its computer analysis. *The computer and literary studies*, pages 153–165.

Mathieu Lafourcade. 2007. Making people play for lexical acquisition with the jeuxdemots prototype. In *SNLP'07: 7th international symposium on natural language processing*, page 7.

Thang Luong, Richard Socher, and Christopher Manning. 2013. Better word representations with recursive neural networks for morphology. In *Proceedings of the Seventeenth Conference on Computational Natural Language Learning*, pages 104–113, Sofia, Bulgaria. Association for Computational Linguistics.

Tomas Mikolov, Kai Chen, Greg Corrado, and Jeffrey Dean. 2013a. Efficient estimation of word representations in vector space. In *1st International Conference on Learning Representations, ICLR 2013,*

Scottsdale, Arizona, USA, May 2-4, 2013, Workshop Track Proceedings.

Tomas Mikolov, Ilya Sutskever, Kai Chen, Gregory S. Corrado, and Jeffrey Dean. 2013b. Distributed representations of words and phrases and their compositionality. In *Advances in Neural Information Processing Systems 26: 27th Annual Conference on Neural Information Processing Systems 2013. Proceedings of a meeting held December 5-8, 2013, Lake Tahoe, Nevada, United States.*, pages 3111–3119.

George A Miller and Walter G Charles. 1991. Contextual correlates of semantic similarity. *Language and cognitive processes*, 6(1):1–28.

Marvin Minsky. 1988. *Society of mind.* Simon and Schuster.

Helen Moss, Lianne Older, and Lianne JE Older. 1996. *Birkbeck word association norms.* Psychology Press.

Neha Nayak, Gabor Angeli, and Christopher D. Manning. 2016. Evaluating word embeddings using a representative suite of practical tasks. In *Proceedings of the 1st Workshop on Evaluating Vector-Space Representations for NLP*, pages 19–23, Berlin, Germany. Association for Computational Linguistics.

Douglas L Nelson, Cathy L McEvoy, and Thomas A Schreiber. 2004. The university of south florida free association, rhyme, and word fragment norms. *Behavior Research Methods, Instruments, & Computers*, 36(3):402–407.

Jeffrey Pennington, Richard Socher, and Christopher D. Manning. 2014. Glove: Global vectors for word representation. In *Empirical Methods in Natural Language Processing (EMNLP)*, pages 1532–1543.

Julien Plu, Kévin Cousot, Mathieu Lafourcade, Raphaël Troncy, and Giuseppe Rizzo. Jeuxdeliens: Word embeddings and path-based similarity for entity linking using the french jeuxdemots lexical semantic network. In *Actes de la conférence Traitement Automatique de la Langue Naturelle, TALN 2018*, page 529.

Kira Radinsky, Eugene Agichtein, Evgeniy Gabrilovich, and Shaul Markovitch. 2011. A word at a time: computing word relatedness using temporal semantic analysis. In *Proceedings of the 20th International Conference on World Wide Web, WWW 2011, Hyderabad, India, March 28 - April 1, 2011*, pages 337–346.

Herbert Rubenstein and John B. Goodenough. 1965. Contextual correlates of synonymy. *Commun. ACM*, 8(10):627–633.

Tobias Schnabel, Igor Labutov, David Mimno, and Thorsten Joachims. 2015. Evaluation methods for unsupervised word embeddings. In *Proceedings of the 2015 Conference on Empirical Methods in Natural Language Processing*, pages 298–307, Lisbon, Portugal. Association for Computational Linguistics.

Robert Speer, Joshua Chin, and Catherine Havasi. 2017. Conceptnet 5.5: An open multilingual graph of general knowledge. In *Proceedings of the Thirty-First AAAI Conference on Artificial Intelligence, February 4-9, 2017, San Francisco, California, USA.*, pages 4444–4451.

Ashish Vaswani, Noam Shazeer, Niki Parmar, Jakob Uszkoreit, Llion Jones, Aidan N. Gomez, Lukasz Kaiser, and Illia Polosukhin. 2017. Attention is all you need. In *Advances in Neural Information Processing Systems 30: Annual Conference on Neural Information Processing Systems 2017, 4-9 December 2017, Long Beach, CA, USA*, pages 6000–6010.

Edwin B. Wilson. 1927. Probable inference, the law of succession, and statistical inference. *Journal of the American Statistical Association*, 22(158):209–212.

Dongqiang Yang and David Martin Powers. 2006. *Verb similarity on the taxonomy of WordNet.* Masaryk University.

Michael Zhai, Johnny Tan, and Jinho D. Choi. 2016. Intrinsic and extrinsic evaluations of word embeddings. In *Proceedings of the Thirtieth AAAI Conference on Artificial Intelligence, February 12-17, 2016, Phoenix, Arizona, USA.*, pages 4282–4283.

Classification of Semantic Paraphasias:
Optimization of a Word Embedding Model

Katy McKinney-Bock and **Steven Bedrick**
Center for Spoken Language Understanding
Oregon Health & Science University
Portland, Oregon, USA
{mckinnka,bedricks}@ohsu.edu

Abstract

In clinical assessment of people with aphasia, impairment in the ability to recall and produce words for objects (*anomia*) is assessed using a confrontation naming task, where a target stimulus is viewed and a corresponding label is spoken by the participant. Vector space word embedding models have had inital results in assessing semantic similarity of target-production pairs in order to automate scoring of this task; however, the resulting models are also highly dependent upon training parameters. To select an optimal family of models, we fit a beta regression model to the distribution of performance metrics on a set of 2,880 grid search models and evaluate the resultant first- and second-order effects to explore how parameterization affects model performance. Comparing to SimLex-999, we show that clinical data can be used in an evaluation task with comparable optimal parameter settings as standard NLP evaluation datasets.

1 Introduction

In clinical assessment of people with aphasia, impairment in the ability to recall and produce words for objects (*anomia*) is assessed using a confrontation naming task, where a target stimulus is viewed and a corresponding label is spoken by the participant. Semantic impairment is measured by a clinician's rating of semantic similarity between the target-production pairs, and involves a defined similarity criteria involving synonymy, association, and hypernymy. Research into word embedding models has shown that different window parameterization settings capture different semantic relations of association/relatedness vs synonymy, functional properties vs topicality, and word embedding models have been adapted to synonymy, association, and hypernymy (Hill et al., 2015; Levy et al., 2015; Levy and Goldberg, 2015; Lison and Kutuzov, 2017). A central question in NLP research is how to use extrinsic evaluation to measure what semantic relations are encoded by a model. In this paper, we engage in the interdiscplinary question of how semantic relations can be modeled in a clinical domain, and present an application of word embedding models for assessing semantic impairment.

The Philadelphia Naming Test (PNT) implements one such naming task that was developed for psycholinguistic and clinical research; the scoring of this test involves a large taxonomy of coding responses based on phonological and semantic similarity of the response to the target object (Roach et al., 1996). The taxonomy is motivated by Dell's two-step model of aphasia, where anomia results from a disruption in accessing both the phonological representation as well as semantic properties of the object (Dell, 1986).

PNT scoring is time-intensive due to the high number of items, and there have been successful attempts to both shorten the number of items on the test via computer adaptive assessment (Hula et al., 2015) as well as automate the scoring of the PNT via automated classification of paraphasias to facilitate the use of the PNT as a tool in clinical practice (Fergadiotis et al., 2016). Our work is part of a broader goal to develop an end-to-end automation of the PNT, from presentation of target items to an individual error profile.

In this paper, we present results of a classification task that identifies semantic paraphasias (errors) on the PNT, using a word embedding model to measure semantic similiarity of a production to the target item. Fergadiotis et al. (2016) showed that word embeddings can be successfully applied to classification of semantic paraphasias in the context of the PNT, and our paper builds on this baseline work by exploring (i) the nature of semantic similarity that their optimal model encodes; (ii) the relationship between the evaluation

52

Proceedings of the 3rd Workshop on Evaluating Vector Space Representations for NLP, pages 52–62
Minneapolis, USA, June 6, 2019. ©2019 Association for Computational Linguistics

synonym	TOILET → "commode"
category coordinate	BANANA → "apple"
superordinate	APPLE → "fruit"
subordinate	FLOWER → "rose"
associated	BENCH → "park"
diminutive	DOG → "doggie"

Table 1: PNT Semantic Error Relations

metric, a large database of PNT target-production pairs, and the distribution of similarity scores in an optimal model.

We present results of parameter optimization tasks and post-hoc analysis of the resulting vector space in optimal and non-optimal models for the downstream application of classifying semantic paraphasias on the PNT, using a novel application of the beta regression model to evaluate grid search parameters. We then compare the evaluation metric of psycholinguistic aphasic data with SimLex-999, a standard NLP evaluation tasks with measured controls for synonymy and association, and explore best practices for adapting models to psycholinguistic, clinical environments.

2 Optimizing for confrontation naming

2.1 Using Clinical Data for Model Evaluation

Canonical word embedding tasks strive to model semantic relations that are similar to those used in the definition of PNT semantic errors such as synonymy and association (e.g. Hill et al. (2015); Levy et al. (2015)), and thus should be well suited for the classification of semantic errors in the PNT. Conventional scoring of the PNT defines a criteria for semantic errors that involves a real word noun production that is in one of six semantic relations with the target word; see Table 1 (Roach et al., 1996).

The PNT consists of 175 items, represented by a set of black-and-white images, and were selected based on a series of controls, involving varying word frequency based on Francis and Kučera (1982), word length (1 to 4 syllables), and high name performance by control participants (Roach et al., 1996). Items in the PNT come from several semantic categories, and avoid landmarks or other recognizable individuals (Mirman et al., 2010). The Moss Aphasia Psycholinguistic Project Database (MAPPD) contains transcribed responses from over 300 administrations of the PNT, and is often used in aphasiological research; in this work, we use a subsample of 152 admin-

istrations selected on the basis of clinical characteristics. The 152 administrations of the PNT are from 99 subjects from 1-195 months post onset of aphasia. Five different sub-types of aphasia were present among the subjects (anomic, Broca, conduction, transcortical sensory, and Wernicke). Some subjects had multiple administrations of the PNT at different months post onset; the range is 1-6 administrations per subject.

The frequency and length controls for targets on the PNT, in addition to the semantic relations that define paraphasic errors on the naming test, establish a paradigm for target-production word pairs that is quite similar to the structure of certain external evaluation datasets developed for word embedding models. For example, SimLex-999 (Hill et al., 2015) is a benchmark dataset for assessing semantic similarity that is based on human ratings of word pairs on a scale of *synonymy*, as opposed to *association/relatedness*. SimLex-999 balances word association strength using the USF Free Association norms, samples from both associated and unassociated word pairs, and controls for features such as the concreteness and part-of-speech of the word pairs. Additionally, the PNT involves human evaluation of these semantic relations – in this case, two trained clinicians – with instructions that train evaluators to look for specific dimensions of semantic similiarity when evaluating whether a word pair is semantically similar (the instructions are very similar to those used by SimLex-999). Comparing results from MAPPD, which depends on a clinician's identification of a word pair as semantically similar, with results from SimLex-999 should establish whether clinical data is a reliable evaluation metric for embedding models.

2.2 Parameterization Affects Semantic Relations in Word Embedding Models

From the NLP literature, parameterization is one consideration that has been shown to have a large effect on the semantic information encoded in word embedding models. In general, larger context windows are associated with more topical similarities, while smaller windows are expected to produce more functional/syntactic similarities (Goldberg, 2015). For Skipgram models, a smaller window size is associated with increased performance on SimLex-999, a word pair similiarity task (Lison and Kutuzov, 2017), and qualitatively less topicality (Levy and Goldberg, 2015). Additionally, there are more domain general considerations when optimizing models to our downstream task. It has been shown that there is an ideal parameter setting for dimensionality of the resulting word vectors that is neither too high nor too low (Landauer and Dumais, 1997; Yin and Shen, 2018).

3 Methods

The current study tests whether model architecture, corpus preparation, and training parameters influence the semantic content of the word embedding model, as measured via the downstream classification task of scoring paraphasic errors on the PNT. We performed a grid search over these sets of parameters, and we evaluate the resultant models on both the PNT dataset as well as the SimLex-999 dataset (Hill et al., 2015), to evaluate and compare what patterns both evaluation methods find in the data. In doing this, we ask whether the items and semantic similarity criteria of the Philadelphia Naming Test are informative in the context of evaluating parameter settings of word embedding models.

3.1 Corpus Preparation Pipelines

Following the method described by Fergadiotis et al. (2016), four versions of the English Gigaword corpus (LDC2011T07) were prepared,[1] with stemming and stopword/punctuation removal as variables (see Table 2).[2] Stemming was done using NLTK's implementation of the Porter stemming algorithm (Porter, 1980; Bird et al., 2009). Stopword removal used the NLTK list of English-language stop words, notably including *can*, which is a PNT item; punctuation was re-

Parameter	Levels
Corpus Preparation	+Stemming, -Stemming
Corpus Preparation	+Stopword Removal, -Stopword Removal
Dimensionality	100, 200, 500, 750
Minimum Word Frequency	100, 250, 500, 750, 1000, 1500, 2000, 3000, 4000, 5000
Context Window Size	1, 2, 3, 4, 5, 10, 15, 20, 25

Table 2: Grid Search Variables

moved with stopwords.[3]

3.2 *word2vec* Training Parameters

At training time, three parameters were varied: the size of the *context window*[4], *dimensionality* of word embedding vectors, and *minimum word frequency* threshold (see Table 2). 1,440 CBOW and 1,440 Skipgram models were trained using Gensim v3.4.0, using the four Gigaword corpora, varying the above-mentioned parameters. The default *word2vec* training parameters were used for both CBOW and Skipgram models, including a negative sampling rate of 5, a negative sampling exponent of 0.75, `cbow_mean=1` (uses the mean rather than the sum of context word vectors), 5 training epochs, alpha = 0.025, a minimum learning rate of .0001, and downsampling word frequency of 0.001.[5]

3.3 Evaluation Tasks

3.3.1 MAPPD Database of Philadelphia Naming Tests

We evaluated the word embedding model using a semantic classification task for all trials in the MAPPD database. To do this, we took the orthographic representation of the visual target item and the produced response to the naming task to be a target-production word pair in the embedding model, and used cosine similarity scores as input to the classifier to determine semantic similarity of

---

[1] A reviewer suggests that multiple corpora could have been included in the grid search, with which we wholeheartedly agree. Our preliminary experiments using pretrained embedding models trained on different corpora (such as a Wikipedia crawl), do not show large differences in performance in terms of optimal parameter settings. We leave a more detailed parameter search over different corpora to future research, and do have reason to expect that corpus selection would be important for this task. With the embeddings described in the present study, we observed word sense issues for certain PNT items, such as *head*, which when trained on newswire text obtains a dominant word sense for *ruler/dictator/chairperson* rather than the body part; work aimed at modeling and addressing issues of word sense is in progress.

[2] Note that the original paper by Fergadiotis et al. had used a version of the Gigaword corpus that had been augmented with additional conversational text; we elected to use the standard "vanilla" version of Gigaword, for reasons of reproducibility. An initial pilot study showed that the changes to the corpus resulted in negligible differences in performance.

[3] For comparability with previous classification experiments, the version of Gigaword with +Stemming, +Stopword Removal was formatted with line breaks after each one article. This may have had an effect on window trimming at training time for this particular variable manipulation. However, the limited second-order interaction of stemming and stopword removal shows that this likely had only a minor effect (see Section 4). Samples from the corpora are in Appendix A.

[4] *word2vec* window is symmetrical on both sides of target word; e.g. window $n = 1$ is [Word1 Target Word2].

[5] A future grid search parameter could include a comparison of *word2vec* output/decoding methods (hierarchical softmax vs. negative sampling), along with their various related hyperparameter settings. We did not vary this in the current study.

target-production pairs in MAPPD. Cosine similarity of the vectors for the target and production were computed from each model on a transformed scale of [0,1]; target/production pairs including an OOV term were assigned a similarity score of 0.[6]

We then used these cosine similarity scores to determine whether, for the purposes of PNT item scoring, a subject's production is sufficiently similar to the target word to count as a semantic paraphasia. Following the approach described by Fergadiotis et al. (2016), we do this via threshold-based classification: word pairs with cosine similiary *above* a pre-identified threshold are classified as paraphasias with semantic relatedness, and word pairs with cosine similiarity below the threshold are classified as not semantically related. This approach has the advantage of being easily integrated into downstream classifiers in a way that is interpretable as well as tunable (by raising or lowering the threshold, we can trivially trade off precision for recall). Furthermore, there exist numerous well-understood methods for optimizing the operating point of the threshold classifier. In this work, we calculated the optimal operating point for a model to be that which maximized the S1 score (the harmonic mean of sensitivity and specificity) in the cosine similiarity space.

In this work, we compared the performance of a large number of trained similarity models. To compare models, we took the set of computed similarity scores from each model and calculated the Area Under the Curve for the Receiver Operating Characteristic (AUC for ROC; Hanley and McNeil (1982)). We take AUC score as a broad, threshold-independent evaluation of model performance (Huang and Ling, 2005) and use this as a criteria for selection of our optimal family of models.

The resulting distribution of AUC scores show clear interactions over parameter settings. We used beta regression (Ferrari and Cribari-Neto, 2004) to model the distribution of the AUC scores

from our grid search, and used the resulting coefficients to find optimal settings for each parameter. Beta regression is used for a response variable that is bounded within the standard unit interval, such as rates or proportions, and is appropriate to use for data that are heteroskedastic and/or asymmetric, as is the case with the distribution of AUC scores resulting from our grid search over word embedding models. It is typical to fit two beta regression models, one for each of the two hyperparameters of the Beta distribution (mode and dispersion) (Simas et al., 2010; Cribari-Neto and Zeileis, 2010).

3.3.2 SimLex-999

Cosine similarity scores for all SimLex-999 word pairs were computed for each of the 2,880 grid search models, and Spearman's rank correlation coefficient was calculated to test the correlation of any given models' similarity scores with the human rating of similarity for synonymy. The resulting models were compared by fitting a beta regression model, scaling $(\rho + 1)/2$ as the response variable to fit the distribution of ρ to the unit interval [0,1] which is required in beta regression (see Ferrari and Cribari-Neto (2004)).

4 Results

4.1 MAPPD Grid Search

Coefficients from a beta regression model are reported individually for each parameter (a table of estimates is provided in Appendex B). Coefficients represent the log-odds of an increase in AUC score per unit change in that parameter. We take the *mean* model as the main heuristic to evaluate how each parameter moves the center of AUC distribution. *Precision* model coefficients are used to evaluate how each parameter changes the dispersion of the data (positive coefficients indicate smaller dispersion). In beta regression, the dispersion (or precision) parameter ϕ increases as the variance of the reponse variable decreases when the mean of the response variable is fixed (response variable in this case is the AUC score) (Ferrari and Cribari-Neto, 2004).

4.1.1 Model Type

AUC scores move in the positive direction for Skipgram models compared with CBOW models ($\beta_{\text{SKIP}} = .067, p < .001$; mean model), indicating that Skipgram models outperform CBOW models when other parameters are held constant. How-

---

[6]A reviewer of this work noted that OOVs could have been treated as missing data for this task. The output of the semantic classifier under consideration in this study is used as a feature in a larger multinomial classifier, which also involves identifying nonwords, such that in our larger error-classification pipeline, nonwords are not assigned a similarity score. In the present study we used a zero value rather than a missing value, to avoid conflating nonwords with OOVs. Additionally, we note that investigations of the resulting distribution of cosine similiarty scores shows a floor of .49, so that OOVs with a zero score are fully distinguishable from low-similarity word pairs in the MAPPD dataset.

ever, the type of word embedding model interacts with corpus preparation and window size, such that the absolute highest performing model is a CBOW model with parameters (+stemmed, +stopword removed, dimensions= 750, window size $n = 1$, frequency threshold= 100). However, Skipgram models show higher dispersion, especially with smaller window sizes.

4.1.2 Corpus Preparation

Stopword removal moves AUC scores in a positive direction when other parameters are held constant ($\beta_{\text{STOPRM}} = .108, p < .001$; mean model). A negative interaction with Skipgram models indicates that stopword removal improves CBOW models more than Skipgram models ($\beta_{\text{SKIP x STOPRM}} = -.060, p < .001$; mean model); however, for both types of models the AUC scores are still pulled in the positive direction when stopwords are removed. Stopword removal also decreases variance in the data, though there are second-order effects with all other parameters that subsequently show increased variance.

Optimal settings for stemming varies by the type of word embedding model. As a main effect, stemming improves model performance ($\beta_{\text{STEM}} = .034, p < .001$; mean model). However, the negative interaction with Skipgram models is significantly large enough that the effect is reversed, and stemming is contraindicated for Skipgram models ($\beta_{\text{SKIP x STEM}} = -0.078, p < .001$; mean model) when other parameters are held constant.

The mean model shows a non-significant effect for the interaction of stemming and stopword removal ($\beta_{\text{STEM x STOPRM}} = .004, p > .05$; mean model). See Appendix C for a heat map of perfomance broken down by corpus preparation.

4.1.3 Frequency Threshold

The frequency threshold has the largest effect on the mean model, in the negative direction ($\beta_{\text{FT}} = -0.191, p < .001$), indicating that the smallest frequency threshold is optimal for all models. This interacts with stemming as well ($\beta_{\text{STEM x FT}} = 0.079, p < .001$); models trained on stemmed Gigaword show less decrease in the mean AUC score than the non-stemmed versions. As frequency threshold decreases, dispersion increases; this is mitigated via second-order effects with Skipgram/CBOW, Stemming, and Stopword removal.

4.1.4 Dimensionality

As dimensionality increases, so do corresponding AUC scores ($\beta_{\text{DIM}} = 0.035, p < .001$). Skipgram models show even higher performance from large dimensionality ($\beta_{\text{SKIP x DIM}} = 0.015, p < .001$).

4.1.5 Window Size

Increasing window size shows a corresponding increase in AUC scores ($\beta_{\text{WIN}} = .027, p < .001$; mean model), but second-order effects show that this holds only for CBOW models. A negative interaction of window size with Skipgram models is large enough that the effect is reversed, and a larger window size is contraindicated for Skipgram models ($\beta_{\text{SKIP x WIN}} = -0.080, p < .001$; mean model).

While CBOW models generally perform better with larger windows, there is one parameter setting for window size that violates the general trend. A heat map of the three parameters is given in Figure 1, which shows that the highest AUC scores occur in the smallest windows. The inverse relationship in performance for CBOW and Skipgram models holds for a window size of [2, 25], but does not when $n=1$ (see Section 5.2).

4.1.6 Summary

The optimal parameter selection is frequency threshold=100 and dimensions=750 for all models. Skipgram models are optimal when the corpus has been stopword removed and not stemmed, with window size $n = 1$. CBOW models perform well when the corpus is stemmed and stopword-removed. While CBOW models generally show top performance as window sizes increase, with the exception that for window size $n = 1$ the CBOW models perform highest.

4.2 SimLex-999

To evaluate models on the SimLex-999 dataset, Spearman's rank correlation coefficient (ρ) was calculated for each model comparing the relationship of model similarity scores and the human similarity judgments. The mean correlation across models, mean$_\rho = .379$ and range$_\rho = (.262, .496)$, is close to the state-of-the-art SimLex-999 score reported for Skipgram *word2vec* models of .37.[7]

There is a significant moderate correlation of AUC scores to Spearman's ρ ($R = .41, p < .001$).

Following the same method for reporting AUC scores, we report only the differences on param-

---

[7] https://fh295.github.io/simlex.html

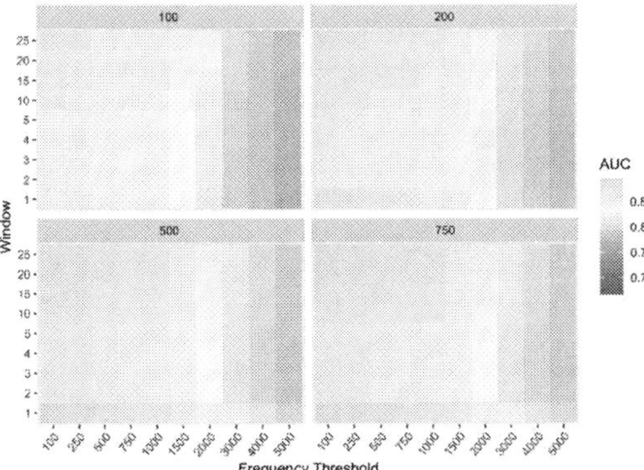

CBOW Models (N=1440)

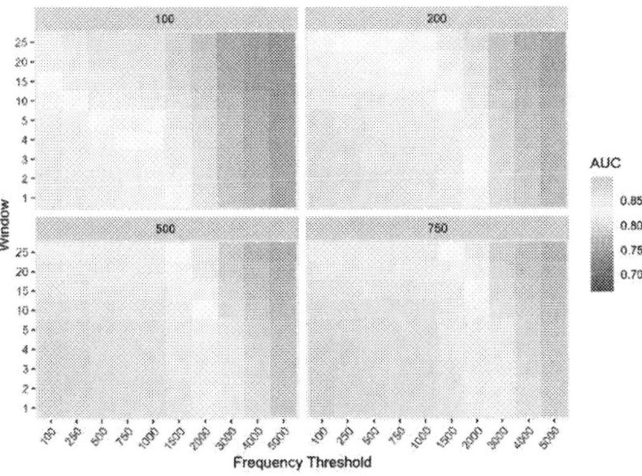

Skipgram Models (N=1440)

Figure 1: Heat Map of AUC scores for CBOW and Skipgram models, by Dimensionality (facet), Window Size, and Frequency Threshold

eterization effects for a beta regression model, fit to scaled SimLex ρ scores (Pseudo-R^2 = .874; a table of estimates is included in Appendix B).

Frequency threshold has much less of an effect on the SimLex task than the clinical MAPPD task. The beta regression model finds less of a negative impact for frequency threshold (β_{FT} = $-.028, p < .001$) than in the MAPPD model. This is due to out-of-vocabulary (OOV) counts, as these are much lower proportionally in SimLex. OOVs impact the MAPPD dataset at a higher rate partly because there is a pool of 175 items that occur, and at differing frequency thresholds some of these items are excluded from training.

Stemming is dispreferred when looking at performance on SimLex CBOW models, (β_{STEM} = $-.084, p < .001$). There is an interaction between stemming and Skipgram models that shows slight improvement in performance when Skipgram models are stemmed over CBOW models ($\beta_{\text{SKIP x STEM}}$ = $0.028, p < .001$), but still dispreferred. This differs from the MAPPD results,

where stemming improves CBOW models.

Interestingly, window size still shows an inverse relation for CBOW and Skipgram models, as in the MAPPD task. Larger window sizes are optimal for CBOW models; smaller window sizes are optimal for Skipgram models. The same exception for $n = 1$ with CBOW models is apparent, with the highest ρ in the smallest window size.

5 Discussion

5.1 Dimensionality, Frequency Threshold and Corpus Preparation

Across all model types, models with high dimensionality and low minimum frequency thresholds proved optimal. Furthermore, stopword removal also produced consistently optimal results, while stemming was optimal for CBOW models but not for Skipgram models.

Stemming proved to be a more complex parameter, and interacted with minimum frequency threshold. Models with a higher frequency threshold performed better with *unstemmed* training data, whereas those with a lower threshold benefited from stemming. This is intuitive, as stemming a corpus will increase the token frequency for observed words while reducing the number of distinct types (e.g. *cat* and *cats* are stemmed to the same form, *cat*) relative to the unstemmed version of the corpus. In the *unstemmed* condition, there will be more distinct token types whose frequency falls below any given minimum frequency threshold, which will result in proportionally more words being removed from the final model's vocabulary than would be the case in the *stemmed* condition. A greater amount of information is therefore removed prior to training, along with an increase in the out-of-vocabulary count when analyzing the PNT data.[8]

5.2 Parameter Optimization: Model Type and the Window *n*=1 Mystery

Window size affects how much linguistic context is available during training time and the semantic properties of resulting word vectors. We find concordance in the literature that Skipgram outperforms CBOW on small window sizes for word pair similarity tasks (Levy et al., 2015) and that Skipgram models show better SimLex performance for

---

[8]Looking at the resulting distribution of cosine similarity scores for comparable high vs. low frequency shows that the OOV count is much higher, while the distribution of non-OOV scores remains similar.

smaller windows (Lison and Kutuzov, 2017); our results show that Skipgram models perform better with smaller window sizes for both MAPPD and on SimLex. However, we also find overall that CBOW models show improved performance over Skipgram models as window size grows to 25, which is a much larger window size than reported in the literature on hyperparameter comparison. A notable exception is that performance for $n = 1$ shows high performance for CBOW models across all parameter settings.

In addition to small context windows, we find Skipgram models to be optimal on the non-stemmed corpora, which decreases the token frequency. Levy et al. (2015) observe that the smoothing in Skipgram models may alleviate PMI's bias towards rare occurrences, improving performance. However, it may still be the case that Skipgram models perform better with a larger variety of lower-frequency tokens overall, as in the non-stemmed corpora. This, combined with a small context window may increase the rarity of word co-occurrences overall with a given target and explain the interaction.

It remains a mystery why CBOW models show high performance with both large windows and the smallest window size $n = 1$. It may be the case that the symmetric bi-gram context returns the densest information context, only matched by window sizes that are quite large. While there are qualitative differences in the information captured by the CBOW window sizes for some items (not reported here due to space), it also appears that the resulting vector space geometry for large and small windows differs even for items where the list of most similar words is very similar.

For example, *jewelry* shares $4/5$ of the five most similar words (*pendant, earring, brooch, jewelry*) for the optimal $n = 1$ and $n = 25$ CBOW model, but the range of cosine similarity scores for the two lists of most similar words differs: $n = 1, (.60, .70)$ vs. $n = 25, (.46, .54)$. However, the optimal operating threshold for these models is approximately the same: $n = 1, S1 = .562$; $n = 25, S1 = .578$. Investigation of neighborhood density with respect to the target words across models trained with different window sizes may result in a very different geometry of the resulting embedding space. Word frequency can bias the resulting vector space of word embedding models (Gong et al., 2018), making direct compar-

ison of word vectors of high and low frequencies problematic. Simple optimization based on operating threshold on the ROC may be insufficient for overall optimization, and transformations of embedding space based on neighborhood density and word frequency an interesting vein of future work.

5.3 MAPPD and SimLex: Using Clinical Datasets for Evaluation

Optimization over the SimLex dataset shows similar parameter settings as MAPPD for dimensionality and window size. Skipgram models are optimal, and a similar pattern of performance across window sizes is observed for Skipgram and CBOW models. Key differences in frequency threshold are related to differences in out-of-vocabulary items. Stemming is dispreferred across the SimLex dataset, which differs from the MAPPD CBOW models. As MAPPD utilizes only a limited vocabulary of nouns, the stemmed corpus might have a smaller effect than on the more morphologically varied SimLex word pairs.

6 Conclusion

Using beta regression to explore how parameterization affects model performance, we show that performance on MAPPD and SimLex-999 datasets depends on similar optimal parameters. The implications, particularly for window size, are that the semantic relations encoded in these word pair datasets are comparable. However, results also reveal the importance of further investigation into the geometry of resulting vector spaces. Patterns of performance demonstrate that the MAPPD dataset, based on a carefully constructed clinical assessment, is useful as an evaluation task for word embedding models and sheds additional insight onto the sensitivity of training parameter selection.

Acknowledgments

We thank Kyle Gorman, Gerasimos Fergadiotis, and Rosemary Ingham for their contributions to this work, as well as the anonymous reviewers for their insightful and helpful comments. We also thank the Oregon Clinical and Translational Research Institute's Biostatistics & Design Program, specifically Jack Wiedrick, for statistical advice. Any errors in this paper's analysis are the authors' alone. This work was supported by the National Institute on Deafness and Other Communication Disorders under award number R01DC015999.

References

Steven Bird, Edward Loper, and Ewan Klein. 2009. *Natural Language Processing with Python*. OReilly Media Inc, Sebastapol, CA.

Francisco Cribari-Neto and Achim Zeileis. 2010. Beta regression in r. *Journal of Statistical Software, Articles*, 34(2):1–24.

G. S. Dell. 1986. A spreading-activation theory of retrieval in sentence production. *Psychological Review*, 93:283–321.

Gerasimos Fergadiotis, Kyle Gorman, and Steven Bedrick. 2016. Algorithmic classification of five characteristic types of paraphasias. *American Journal of Speech-Language Pathology*, 25:S776–S787.

S.L.P. Ferrari and F. Cribari-Neto. 2004. Beta regression for modelling rates and proportions. *Journal of Applied Statistics*, 31(7):799–815.

W. Francis and H. Kučera. 1982. *Frequency analysis of English usage: Lexicon and grammar*. Boston: Houghton Mifflin.

Yoav Goldberg. 2015. A primer on neural network models for natural language processing. *CoRR*, abs/1510.00726.

Chengyue Gong, Di He, Xu Tan, Tao Qin, Liwei Wang, and Tie-Yan Liu. 2018. Frage: Frequency-agnostic word representation. In S. Bengio, H. Wallach, H. Larochelle, K. Grauman, N. Cesa-Bianchi, and R. Garnett, editors, *Advances in Neural Information Processing Systems 31*, pages 1334–1345. Curran Associates, Inc.

J. A. Hanley and B. J. McNeil. 1982. The meaning and use of the area under a receiver operating characteristic (roc) curve. *Radiology*, 143:29–36.

Felix Hill, Roi Reichart, and Anna Korhonen. 2015. Simlex-999: Evaluating semantic models with (genuine) similarity estimation. *Computational Linguistics*, 41(4):665–695.

Jin Huang and Charles X Ling. 2005. Using auc and accuracy in evaluating learning algorithms. *IEEE Transactions on knowledge and Data Engineering*, 17(3):299–310.

William Hula, Stacey Kellough, and Gerasimos Fergadiotis. 2015. Development and simulation testing of a computerized adaptive version of the philadelphia naming test. *Journal of speech, language, and hearing research : JSLHR*, 58.

T. K. Landauer and S. T. Dumais. 1997. A solution to plato's problem: The latent semantic analysis theory of acquisition, induction, and representation of knowledge. *Psychological Review*, 104(2):211–240.

Omer Levy and Yoav Goldberg. 2015. Dependency-based word embeddings. In *Proceedings of the 52nd Annual Meeting of the Association for Computational Linguistics (Short Papers)*, pages 302–308.

Omer Levy, Yoav Goldberg, and Ido Dagan. 2015. Improving distributional similarity with lessons learned from word embeddings. *Transactions of the Association for Computational Linguistics*, 3:211–225.

Pierre Lison and Andrey Kutuzov. 2017. Redefining context windows for word embedding models: An experimental study. *CoRR*, abs/1704.05781.

D. Mirman, A. Brecher, G.M. Walker, P. Sobel, G.S. Dell, and M.F. Schwartz. 2010. A large, searchable, web-based database of aphasic performance on picture naming and other tests of cognitive function. *Cognitive Neuropsychology*, 27(6):495–504.

M.F. Porter. 1980. An algorithm for suffix stripping. *Program*, 14(3):130–137.

A. Roach, M.F. Schwartz, N. Martin, R.S. Grewal, and A. Brecher. 1996. The philadelphia naming test: Scoring and rationale. *Clinical Aphasiology*, 24:121–133.

A.B. Simas, W. Barreto-Souza, and A.V. Rocha. 2010. Improved estimators for a general class of beta regression models. *Computational Statistics and Data Analysis*, 54(2):348–366.

Zi Yin and Yuanyuan Shen. 2018. On the dimensionality of word embedding. In S. Bengio, H. Wallach, H. Larochelle, K. Grauman, N. Cesa-Bianchi, and R. Garnett, editors, *Advances in Neural Information Processing Systems 31*, pages 887–898.

A   Samples from Gigaword Corpora

+Stemming, +Stopword Removal

TRIBUT POUR AROUND WORLD LATE LABOUR PARTI LEADER JOHN SMITH DIE EARLIER MASSIV HEART ATTACK AGE WASHINGTON US STATE DEPART ISSU STATEMENT REGRET UNTIM DEATH SCOTTISH BARRIST PARLIAMENTARIAN SMITH THROUGHOUT DISTINGUISH CAREER GOVERN OPPOSIT LEFT PROFOUND IMPRESS HISTORI PARTI COUNTRI STATE DEPART SPOKESMAN MICHAEL MCCURRI SAID SECRETARI STATE WARREN CHRISTOPH EXTEND DEEPEST CONDOL SMITH SMITH CHILDREN

+Stemming, −Stopword Removal

TRIBUT POUR IN FROM AROUND THE WORLD *DAY* TO THE LATE LABOUR PARTI LEADER JOHN SMITH , WHO DIE EARLIER FROM A MASSIV HEART ATTACK

AGE # .

IN WASHINGTON , THE US STATE DE-
PART ISSU A STATEMENT REGRET " THE
UNTIM DEATH " OF THE RAPIER-TONGU
SCOTTISH BARRIST AND PARLIAMENTAR-
IAN .

" MR. SMITH , THROUGHOUT HIS DIS-
TINGUISH CAREER IN GOVERN AND IN
OPPOSIT , LEFT A PROFOUND IMPRESS
ON THE HISTORI OF HIS PARTI AND HIS
COUNTRI , " STATE DEPART SPOKESMAN
MICHAEL MCCURRI SAID .

" SECRETARI (OF STATE WARREN)
CHRISTOPH EXTEND HIS DEEPEST CON-
DOL TO MRS. SMITH AND TO THE SMITH
CHILDREN . "

−Stemming, +Stopword Removal

tributes poured around world late labour party
leader john smith died earlier massive heart attack
aged

washington us state department issued statement regretting untimely death scottish barrister
parliamentarian

smith throughout distinguished career government opposition left profound impression
history party country state department spokesman
michael mccurry said

secretary state warren christopher extends
deepest condolences smith smith children

−Stemming, −Stopword Removal

tributes poured in from around the world *day* to
the late labour party leader john smith , who died
earlier from a massive heart attack aged # .

in washington , the us state department issued a statement regretting " the untimely death
" of the rapier-tongued scottish barrister and
parliamentarian .

" mr. smith , throughout his distinguished
career in government and in opposition , left a
profound impression on the history of his party
and his country , " state department spokesman
michael mccurry said .

B Table of Estimates for Beta Regression Models

Parameter	MAPPD Mean Model Coefficient	SE	Precision Model Coefficient	SE	SimLex-999 Mean Model Coefficient	SE
Intercept	1.617***	(0.006)	7.778***	(0.155)	0.692***	(0.004)
SKIP	0.067***	(0.006)	-0.582***	(0.148)	0.129***	(0.004)
STEM	0.034***	(0.006)	0.119	(0.148)	-0.084***	(0.004)
STOPRM	0.108***	(0.005)	0.364*	(0.148)	0.105***	(0.004)
DIM	0.035***	(0.001)	0.056*	(0.027)	0.027***	(0.001)
WIN	0.027***	(0.003)	0.098	(0.089)	0.020***	(0.002)
FREQTHRESH	-0.191***	(0.002)	-0.118**	(0.046)	-0.028***	(0.001)
SKIP x STEM	-0.078***	(0.004)	0.053	(0.105)	0.028***	(0.003)
SKIP x STOPRM	-0.060***	(0.004)	-0.013	(0.105)	-0.077***	(0.003)
SKIP x DIM	0.015***	(0.001)	0.035	(0.021)	0.003***	(0.001)
SKIP x WIN	-0.080***	(0.002)	-0.236***	(0.064)	-0.067***	(0.002)
SKIP x FREQTHRESH	0.003*	(0.001)	0.109***	(0.033)	0.005***	(0.001)
STEM x STOPRM	0.004	(0.004)	-0.274**	(0.105)	-0.017***	(0.003)
STEM x DIM	-0.002**	(0.001)	-0.015	(0.021)	0.001	(0.001)
STEM x WIN	0.006*	(0.002)	-0.014	(0.064)	-0.003*	(0.002)
STEM x FREQTHRESH	0.079***	(0.001)	0.162***	(0.033)	0.013***	(0.001)
STOPRM x DIM	-0.006***	(0.001)	-0.062**	(0.021)	-0.002***	(0.001)
STOPRM x WIN	-0.016***	(0.002)	-0.164*	(0.064)	-0.020***	(0.002)
STOPRM x FREQTHRESH	0.000	(0.001)	0.118***	(0.033)	0.001	(0.001)
DIM x WIN	-0.002***	(0.000)	0.055***	(0.013)	-0.002***	(0.000)
DIM x FREQTHRESH	-0.004***	(0.000)	-0.029***	(0.006)	-0.000	(0.000)
WIN x FREQTHRESH	0.004***	(0.001)	-0.027	(0.020)	0.004***	(0.001)
Pseudo-R^2	0.965				0.874	
N	2880				2880	

Table 3: Table of Estimates for Beta Regression for Mean (μ) and Precision (ϕ). 'x' denotes second-order effects.
$*p < .05 / **p < .01 / ***p < .001$

C   MAPPD Grid Search Results, by Corpus Preparation Type

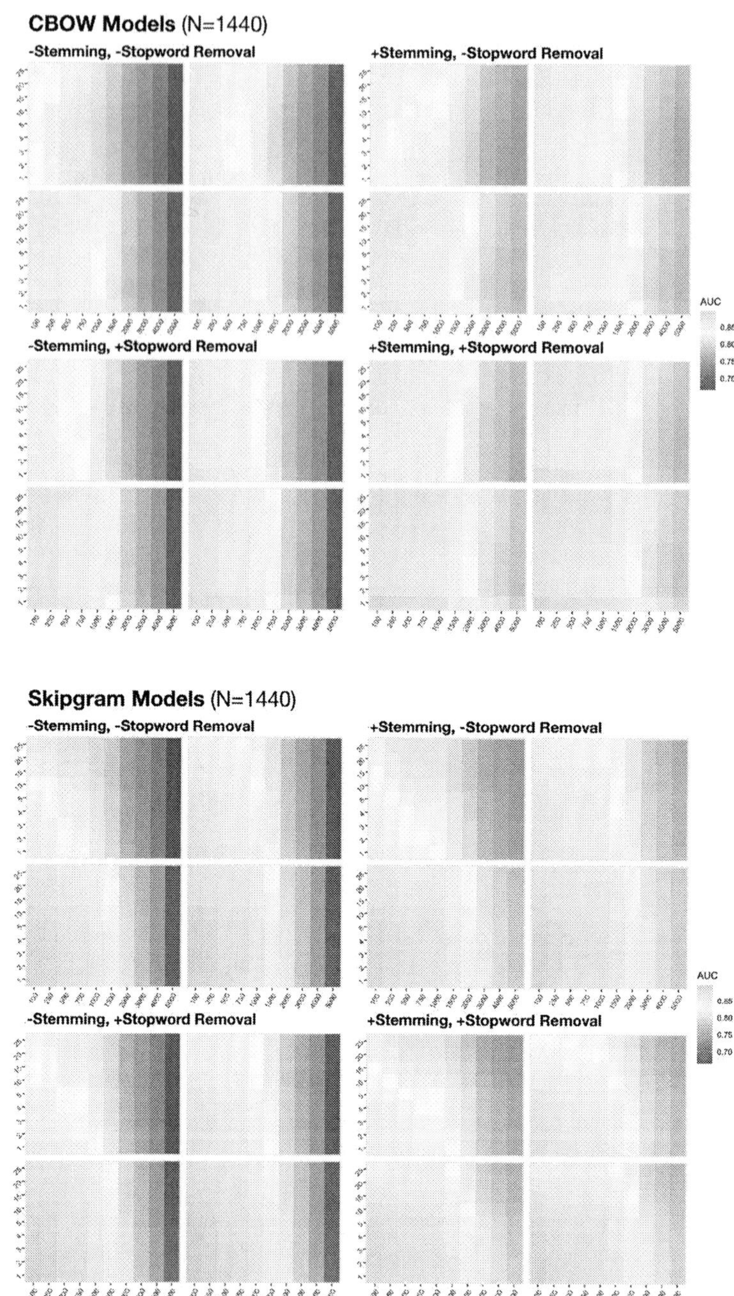

Figure 2: Heat Map of AUC scores for CBOW and Skipgram models, by Corpus Preparation Type (plot), Dimensionality (facet), Window Size, and Frequency Threshold

CODAH: An Adversarially-Authored Question Answering Dataset for Common Sense

Michael Chen   **Mike D'Arcy**   **Alisa Liu**   **Jared Fernandez**   **Doug Downey**

Department of Computer Science
Northwestern University
Evanston, IL 60208

{y-chen, m.m.darcy, alisa, jared.fern}@u.northwestern.edu
ddowney@eecs.northwestern.edu

Abstract

Commonsense reasoning is a critical AI capability, but it is difficult to construct challenging datasets that test common sense. Recent neural question answering systems, based on large pre-trained models of language, have already achieved near-human-level performance on commonsense knowledge benchmarks. These systems do not possess human-level common sense, but are able to exploit limitations of the datasets to achieve human-level scores.

We introduce the CODAH dataset, an adversarially-constructed evaluation dataset for testing common sense. CODAH forms a challenging extension to the recently-proposed SWAG dataset, which tests commonsense knowledge using sentence-completion questions that describe situations observed in video. To produce a more difficult dataset, we introduce a novel procedure for question acquisition in which workers author questions designed to target weaknesses of state-of-the-art neural question answering systems. Workers are rewarded for submissions that models fail to answer correctly both before *and* after fine-tuning (in cross-validation). We create 2.8k questions via this procedure and evaluate the performance of multiple state-of-the-art question answering systems on our dataset. We observe a significant gap between human performance, which is 95.3%, and the performance of the best baseline accuracy of 65.3% by the OpenAI GPT model.

1 Introduction

Enabling commonsense reasoning in machines is a longstanding challenge in AI. The rise of data-driven methods has led to interest in developing large datasets for commonsense reasoning over text.

The Situations With Adversarial Generations (SWAG) dataset (Zellers et al., 2018) introduced a large-scale benchmark for commonsense question answering in the form of multiple choice sentence completion questions describing situations as observed in video. However, while SWAG was constructed to be resistant to certain baseline algorithms, powerful subsequent methods were able to perform very well on the dataset. In particular, the development of the transformer architecture (Vaswani et al., 2017) has led to powerful pre-trained language model representations, including the OpenAI Transformer Language Model (Radford et al., 2018) and the Bidirectional Encoder Representations from Transformers (BERT) model (Devlin et al., 2018). BERT achieved new state-of-the-art performance on SWAG that exceeded even that of a human expert. However, BERT does not possess human-level common sense in general, as our experiments demonstrate. It is instead able to exploit regularities in the SWAG dataset to score high. This motivates the construction of additional datasets that pose new challenges, and serve as more reliable benchmarks for commonsense reasoning systems.

In this work, we introduce the **CO**mmonsense **D**ataset **A**dversarially-authored by **H**umans (**CODAH**) for commonsense question answering in the style of SWAG multiple choice sentence completion. We propose a novel method for question generation, in which human annotators are educated on the workings of a state-of-the-art question answering model, and are asked to submit questions that adversarially target the weaknesses. Annotators are rewarded for submissions in which the model fails to identify the correct sentence completion both before *and* after fine-tuning on a sample of the submitted questions, encouraging the creation of questions that are not easily learnable.

We experimentally demonstrate that CODAH's generation procedure produces a dataset with a

Proceedings of the 3rd Workshop on Evaluating Vector Space Representations for NLP, pages 63–69
Minneapolis, USA, June 6, 2019. ©2019 Association for Computational Linguistics

large gap between system performance and human expert accuracy, even when using state-of-the-art pre-trained language models with and without fine-tuning on the large SWAG dataset. Using a model initially fine-tuned on SWAG, we find that the OpenAI GPT-1 and BERT neural question answering models yield 65.3% and 64.5% accuracy, respectively, on the CODAH dataset in cross-validation. Thus, cross-validating on CODAH can form a challenging additional evaluation for SWAG-style commonsense QA systems. Human evaluators achieve 95.3% accuracy, which is substantially higher than the 85.0% (Zellers et al., 2018) and 87.7% (Ghaeini et al., 2018) human performance on the SWAG and SNLI natural language inference tasks. The high human performance suggests that answers to the CODAH questions are in fact commonsense knowledge. Finally, we also analyze differences in performance across questions that target different types of commonsense reasoning, including quantitative, negation, and object reference, showing consistency in performance for BERT and GPT on the proposed categories.

2   Related Work

Prior work in question answering has largely focused on the development of reading comprehension-based question answering and resulted in the creation of several large datasets for factoid extraction such as SQuAD (Rajpurkar et al., 2016, 2018) and the Google Natural Questions datasets (Kwiatkowski et al., 2019). In these tasks, extraction of correct answers from the provided context requires little external world knowledge, understanding of intents, or other commonsense knowledge.

Earlier work has established multiple benchmarks for natural language inference and linguistic entailment with the release SNLI (Bowman et al., 2015) and MultiNLI datasets (Williams et al., 2018). In these tasks, systems must identify whether a hypothesis agrees with or contradicts a provided premise. In these datasets, determining entailment solely relies upon the provided premise and does not require a question answering system to utilize external knowledge. More recently, the SWAG dataset (Zellers et al., 2018) directly targets natural language inference that leverages commonsense knowledge. SWAG multiple choice completion questions are con-

structed using a video caption as the ground truth with incorrect counterfactuals created using adversarially-filtered generations from an LSTM language model. State-of-the-art models for natural language inference have rapidly improved and approach human performance, which leaves little room for continued improvement on current benchmarks.

Generation of adversarial examples has also been used to increase the robustness of NLP systems as part of the *Build it, Break It, The Language Edition* Workshop (Ettinger et al., 2017). In this workshop, builders designed systems for Sentiment Analysis and Question Answer Driven Semantic Role Labeling tasks and were evaluated on the accuracy of their models on adversarial test cases designed by breakers. Whereas *Build It Break It* adversarial generation required submissions to match the format of a starter dataset and offered limited adversarial access to the target NLP systems, the CODAH construction procedure allows for entirely new questions and provide adversaries with a target model throughout the submission process, allowing workers to experiment.

3   The CODAH Dataset

Our dataset contains multiple choice sentence completion questions in the format of the SWAG dataset. Examples of the questions are shown in Table 1. Each question consists of a prompt sentence, the subject of the subsequent sentence, and four candidate completions, such that exactly one candidate completion is consistent with common sense. This task definition allows for easy evaluation by many state-of-the-art models, such as BERT and GPT-1, and enables us to utilize the large SWAG dataset for pre-training. The full dataset is available at `https://github.com/Websail-NU/CODAH`.

3.1   Question Production

We collected questions via a Web-based system. Participants were asked to compose a complete question, including the prompt, subject, and the four candidate completions. They would then be presented with the response of a pre-trained BERT model to their question. The pre-trained model consisted of a BERT-base model fine-tuned on the SWAG training set for 3 epochs with a batch size of 8. This model achieved 80.68% accuracy on the SWAG validation set. The ability to obtain

Category	Description	Example
Idioms	Including phrases whose meaning cannot be readily interpreted from the meaning of constituent parts	**A man on his first date wanted to break the ice. He** drank all of his water. threw the ice at the wall. looked at the menu. **made a corny joke.**
Negation	Including negators to dictate the meaning of the sentence	**The man's rebuttal was clearly not nonsensical. The rebuttal** has nothing to do with sense. **had some reasons associated with it.** did not make any sense. was funny.
Polysemy	Testing the understanding of multiple meanings of a single word	**An architect retrieves his compass. He** computes the area of a circle explores the open sea **draws building dimensions on a canvas** uses his compass to find the north cardinal direction
Reference	Requiring understanding of reference to one of multiple subjects	**Rose is walking the dog while Joseph cooks dinner. Rose** is following a new recipe. **enjoys the fresh air.** wags her tail with joy. cuts tomatoes for the soup.
Quantitative Reasoning	Involving basic arithmetic calculations or comparisons	**A woman is walking two dogs and carrying a cat on her way to her car. She** **puts all three animals in the back seat before driving off.** puts all four animals in the back seat before driving off. puts both animals in the back seat before driving off. puts all nine animals in the back seat before driving off.

Table 1: Question categories, descriptions, and examples

real-time feedback about the model's answers allowed participants to explore areas of weakness and design challenging questions. All submitted questions were added to the dataset, whether they fooled the baseline model or not.

Annotators were provided explicit incentives to produce questions that the model answered incorrectly. The vast majority of submissions were contributed by university computer science students, who were familiar with neural network question answering systems. Students were rewarded with extra credit points for submitting valid questions that fooled the baseline model. Further, students could earn an equal number of extra credit points for questions that fooled the model when evaluated in cross-validation, after fine-tuning on other submitted questions. This protocol was designed to encourage the creation of challenging and valid commonsense questions that are also free from stylistic annotation artifacts or redundancy, which would reduce the difficulty of the questions after fine-tuning and reduce the returns on their submissions. A small portion of the dataset was submitted anonymously by other individuals.

We received a total of 4,149 raw questions, which were read and cleaned by four annotators (the authors). During cleaning, the answer choice order was shuffled and model's output answer were hidden from the annotator. We removed submissions with multiple or no distinctive commonsense answers, spelling or grammatical errors, incorrect answers, as well as duplicate submissions. The remaining questions were judged natural and easily answerable from common sense with minimal ambiguity and dispute. The cleaning operation produced our current 2,801-question dataset.

Our 2,801-question dataset contains submissions from 116 named participants. The median, mean and standard deviation of the number of valid questions submitted by named individuals are 20.00, 21.38, and 13.86. The most prolific contributor submitted 86 questions. Anonymous participants contributed 321 questions, which is 11% of the final dataset.

4 Experiments

We evaluate the dataset on state-of-the-art neural question answering systems built on the BERT and GPT-1 architecture and provide multiple baselines. The models and experiment setups are discussed below. We also analyze the questions to identify distinctive categories of commonsense reasoning that provide a finer-grained understanding of model performances. In addition, the ablation experiments on dataset size and the use of fine-tuning on SWAG data allow us to further understand the impact of the relatively small size of CODAH.

4.1 Question Categorization

One of our goals is to analyze how system and human performance varies across questions in CODAH that employ different types of common sense. Therefore, we identified a small number of unambiguous categories of common sense, such as questions involving quantitative reasoning or negation. These categories only apply to a portion of the questions in our dataset, but have the advantage of being unambiguous and in many cases predictive of low system performance. In earlier attempts to devise categories to cover *all* questions, similar to analysis performed for textual entailment (LoBue and Yates, 2011), we found the inter-annotator agreement on such complete categorizations to be substantially lower (at <0.4), even after iterating on category definitions.

We manually inspected all questions in our dataset and annotated each with one or more category labels, representing all types of reasoning required to identify the correct answer and eliminate incorrect ones. The descriptions and examples of these categories are found in Table 1. Four human annotators (the authors) categorized the questions, and we calculated a Feiss' Kappa score of 0.63 between the annotators over an additional 50 questions. Table 2 shows the distribution of labels over the entire dataset.

Category	Count	Percentage
Idioms	249	8.8
Reference	133	4.8
Polysemy	108	3.9
Negation	116	4.1
Quantitative	87	3.1
Other	2108	75.3
Total	2801	

Table 2: Distribution of question categories.

4.2 Models

4.2.1 BERT

We evaluate a pre-trained BERT-Large implemented in PyTorch on the CODAH dataset. This model consists of a 24-layer network, with 1,024 hidden units per layer, 16-heads and a total of 340M parameters. For fine-tuning, settings were determined as described in Devlin et al. (2018): a batch size of 16, learning rate of 2e-5, and linear learning rate decay over 3 epochs (with a learning rate warmup over the first 10% of training).

4.2.2 OpenAI GPT-1

We also evaluate a pre-trained GPT model implemented in PyTorch. As described in Radford et al. (2018), this model consists of a 12-layer decoder transformer with 12 attention heads and 3,072-dimensional hidden states. Our fine-tuning configuration is the same as described in the original paper: a batch size of 32, learning rate of 6.25e-5, linear learning rate decay over 3 epochs (with warmup over 0.2% of training), and λ of 0.5 (where λ is a tuning coefficient that balances language-modeling loss and multiple-choice loss).

4.3 Model Evaluation

We evaluate the models on several different train and test configurations described below. The CODAH dataset is evaluated in 5-fold stratified cross-validation which balances the distribution of question categories in each fold.

- **CODAH:** Cross-validation fine-tuning on the CODAH dataset. The CODAH 80% experiment represents the standard cross-validation setting on the full dataset, training on 80% of the data in each fold and evaluating on the remaining 20%. The 60%, 40% and 20% ablation experiments are trained on a smaller portion of the CODAH dataset for each fold, but are evaluated in on the same test set which consists of 20% of the full dataset. The question categories are balanced in both training set and test set. This makes the results from the experiments more comparable with each other. Three trials are conducted for all settings; the mean and standard deviation of the model accuracy are reported in Table 3.

- **SWAG+CODAH:** Fine-tuned on SWAG first, then fine-tuned again in cross-validation on CODAH. Ablation experiments are conducted in the same way as in the CODAH-only setting above, with the same dataset splits for training. The mean and standard deviation of the three trials are reported in Table 3.

- **SWAG only:** Fine-tuned on SWAG and evaluated on CODAH. Only one trial is conducted.

- **Answer only:** Cross-validation fine-tuning on the full CODAH dataset with the questions left blank (in both training and testing). Only one trial is conducted.

Results for the above configurations are shown in Table 3. As a baseline, we evaluate both models on the full SWAG training and validation sets, providing an accuracy of 83.7% on BERT and 80.2% on GPT. To adjust for the difference in size between our dataset and SWAG, we also train the models on a sample of 2,241 SWAG questions (the size of the training set in each of CODAH's cross-validation folds) and evaluate them on the full SWAG validation set. This produces an accuracy of 28.7% for BERT and 63.6% for GPT.

Experiment	BERT %	GPT-1 %
CODAH 80%	49.6 (5.21)	62.4 (0.66)
CODAH 60%	42.8 (13.6)	60.8 (0.50)
CODAH 40%	42.3 (2.23)	57.1 (0.48)
CODAH 20%	39.6 (7.19)	49.5 (0.59)
SWAG+CODAH 80%	64.5 (3.46)	65.3 (0.55)
SWAG+CODAH 60%	67.3 (0.62)	63.6 (0.85)
SWAG+CODAH 40%	64.8 (0.62)	60.6 (0.37)
SWAG+CODAH 20%	60.3 (2.98)	56.3 (0.51)
SWAG only	42.1	38.1
CODAH (Answer only)	28.4	53.9

Table 3: Accuracy of BERT and GPT on different training settings when tested on CODAH. Numbers in parentheses represent the standard deviation.

4.4 Human Evaluation

For each category, we measure the accuracy of the BERT and GPT models trained on SWAG+CODAH. We also measure human accuracy as a baseline. Human accuracy was calculated as the mean accuracy of three human annotators, covering 707 dataset questions in total. Human annotators answered 95.3% of questions correctly, presenting a 7-fold reduction in error compared to the fine-turned BERT model. Inter-annotator agreement was computed over a set of 50 additional questions with a pairwise average Cohen-Kappa score of 0.89, which is interpreted as almost perfect agreement by some guidelines. Table 4 displays the accuracy of the human annotators and neural networks on each category.

5 Discussion

Based on our experiments, we find that model performance on CODAH is substantially lower

Category	Human %	BERT %	GPT-1 %
Idioms	97.5	69.5 (4.44)	72.6 (1.33)
Reference	100	63.1 (4.08)	71.0 (2.04)
Polysemy	91.7	62.9 (4.93)	55.2 (3.40)
Negation	100	60.0 (5.37)	60.5 (2.14)
Quantitative	97.6	51.5 (1.82)	49.5 (3.80)
Other	94.9	64.9 (4.33)	65.7 (0.54)
Total	95.3	64.5 (3.46)	65.3 (0.55)

Table 4: Class-wise and overall accuracy of human annotators and neural network models, sorted by BERT performance on the proposed categories. Numbers in parentheses represent the standard deviation.

than those seen on SWAG, which has seen models achieve over 85% accuracy. We observed a decrease of 19.2% on BERT and 14.9% on the OpenAI GPT-1 models between the accuracy on SWAG and the accuracy on our SWAG+CODAH setting. This is especially significant since human error on CODAH is 4.7%—less than a third of the 15% expert error on the SWAG dataset. This suggests that CODAH is challenging to our QA systems because of the difficult commonsense reasoning involved, and not because of ambiguity or intractability in the dataset.

5.1 Question Categories

The logic categories including Quantitative and Negation are especially difficult for our models, seeing some of the lowest accuracies from both models, in contrast to the 99.0% weighted average human accuracy on these categories. Surprisingly, both models performed very well on the Idioms category, suggesting that our neural systems may be capable of learning idioms just like other semantic knowledge. Further identification of additional distinctive and interesting categories that cover the entire dataset may prove very useful in directing our efforts towards aspects of our commonsense QA systems that require the most attention.

5.2 Annotation Artifacts

Annotation artifacts are known to exist in many datasets and may be exploited by supervised models to achieve inflated performances (Gururangan et al., 2018). In CODAH, we did not explicitly filter questions with artifacts or try to detect them. We instead incentivize the question authors, who have some knowledge of how the learners work, to avoid introducing noticeable artifacts in their submissions, as explained in Section 3.1. Our results show that artifacts do not provide sufficient signal for state-of-the-art neural models to come close to human-level accuracy on our data.

5.3 Answer-Only Baseline

In the answer-only experiment (where questions are omitted during training and testing), we found that BERT achieves 28.4% accuracy, only slightly above random, whereas GPT-1 achieves 53.9% accuracy, which is the equivalent of narrowing four random options down to two. By comparing this to the CODAH experiment setting, we can interpret these results as an indication of the extent to which the signal was in the answers. While this could be due to artifacts, such as the right answer commonly being of a certain length, we also observed that in many cases, distinguishing between reasonable and ridiculous answers (without seeing the premise) is a part of commonsense reasoning. For example, a commonsense reasoner would be able to rule out the choice "picks up his phone and calls his mom to tell her he doesn't have his phone" without seeing the premise, as a contradiction is contained in the answer. Similarly, "kicks a field goal, celebrates by transforming into a fish, and then quits football" is unlikely to be veracious regardless of the hidden subject.

5.4 Dataset Size

Our experiments show that CODAH forms a challenging extension to the existing SWAG dataset. Even when we train a system to perform near human-level on SWAG, and then fine-tune on CODAH, the system still struggles to answer CODAH questions correctly. However, CODAH is also smaller than SWAG. Our results do *not* suggest that CODAH questions are more difficult than SWAG questions if dataset size is equalized. When we restrict to a subset of SWAG of the same number of questions as CODAH, we find that SWAG has comparable accuracy for GPT (63.6% on reduced-size SWAG vs 62.4% for CODAH) and much lower accuracy for BERT (28.7% vs 49.6%). This shows that CODAH questions are distinct from and complementary to SWAG questions, but taken in isolation are not necessarily more challenging.

Our results suggest two recommendations for dataset construction which we hope to evaluate in future work. The first is, rather than using a single protocol to collect one monolithic dataset, the community may be able to obtain more challenging data by aggregating a variety of distinct, independently-gathered datasets that follow a similar format. For example, pre-training on SWAG and evaluating on CODAH forms a more challenging benchmark than training and testing on SWAG alone. Secondly, if we wish to use our adversarial collection approach to grow CODAH to tens of thousands of examples, we should update our system as new data arrives, so that contributors are able to tune their questions to remain difficult for the strongest, most up-to-date version of the system. Under such a data collection scheme, we may need to increase the reward for fooling the model in cross-validation compared to that for fooling the current model (whereas, these two rewards were equal in CODAH), in order to disincentivize adversarial attacks that manipulate the current model to make it easy to fool on subsequent questions.

Our experiments on different sizes of CODAH produce very different results for BERT and GPT. Unsurprisingly, GPT performance improves with more data on both the CODAH-only and SWAG+CODAH experiments, with the rate of improvement slowing down as data size increases. However, the BERT results are more challenging to interpret. On the CODAH-only setting, BERT appears to improve with data size, but the extremely high variance prevents us from being certain of any trend in BERT's performance on this setting. The variance is lower in the SWAG+CODAH setting and accuracy increases as data size goes from 20% to 60%, but accuracy decreases between SWAG+CODAH-60% and SWAG+CODAH-80% settings (although the SWAG+CODAH-80% setting has high variance and the true mean may be higher). The inconsistency in improvement with more CODAH data after training on SWAG+CODAH-60% for BERT and the reduced rate of performance gain for GPT suggest that it is unclear whether the performance of all models will improve dramatically with an even larger CODAH dataset size.

6 Conclusion

We present CODAH, a commonsense question answering dataset that is adversarially-constructed by allowing humans to view feedback from a pre-trained model and use this information to design challenging commonsense questions. Our experimental results show that CODAH questions present a complementary extension of the

SWAG dataset, testing additional modes of common sense.

We identify specific categories of commonsense questions to determine types of reasoning that are more challenging for existing models. In particular, we note that Quantitative questions have low accuracy for both BERT and GPT. A more detailed analysis into why models struggle to reason about numbers as well as development of more detailed categories of commonsense reasoning are items for future work.

Acknowledgments

We thank the anonymous reviewers, Yiben Yang, and Chandra Bhagavatula for helpful comments and feedback. We also thank the students of Northwestern EECS 349 Fall 2018, whose creativity and insight made this work possible. This work was supported in part by NSF Grant IIS-1351029 and the Allen Institute for Artificial Intelligence.

References

Samuel R Bowman, Gabor Angeli, Christopher Potts, and Christopher D Manning. 2015. A large annotated corpus for learning natural language inference. In *Proceedings of the 2015 Conference on Empirical Methods in Natural Language Processing*, pages 632–642.

Jacob Devlin, Ming-Wei Chang, Kenton Lee, and Kristina Toutanova. 2018. Bert: Pre-training of deep bidirectional transformers for language understanding. *arXiv preprint arXiv:1810.04805*.

Allyson Ettinger, Sudha Rao, Hal Daumé III, and Emily M Bender. 2017. Towards linguistically generalizable nlp systems: A workshop and shared task. In *Proceedings of the First Workshop on Building Linguistically Generalizable NLP Systems*, pages 1–10.

Reza Ghaeini, Sadid A Hasan, Vivek Datla, Joey Liu, Kathy Lee, Ashequl Qadir, Yuan Ling, Aaditya Prakash, Xiaoli Fern, and Oladimeji Farri. 2018. Dr-bilstm: Dependent reading bidirectional lstm for natural language inference. In *Proceedings of the 2018 Conference of the North American Chapter of the Association for Computational Linguistics: Human Language Technologies, Volume 1 (Long Papers)*, volume 1, pages 1460–1469.

Suchin Gururangan, Swabha Swayamdipta, Omer Levy, Roy Schwartz, Samuel Bowman, and Noah A Smith. 2018. Annotation artifacts in natural language inference data. In *Proceedings of the 2018 Conference of the North American Chapter of the Association for Computational Linguistics: Human Language Technologies, Volume 2 (Short Papers)*, pages 107–112.

Tom Kwiatkowski, Jennimaria Palomaki, Olivia Redfield, Michael Collins, Ankur Parikh, Chris Alberti, Danielle Epstein, Illia Polosukhin, Matthew Kelcey, Jacob Devlin, Kenton Lee, Kristina N. Toutanova, Llion Jones, Ming-Wei Chang, Andrew Dai, Jakob Uszkoreit, Quoc Le, and Slav Petrov. 2019. Natural questions: a benchmark for question answering research. *Transactions of the Association of Computational Linguistics*.

Peter LoBue and Alexander Yates. 2011. Types of common-sense knowledge needed for recognizing textual entailment. In *Proceedings of the 49th Annual Meeting of the Association for Computational Linguistics: Human Language Technologies*, pages 329–334.

Alec Radford, Karthik Narasimhan, Tim Salimans, and Ilya Sutskever. 2018. Improving language understanding by generative pre-training.

Pranav Rajpurkar, Robin Jia, and Percy Liang. 2018. Know what you don't know: Unanswerable questions for squad. In *Proceedings of the 56th Annual Meeting of the Association for Computational Linguistics (Volume 2: Short Papers)*, pages 784–789.

Pranav Rajpurkar, Jian Zhang, Konstantin Lopyrev, and Percy Liang. 2016. Squad: 100,000+ questions for machine comprehension of text. In *Proceedings of the 2016 Conference on Empirical Methods in Natural Language Processing*, pages 2383–2392.

Ashish Vaswani, Noam Shazeer, Niki Parmar, Jakob Uszkoreit, Llion Jones, Aidan N Gomez, Łukasz Kaiser, and Illia Polosukhin. 2017. Attention is all you need. In *Advances in Neural Information Processing Systems*, pages 5998–6008.

Adina Williams, Nikita Nangia, and Samuel Bowman. 2018. A broad-coverage challenge corpus for sentence understanding through inference. In *Proceedings of the 2018 Conference of the North American Chapter of the Association for Computational Linguistics: Human Language Technologies, Volume 1 (Long Papers)*, volume 1, pages 1112–1122.

Rowan Zellers, Yonatan Bisk, Roy Schwartz, and Yejin Choi. 2018. Swag: A large-scale adversarial dataset for grounded commonsense inference. In *Proceedings of the 2018 Conference on Empirical Methods in Natural Language Processing*, pages 93–104.

Syntactic Interchangeability in Word Embedding Models

Daniel Hershcovich   **Assaf Toledo**   **Alon Halfon**   **Noam Slonim**

IBM Research

daniel.hershcovich@gmail.com,
assaf.toledo@ibm.com,
{alonhal,noams}@il.ibm.com

Abstract

Nearest neighbors in word embedding models are commonly observed to be semantically similar, but the relations between them can vary greatly. We investigate the extent to which word embedding models preserve syntactic interchangeability, as reflected by distances between word vectors, and the effect of hyper-parameters—context window size in particular. We use part of speech (POS) as a proxy for syntactic interchangeability, as generally speaking, words with the same POS are syntactically valid in the same contexts. We also investigate the relationship between interchangeability and similarity as judged by commonly-used word similarity benchmarks, and correlate the result with the performance of word embedding models on these benchmarks. Our results will inform future research and applications in the selection of word embedding model, suggesting a principle for an appropriate selection of the context window size parameter depending on the use-case.

1 Introduction

Word embedding algorithms (Mikolov et al., 2013; Pennington et al., 2014; Levy et al., 2015) attempt to capture the semantic space of words in a metric space of real-valued vectors. While it is common knowledge that the hyper-parameters used to train these models affects the semantic properties of the distances arising from them (Bansal et al., 2014; Lin et al., 2015; Goldberg, 2016; Lison and Kutuzov, 2017), and indeed, it has been shown that they capture many different semantic relations (Yang and Powers, 2006; Agirre et al., 2009), little has been done to *quantify* the effect of model hyper-parameters on output tendencies. Here we begin to answer this question, evaluating fastText (Bojanowski et al., 2017) on benchmarks designed to measure how well a model captures the degree of similarity between words (§2).

In our experiments, we investigate how *syntactic interchangeability* of words, represented by their part of speech (§3), is expressed in word embedding models and evaluation benchmarks.

Based on the distributional hypothesis (Harris, 1954), word embeddings are learned from text by first extracting co-occurrences—finding, for each word token, all words within a context window around it, whose size (or maximal size) is a hyper-parameter of the training algorithm. Word vectors are then learned by predicting these co-occurrences or factorizing a co-occurrence matrix.

We discover a clear relationship between the context window size hyper-parameter and the performance of a word embedding model in estimating the similarity between words. To try to explain this relationship, we quantify how syntactic interchangeability is reflected in each benchmark, and its relation to the context window size. Our experiments reveal that context window size is negatively correlated with the number of same-POS words among the nearest neighbors of words, but that this fact is not enough to explain the complex interaction between context window size and performance on word similarity benchmarks.[1]

2 Word Similarity and Relatedness

Many benchmarks have been proposed for the evaluation of unsupervised word representations. In general, they can be divided into intrinsic and extrinsic evaluation methods (Schnabel et al., 2015; Chiu et al., 2016; Jastrzebski et al., 2017; Alshargi et al., 2018; Bakarov, 2018). While most datasets report the semantic similarity between words, many datasets actually capture semantic relatedness (Hill et al., 2015; Avraham and Goldberg, 2016), or more complex relations such as analogy or the ability to

---

[1]Our code and data are available at https://github.com/danielhers/interchangeability.

Proceedings of the 3rd Workshop on Evaluating Vector Space Representations for NLP, pages 70–76
Minneapolis, USA, June 6, 2019. ©2019 Association for Computational Linguistics

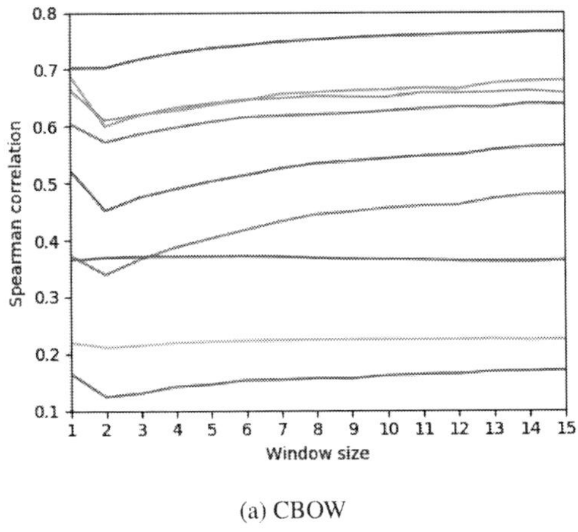
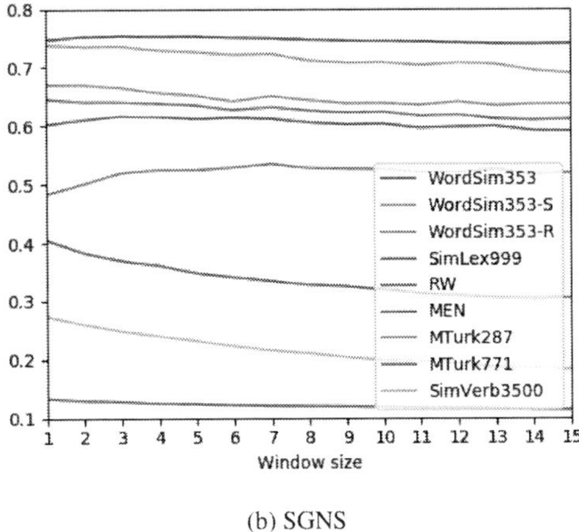

(a) CBOW   (b) SGNS

Figure 1: Performance of the CBOW (a) and SGNS (b) algorithms on each benchmark, for each window size, measured by Spearman correlation between the benchmark score and the word embedding cosine similarity.

categorize words based on the distributed representation encoded in word embeddings. We focus on similarity and relatedness, and evaluate word embedding models on several common benchmarks.

2.1 Data

We learn word embeddings from English Wikipedia, using a dump from May 1, 2017.[2] The data is preprocessed using a publicly available preprocessing script,[3] extracting text, removing nonalphanumeric characters, converting digits to text, and lowercasing the text.

Benchmarks. We use the following benchmarks: WordSim-353 (Finkelstein et al., 2001) and its partition into WordSim-353-Sim (Agirre et al., 2009) and WordSim-353-Rel (Zesch et al., 2008), SimLex999 (Hill et al., 2015), Rare Words (RW; Luong et al., 2013), MEN (Bruni et al., 2012), MTurk-287 (Radinsky et al., 2011), MTurk-771 (Halawi et al., 2012), and SimVerb-3500 (Gerz et al., 2016). See Table 1 for the size of each benchmark.

2.2 Hyper-parameters

We use fastText (Bojanowski et al., 2017) to learn 300-dimensional word embedding models, using both the CBOW (continuous bag-of-words) and SGNS (skip-gram with negative sampling) algorithms (Mikolov et al., 2013). The context window size varies from 1 up to 15. We include only all

words occurring 500 times or more (including function words), to avoid very rare words or uncommon spelling errors from skewing the results. All other hyper-parameters are set to their default values.

2.3 Evaluation on Benchmarks

To investigate the effect of window size on a model's performance on the benchmarks, we evaluate each model on each benchmark, using cosine similarity as the model's prediction for each pair. The performance is measured by Spearman correlation between the benchmark score and the word embedding cosine similarity (Levy et al., 2015).

Results. Figure 1 displays the performance of the CBOW and SGNS algorithms on each benchmark, with window sizes 1 to 15. Apart from a small dip between windows 1 and 2 for CBOW, the performance is either nearly constant, or changes nearly monotonically with window size in each setting.

The relative improvement (or deterioration), in percents, with the increase of window size from 2 to 15, are shown in Table 1 (Δwin $= 2 \to 15(\%)$). Interestingly, CBOW exhibits a positive correlation of window size with model's performance for all benchmarks but SimLex999, while performance for SGNS barely changes with window size, except for SimLex999 and SimVerb3500, where we see a strong *negative* correlation.

Discussion. In SimLex999 and in SimVerb3500, the words in each pair have the same part of speech by design (in particular, SimVerb3500 only contains verbs). Hypothesizing that the effect of win-

---

71

Benchmark	Size	Δwin $= 2 \to 15(\%)$		# Related		# Unrelated		p-value
		CBOW	SGNS	All	Same-POS	All	Same-POS	
WordSim353	353	24	-3	122	107	53	40	0.038
WordSim353-S	203	13	-6	60	53	53	40	0.061
WordSim353-R	252	42	4	104	89	39	31	0.26
SimLex999	999	-1	-20	234	199	334	295	0.897
RW	2034	37	-12	944	555	262	144	0.149
MEN	3000	9	-2	791	564	781	439	$3 \cdot 10^{-10}$
MTurk287	287	8	-5	49	39	119	68	0.004
MTurk771	771	12	-5	204	153	200	146	0.365
SimVerb3500	3500	6	-30	633	265	1217	566	0.974

Table 1: Analysis of interchangeability (by same-POS) in word similarity and relatedness benchmarks. Δwin $= 2 \to 15(\%)$ is the relative change, in percents, of the model's performance (by Spearman correlation) when going from window size 2 to window size 15, for the CBOW and SGNS algorithms (§2.3). *Related* and *Unrelated* are the top and bottom 30% of the pairs, by benchmark score, respectively. *P-value* is calculated using the hypergeometric test, comparing the enrichment of interchangeable pairs within related pairs, with a background of all related and unrelated pairs (§3.1).

dow size is related to the model's implicitly learned concept of part of speech, we investigate this idea in the next section.

3 Syntactic Interchangeability

A word's part of speech (also known as syntactic category) is determined by syntactic distribution, and conveys information about how a word functions in the sentence (Carnie, 2002). We can generally substitute each word in a sentence with various words that are of the same part of speech, but not words that are of different parts of speech. While the same syntactic function can sometimes be fulfilled by words of various parts of speech or possibly longer phrases (such as adverbs and prepositional phrases, or multi-word expressions), part of speech is nonetheless a very good proxy for syntactic distribution (Mohammad and Pedersen, 2004).

Related to our work, Vulić et al. (2017) introduced a framework for automatic selection of specific context configurations for word embedding models per part of speech, improving performance on the SimLex999 benchmark. We take a different approach, investigating existing word embedding models and the way in which part of speech is reflected in them.

We define two words to be (syntactically) *interchangeable* if they share the same part of speech. We quantify interchangeability as a property of a word embedding model, as the proportion of words with the same part of speech within the list of nearest neighbors (that is, the most similar words according to the model) for each word in a pre-determined vocabulary. The higher the interchangeability ratio is, the more importance we assume the model implicitly places on interchangeability for the calculation of word similarity.

3.1 Interchangeability Analysis in Word Similarity Benchmarks

While all benchmarks we experiment with assign a score along a scale to each pair (calculated from human scoring), for our experiment we would like to use a binary annotation of whether a pair is related or not. For this purpose, we divide the whole range of scores, for each benchmark, to three parts: the lowest 30% of the range between the lowest and highest scores is considered "unrelated", the top 30% as "related", and the middle 40% are ignored.

Interchangeability enrichment. Given the binary classification obtained from the human-annotated scores for each benchmark, we can find the enrichment of interchangeable pairs among related pairs. We use spaCy 2.0.11[4] (with the `en_core_web_sm` model) to annotate the POS for each word in each benchmark pair (tagging them in isolation to select the most probable POS), and look at the set of same-POS pairs in the benchmark. For each of the benchmarks, we calculate a p-value using the hypergeometric test, comparing the enrichment of same-POS pairs within related pairs, with a background distribution of all related and unrelated pairs (ignoring ones in the middle 40% range of scores).

Results. Table 1 shows the enrichment of interchangeable pairs among related and unrelated pairs for each benchmark. For WordSim353, MEN and MTurk287, the set of related pairs contains significantly more interchangeable pairs than the background set ($p < 0.05$),[5] suggesting that these benchmarks are particularly sensitive to POS.

3.2 Nearest Neighbor Analysis

To try and relate the results from §2.3 and §3.1, we measure the relation between window size and interchangeability by analyzing nearest neighbors in word embedding models. In our experiment, the *nearest neighbors* of a word are the words with the highest cosine similarity between their vectors.

Collecting pivots. We create a word list for each of the three most common parts of speech: nouns, adjectives and verbs. For each POS, we list all lemmas of all synsets of that POS from WordNet (Miller, 1998). To "purify" the lists and avoid noise from homonyms, we remove from each list any lemma that also belongs to a synset from another POS. As a further cleaning step, we use spaCy to tag each word, and only keep words for which the spaCy POS agrees with the WordNet POS. Without context, spaCy will likely choose the most common POS based on its training corpus, which is different from WordNet, increasing the robustness.

This process results in 6407 *uniquely-noun*, 2784 *uniquely-adjective* and 1460 *uniquely-verb* words, which we refer to as our *pivot lists*.

Algo-rithm	NOUN			ADJ			VERB		
	1	15	r	1	15	r	1	15	r
CBOW	79	70	-0.96	72	48	-0.93	55	41	-0.91
SGNS	78	66	-0.95	66	39	-0.94	51	41	-0.92

Table 2: Percentage of interchangeable neighbors per pivot POS for the smallest (1) and largest (15) windows in our experiment, for the CBOW and SGNS algorithms. The number of interchangeable neighbors has a strong negative Pearson correlation (r) with window size for windows 1 to 15 ($p < 0.01$, two-tailed t-test).

Calculating nearest neighbor POS. We find the 100 nearest neighbors for each word in our pivot lists, according to each fastText model with windows 1 through 15. We filter these neighbors to keep only words in the spaCy vocabulary, and inspect the remaining top 10. Again using spaCy, we tag the POS of each neighbor in the result. We subsequently calculate a histogram, for each POS x, of its *neighbor-POS y*, that is, the POS assigned to the neighbors of words with POS x.

Results. Table 2 shows the results of this experiment. For nouns, adjectives and verbs, we consistently see a decrease in the number of same-POS neighbors when we increase the window size, relative to the total number of nearest neighbors.

Figure 2 shows the the absolute number of neighbors per algorithm, pivot POS and neighbor POS, for all window sizes we experimented with. The number of nearest neighbors of the same POS is consistently decreasing with window size, while the number of nearest neighbors of other POS are increasing or unaffected.

Discussion. The results clearly suggest that for *both* CBOW and SGNS, models with a larger window size are less likely to consider words of the same POS as strongly related. That is, syntactic interchangeability is negatively correlated with window size. This is in sharp contrast to our results from §2.3, where performance for CBOW on almost all benchmarks (among them WordSim353, MEN and MTurk287, for which we showed that syntactic interchangeability plays a role) consistently *improved* with window size. We also find the conclusion to contradict the impression regarding SGNS, where SimLex999 and SimVerb3500 showed worse performance for larger windows: if

---

[4]`https://spacy.io`

[5]The fact that not all pairs in SimLex999 and SimVerb3500 are judged as interchangeable in our experiment is due to ambiguity: for some words, spaCy selected a POS which is not the one intended when constructing the benchmark.

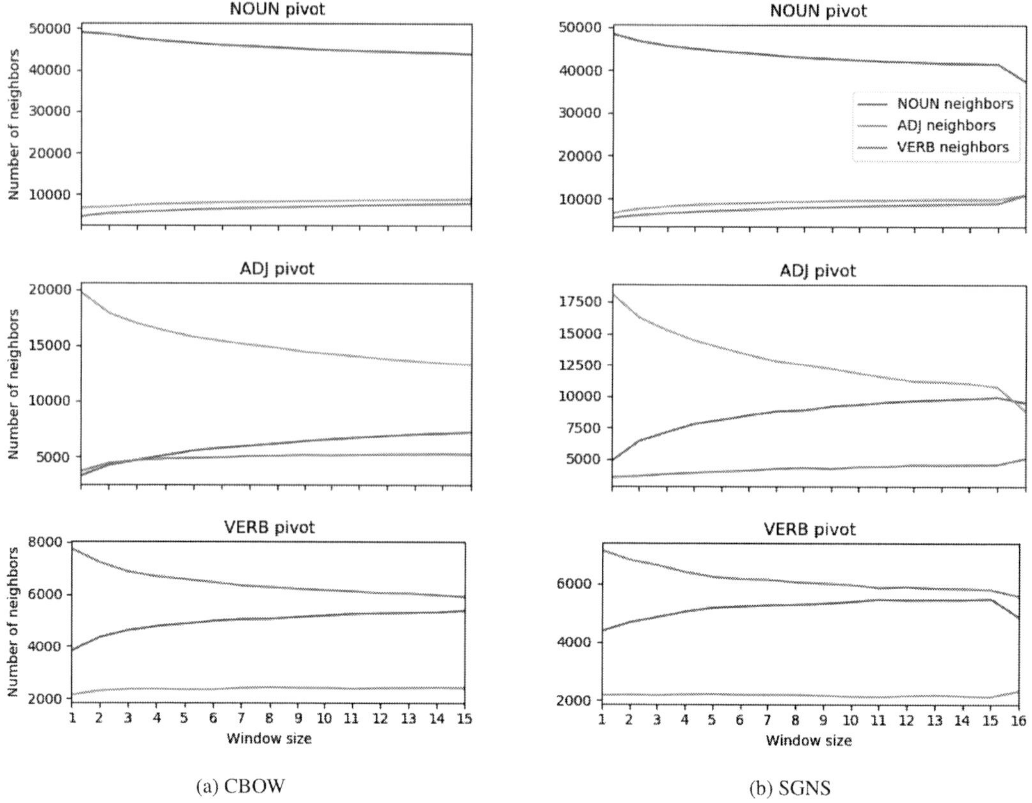

Figure 2: Number of neighbor per POS for each pivot POS and for each window size, for the CBOW (a) and SGNS (b) algorithms. The number of same-POS neighbors is consistently decreasing with window size.

POS should not play a role in these benchmarks, then models with a bias toward syntactic interchangeability (i.e., models with lower windows) should perform *worse* on these benchmarks.

4 Conclusion

We investigated the effect of the context window size hyper-parameter on the performance on word similarity benchmarks. We showed that (1) increasing the window size results in a lower probability of interchangeable nearest neighbors for both CBOW and SGNS algorithms; (2) in some widely used benchmarks, syntactic interchangeability increases the probability of similarity or relatedness; (3) increasing the window size typically improves performance in predicting similarity or relatedness for CBOW, but has little impact on SGNS.

SimLex999 and SimVerb3500 proved to be exceptions to both (2) and (3), since all pairs in them are interchangeable by construction, but on them, increasing the window size has no effect for CBOW and negative impact for SGNS.

This contradiction is presented as a challenge to the community, and could perhaps be explained by other factors affected by window size.

Our investigation focused on a specific relation between words, namely whether they share a part of speech. Many other relations are of interest to the NLP community, such as syntactic dependency relations, and semantic relations like hypernymy and synonymy. Furthermore, a similar analysis could be applied to other word embedding hyper-parameters, such as the vector dimension. While we used a constant vector dimension of 300 in our experiments, it is an open question whether models with different vector dimensions differ with respect to their tendency to capture different word relations. Future work will extend our analysis to other relations and hyper-parameters.

Acknowledgments

We thank the anonymous reviewers for their helpful comments.

References

Eneko Agirre, Enrique Alfonseca, Keith Hall, Jana Kravalova, Marius Paşca, and Aitor Soroa. 2009. A study on similarity and relatedness using distributional and wordnet-based approaches. In *Proceedings of Human Language Technologies: The 2009 Annual Conference of the North American Chapter of the Association for Computational Linguistics*, pages 19–27. Association for Computational Linguistics.

Faisal Alshargi, Saeedeh Shekarpour, Tommaso Soru, Amit Sheth, and Uwe Quasthoff. 2018. Concept2vec: Metrics for evaluating quality of embeddings for ontological concepts. *arXiv preprint arXiv:1803.04488*.

Oded Avraham and Yoav Goldberg. 2016. Improving reliability of word similarity evaluation by redesigning annotation task and performance measure. *arXiv preprint arXiv:1611.03641*.

Amir Bakarov. 2018. A survey of word embeddings evaluation methods. *arXiv preprint arXiv:1801.09536*.

Mohit Bansal, Kevin Gimpel, and Karen Livescu. 2014. Tailoring continuous word representations for dependency parsing. In *Proceedings of the 52nd Annual Meeting of the Association for Computational Linguistics (Volume 2: Short Papers)*, volume 2, pages 809–815.

Piotr Bojanowski, Edouard Grave, Armand Joulin, and Tomas Mikolov. 2017. Enriching word vectors with subword information. *Transactions of the Association for Computational Linguistics*, 5:135–146.

Elia Bruni, Gemma Boleda, Marco Baroni, and Nam-Khanh Tran. 2012. Distributional semantics in technicolor. In *Proceedings of the 50th Annual Meeting of the Association for Computational Linguistics: Long Papers-Volume 1*, pages 136–145. Association for Computational Linguistics.

Andrew Carnie. 2002. *Syntax: A Generative Introduction (Introducing Linguistics)*. Blackwell Publishing.

Billy Chiu, Anna Korhonen, and Sampo Pyysalo. 2016. Intrinsic evaluation of word vectors fails to predict extrinsic performance. In *Proceedings of the 1st Workshop on Evaluating Vector-Space Representations for NLP*, pages 1–6.

Lev Finkelstein, Evgeniy Gabrilovich, Yossi Matias, Ehud Rivlin, Zach Solan, Gadi Wolfman, and Eytan Ruppin. 2001. Placing search in context: The concept revisited. In *Proceedings of the 10th international conference on World Wide Web*, pages 406–414. ACM.

Daniela Gerz, Ivan Vulić, Felix Hill, Roi Reichart, and Anna Korhonen. 2016. SimVerb-3500: A Large-Scale Evaluation Set of Verb Similarity. In *EMNLP*.

Yoav Goldberg. 2016. A primer on neural network models for natural language processing.

Guy Halawi, Gideon Dror, Evgeniy Gabrilovich, and Yehuda Koren. 2012. Large-scale learning of word relatedness with constraints. In *Proceedings of the 18th ACM SIGKDD international conference on Knowledge discovery and data mining*, pages 1406–1414. ACM.

Zellig S Harris. 1954. Distributional structure. *Word*, 10(2-3):146–162.

Felix Hill, Roi Reichart, and Anna Korhonen. 2015. Simlex-999: Evaluating semantic models with (genuine) similarity estimation. *Computational Linguistics*, 41(4):665–695.

Stanisław Jastrzebski, Damian Leśniak, and Wojciech Marian Czarnecki. 2017. How to evaluate word embeddings? on importance of data efficiency and simple supervised tasks. *arXiv preprint arXiv:1702.02170*.

Omer Levy, Yoav Goldberg, and Ido Dagan. 2015. Improving distributional similarity with lessons learned from word embeddings. *Transactions of the Association for Computational Linguistics*, 3:211–225.

Chu-Cheng Lin, Waleed Ammar, Chris Dyer, and Lori Levin. 2015. Unsupervised pos induction with word embeddings. *arXiv preprint arXiv:1503.06760*.

Pierre Lison and Andrey Kutuzov. 2017. Redefining context windows for word embedding models: An experimental study. In *Proceedings of the 21st Nordic Conference on Computational Linguistics*, pages 284–288. Association for Computational Linguistics.

Thang Luong, Richard Socher, and Christopher Manning. 2013. Better word representations with recursive neural networks for morphology. In *Proceedings of the Seventeenth Conference on Computational Natural Language Learning*, pages 104–113.

Tomas Mikolov, Kai Chen, Greg Corrado, and Jeffrey Dean. 2013. Efficient estimation of word representations in vector space. *arXiv preprint arXiv:1301.3781*.

George Miller. 1998. *WordNet: An electronic lexical database*. MIT press.

Saif Mohammad and Ted Pedersen. 2004. Combining lexical and syntactic features for supervised word sense disambiguation. In *Proceedings of the Eighth Conference on Computational Natural Language Learning (CoNLL-2004) at HLT-NAACL 2004*.

Jeffrey Pennington, Richard Socher, and Christopher Manning. 2014. GloVe: Global vectors for word representation. In *Proceedings of the 2014 conference on empirical methods in natural language processing (EMNLP)*, pages 1532–1543.

Kira Radinsky, Eugene Agichtein, Evgeniy Gabrilovich, and Shaul Markovitch. 2011. A word at a time: computing word relatedness using temporal semantic analysis. In *Proceedings of the 20th international conference on World wide web*, pages 337–346. ACM.

Tobias Schnabel, Igor Labutov, David Mimno, and Thorsten Joachims. 2015. Evaluation methods for unsupervised word embeddings. In *Proceedings of the 2015 Conference on Empirical Methods in Natural Language Processing*, pages 298–307.

Ivan Vulić, Roy Schwartz, Ari Rappoport, Roi Reichart, and Anna Korhonen. 2017. Automatic selection of context configurations for improved class-specific word representations. In *Proceedings of the 21st Conference on Computational Natural Language Learning (CoNLL 2017)*, pages 112–122, Vancouver, Canada. Association for Computational Linguistics.

Dongqiang Yang and David Martin Powers. 2006. Verb similarity on the taxonomy of wordnet. In *Proceedings of GWC*.

Torsten Zesch, Christof Müller, and Iryna Gurevych. 2008. Using wiktionary for computing semantic relatedness. In *AAAI*, volume 8, pages 861–866.

Evaluation of Morphological Embeddings for English and Russian Languages

Vitaly Romanov
Innopolis University, Innopolis,
Russia
v.romanov@innopolis.ru

Albina Khusainova
Innopolis University, Innopolis,
Russia
a.khusainova@innopolis.ru

Abstract

This paper evaluates morphology-based embeddings for English and Russian languages. Despite the interest and introduction of several morphology-based word embedding models in the past and acclaimed performance improvements on word similarity and language modeling tasks, in our experiments, we did not observe any stable preference over two of our baseline models - SkipGram and FastText. The performance exhibited by morphological embeddings is the average of the two baselines mentioned above.

1 Introduction

One of the most significant shifts in the area of natural language processing is to the practical use of distributed word representations. Collobert et al. (2011) showed that a neural model could achieve close to state-of-the-art results in Part of Speech (POS) tagging and chunking by relying almost only on word embeddings learned with a language model. In modern language processing architectures, high quality pre-trained representations of words are one of the major factors of the resulting model performance.

Although word embeddings became ubiquitous, there is no single benchmark on evaluating their quality (Bakarov, 2018), and popular intrinsic evaluation techniques are subject to criticism (Gladkova and Drozd, 2016). Researchers very often rely on intrinsic evaluation, such as semantic similarity or analogy tasks. While intrinsic evaluations are simple to understand and conduct, they do not necessarily imply the quality of embeddings for all possible tasks (Gladkova et al., 2016).

In this paper, we turn to the evaluation of morphological embeddings for English and Russian languages. Over the last decade, many approaches tried to include subword information into word representations. Such approaches involve additional techniques that perform segmentation of a word into morphemes (Arefyev N.V., 2018; Virpioja et al., 2013). The presumption is that we can potentially increase the quality of distributional representations if we incorporate these segmentations into the language model (LM).

Several approaches that include morphology into word embeddings were proposed, but the evaluation often does not compare proposed embedding methodologies with the most popular embedding vectors - Word2Vec, FastText, Glove. In this paper, we aim at answering the question of whether morphology-based embeddings can be useful, especially for languages with rich morphology (such as Russian). Our contribution is the following:

1. We evaluate simple SkipGram-based (SG-based) morphological embedding models with new intrinsic evaluation BATS dataset (Gladkova et al., 2016)

2. We compare relative gain of using morphological embeddings against Word2Vec and FastText for English and Russian languages

3. We test morphological embeddings on several downstream tasks other than language modeling, i.e., mapping embedding spaces, POS tagging, and chunking

The rest of the paper is organized as follows. Section 2 contains an overview of existing approaches for morphological embeddings and methods of their evaluation. Section 3 explains embedding models that we have tested. Section 4 explains our evaluation approaches. Section 5 describes results.

Proceedings of the 3rd Workshop on Evaluating Vector Space Representations for NLP, pages 77–81
Minneapolis, USA, June 6, 2019. ©2019 Association for Computational Linguistics

2   Related work

The idea to include subword information into word representation is not new. The question is how does one obtain morphological segmentation of words. Very often, researchers rely on the unsupervised morphology mining tool Morfessor (Virpioja et al., 2013).

Many approaches use simple composition, e.g., sum, of morpheme vectors to define a word embedding. Botha and Blunsom (2014) were one of the first to try this approach. They showed a considerable drop in perplexity of log-bilinear language model and also tested their model on word similarity and downstream translation task. The translation task was tested against an n-gram language model. Similarly, Qiu et al. (2014) tweak CBOW model so that besides central word it can predict target morphemes in this word. Final embeddings of morphemes are summed together into the word embedding. They test vectors on analogical reasoning and word similarity, showing that incorporating morphemes improves semantic similarity. El-kishky et al. (2018) develop their own morpheme segmentation algorithm and test the resulting embeddings on the LM task with SGNS objective. Their method achieved lower perplexity than FastText and SG.

A slightly different approach was taken by Cotterell and Schütze (2015) who optimized a log-bilinear LM model with a multitask objective, where the second objective is to guess the next morphological tag. They test resulting vector similarity against string distance (morphologically close words have similar substrings) and find that their vectors surpass Word2Vec by a large margin.

Bhatia et al. (2016) construct a hierarchical graphical model that incorporates word morphology to predict the next word and then optimize the variational bound. They compare their model with Word2Vec and the one described by Botha and Blunsom (2014). They found that their method improves results on word similarity but is inferior to approach by Botha and Blunsom (2014) in POS tagging.

Another group of methods tries to incorporate arbitrary morphological information into embedding model. Avraham and Goldberg (2017) observe that it is impossible to achieve both high semantic and syntactic similarity on the Hebrew language. Instead of morphemes, they use other linguistic tags for the word, i.e., lemma, the word itself, and morphological tag. Chaudhary et al. (2018) took the next level of a similar approach. Besides including morphological tags, they include morphemes and character n-grams, and study the possibility of embedding transfer from Turkish to Uighur and from Hindi to Bengali. They test the result on NER and monolingual machine translation.

Another approach that deserves being mentioned here is FastText by Bojanowski et al. (2017). They do not use morphemes explicitly, but instead rely on subword character n-grams, that store morphological information implicitly. This method achieves high scores on both semantic and syntactic similarities, and by far is the most popular word embedding model that also captures word morphology.

There are also approaches that investigate the impact of more complex models like RNN and LSTM. Luong et al. (2013) created a hierarchical language model that uses RNN to combine morphemes of a word to obtain a word representation. Their model performed well on word similarity task. Similarly, Cao and Rei (2016) create Char2Vec BiLSTM for embedding words and train a language model with SG objective. Their model excels at the syntactic similarity.

3   Embedding techniques

In this work, we test three embedding models on English and Russian languages: SkipGram, FastText, and MorphGram. The latter one is similar to FastText with the only difference that instead of character n-grams we model word morphemes. This approach was often used in previous research.

All three models are trained using the negative sampling objective

$$\frac{1}{T} \sum_{t=1}^{T} \sum_{-m \leq j \leq m, j \neq 0} \log \sigma(s(w_j, w_t)) +$$

$$\sum_{i=1}^{k} E_{w \sim P_n(w_t)} \left[\log \sigma(s(w, w_t)) \right] \quad (1)$$

In the case of SG, the similarity function s is the inner product of corresponding vectors. FastText and MorphGram are using subword units. We use the same approach to incorporate subword information into the word vector for both models:

$$s(w_j, w_t) = \sum_{s \in \mathcal{S}_{w_t}} v_s^T v_{w_j}$$

where $\mathcal{S}_{w_t}$ is the set of word segmentations into n-grams or morphemes. We use Gensim[1] as the implementation for all models (Řehůřek and Sojka, 2010). For MorphGram, we utilize FastText model and substitute the function that computes character n-grams for the function that performs morphological segmentation.

4 Experiments and Evaluation

To understand the effect of using morphemes for training word embeddings, we performed intrinsic and extrinsic evaluations of SG, FastText, and MorphGram model for two languages - English and Russian. Russian language, in contrast to English, is characterized by rich morphology, which makes this pair of languages a good choice for exploring the difference in the effect of morphology-based models.

4.1 Data and Training Details

We used the first 5GB of unpacked English and Russian Wikipedia dumps[2] as training data.

For training both SG and FastText we used Gensim library, for MorphGram - we adapted Gensim's implementation of FastText by breaking words into morphemes instead of n-grams, all other implementation details left unchanged. Training parameters remain the same as in the original FastText paper, except the learning rate was set to 0.05 at the beginning of the training, and vocabulary size was constrained to 100000 words. Morphemes for English words were generated with polyglot[3], and for Russian - with seq2seq segmentation tool[4].

When reporting our results in tables, we will refer for FastText as FT and MorphGram as Morph.

4.2 Similarity

One of the intrinsic evaluations often used for word embeddings is a similarity test - given word pairs with human judgments of similarity degree

	SG	FT	Morph
en	**0.37**	0.35	0.36
ru	**0.24**	0.19	0.19

Table 1: Correlation between human judgments and model scores for similarity datasets, Spearman's ρ.

		SG	FT	Morph
en	Google Semantic	**65.34**	48.75	57.52
	Google Syntactic	55.88	**75.10**	61.16
	BATS	29.67	**33.33**	32.71
ru	Translated Semantic	**39.11**	25.59	34.69
	Translated Syntactic	32.71	**59.29**	43.68
	Synthetic	24.52	**36.78**	27.06

Table 2: Accuracy of models on different analogies tasks.

for words in each pair, human judgments are compared with model scores—the more is the correlation, the better model "understands" semantic similarity of words. We used SimLex-999 (Hill et al., 2015) dataset—the original one for English and its translated by Leviant and Reichart (2015) version for Russian, for evaluating trained embeddings. Out-of-vocabulary words were excluded from tests for all models. The results are presented in Table 1.

We see that SG beats the other two models on similarity task for both languages, and MorphGram performs almost the same as Fasttext.

4.3 Analogies

Another type of intrinsic evaluations is analogies test, where the model is expected to answer questions of the form A is to B as C is to D, D should be predicted. For English, we used Google analogies dataset introduced by Mikolov et al. (Mikolov et al., 2013a) and BATS collection (Gladkova et al., 2016). For Russian, we used a partial translation[5] of Mikolov's dataset, and a synthetic dataset by Abdou et al. (2018).

Again, we excluded all out-of-vocabulary words from tests. We report accuracy for different models in Table 2.

Interestingly, MorphGram is between SG and FastText in semantic categories for both languages, and between FastText and SG for syntactic categories for English.

---

[1] https://radimrehurek.com/gensim
[2] https://dumps.wikimedia.org/
[3] https://polyglot.readthedocs.io/en/latest/index.html
[4] https://github.com/kpopov94/morpheme_seq2seq
[5] https://rusvectores.org/static/testsets/

	SG	FT	Morph
ru-en *1-nn*	**56.27**	55.58	53.51
ru-en *10-nn*	**78.96**	78.82	77.03

Table 3: Accuracy of supervised mapping from Russian to English using different models, searching among first and ten nearest neighbors.

4.4 Mapping Embedding Spaces

Here we introduce a new type of evaluation—it focuses on a cross-lingual task of mapping two embedding spaces for different languages. The core idea is to transform embedding spaces such that after this transformation the vectors of words in one language appear close to the vectors of their translations in another language. We were interested to see if using morphemes has any benefits to perform this kind of mapping.

We map embeddings using a train seed dictionary (dictionary with word meanings) and state of the art supervised mapping method by Artetxe et al. (2018), and calculate the accuracy of the mapping on the test dictionary. In short, the essence of this method is to find optimal orthogonal transforms for both embedding spaces to map them to a shared space based on a seed dictionary, plus some additional steps such as embeddings normalization. For each model—SG, FastText, and MorphGram, we mapped Russian and English embeddings trained using this model. We used the original implementation[6] for mapping (supervised option), and ground-truth train/test dictionaries provided by Facebook for their MUSE[7] library. We report 1-nn and 10-nn accuracy: whether the correct translation was found as a first nearest neighbor or among 10 nearest neighbors of a word in the mapped space. See the results in Table 3.

We observe no positive impact of using MorphGram for mapping word embedding spaces.

4.5 POS Tagging and Chunking

Other tasks where incorporation of morphology can be crucial are the tasks of POS Tagging and chunking. We use a simple CNN-based architecture introduced in (Collobert et al., 2011), with one projection layer, one convolutional layer, and the final logit layer. The only input features we use are the embeddings from corresponding mod-

	SG	FT	Morph
en	**0.9824**	0.9754	0.9722
ru	0.8817	**0.8899**	0.8871

Table 4: Accuracy on POS task

	SG	FT	Morph
en	0.8966	**0.9034**	0.8985
ru	0.8442	**0.8548**	0.8534

Table 5: Accuracy on Chunk task

els. The English language embeddings are tested with Conll2000 dataset which contains 8935 training sentences and 44 unique POS tags. The dataset for the Russian language contains 49136 sentences and 458 unique POS tags. Due to time constraint, we train models only for a fixed number of epochs: 50 for English and 20 for Russian (iterations reduced due to a larger training set). The results for POS and chunking are given in Tables 4 and 5 correspondingly. It is interesting to note that SG embeddings perform better for English on POS task, but for Russian, embeddings that encode more syntactic information always perform better.

5 Results

In this paper, we compared three word embedding approaches for English and Russian languages. The main inquiry was about the relevance of providing morphological information to word embeddings. Experiments showed that morphology-based embeddings exhibit qualities intermediate between semantic driven embedding approaches as SkipGram and character-driven one as FastText. Morphological embeddings studied here showed average performance on both semantic and syntactic tests. We also studied the application of morphological embeddings on two downstream tasks: POS tagging and chunking. For English language, SG provided the best results for POS, whereas FastText gave the best result on chunking task. For Russian, FastText showed better performance on both tasks. Morphological embeddings, again, showed average results. We recognize that the difference in the results on downstream task can be considered marginal. We also did not observe improvements from morphological embeddings on word similarity dataset compared to other models.

---

[6]https://github.com/artetxem/vecmap
[7]https://github.com/facebookresearch/MUSE

References

Mostafa Abdou, Artur Kulmizev, and Vinit Ravishankar. 2018. Mgad: Multilingual generation of analogy datasets. In *Proceedings of the Eleventh International Conference on Language Resources and Evaluation (LREC-2018)*.

Popov K.P. Arefyev N.V., Gratsianova T.Y. 2018. 24rd International Conference on Computational Linguistics and Intellectual Technologies.

Mikel Artetxe, Gorka Labaka, and Eneko Agirre. 2018. Generalizing and improving bilingual word embedding mappings with a multi-step framework of linear transformations. In *Thirty-Second AAAI Conference on Artificial Intelligence*.

Oded Avraham and Yoav Goldberg. 2017. The interplay of semantics and morphology in word embeddings. *arXiv preprint arXiv:1704.01938*.

Amir Bakarov. 2018. A survey of word embeddings evaluation methods. *arXiv preprint arXiv:1801.09536*.

Parminder Bhatia, Robert Guthrie, and Jacob Eisenstein. 2016. Morphological priors for probabilistic neural word embeddings. *arXiv preprint arXiv:1608.01056*.

Piotr Bojanowski, Edouard Grave, Armand Joulin, and Tomas Mikolov. 2017. Enriching word vectors with subword information. *Transactions of the Association for Computational Linguistics*, 5:135–146.

Jan Botha and Phil Blunsom. 2014. Compositional morphology for word representations and language modelling. In *International Conference on Machine Learning*, pages 1899–1907.

Kris Cao and Marek Rei. 2016. A joint model for word embedding and word morphology. *arXiv preprint arXiv:1606.02601*.

Aditi Chaudhary, Chunting Zhou, Lori Levin, Graham Neubig, David R. Mortensen, and Jaime G. Carbonell. 2018. Adapting Word Embeddings to New Languages with Morphological and Phonological Subword Representations.

Ronan Collobert, Jason Weston, Léon Bottou, Michael Karlen, Koray Kavukcuoglu, and Pavel Kuksa. 2011. Natural language processing (almost) from scratch. *Journal of Machine Learning Research*, 12(Aug):2493–2537.

Ryan Cotterell and Hinrich Schütze. 2015. Morphological word-embeddings. In *Proceedings of the 2015 Conference of the North American Chapter of the Association for Computational Linguistics: Human Language Technologies*, pages 1287–1292.

Ahmed El-kishky, Frank Xu, Aston Zhang, Stephen Macke, and Jiawei Han. 2018. Entropy-Based Subword Mining with an Application to Word Embeddings. pages 12–21.

Anna Gladkova and Aleksandr Drozd. 2016. Intrinsic evaluations of word embeddings: What can we do better? In *Proceedings of the 1st Workshop on Evaluating Vector-Space Representations for NLP*, pages 36–42.

Anna Gladkova, Aleksandr Drozd, and Satoshi Matsuoka. 2016. Analogy-based detection of morphological and semantic relations with word embeddings: What works and what doesn't. In *Proceedings of the NAACL-HLT SRW*, pages 47–54, San Diego, California, June 12-17, 2016. ACL.

Felix Hill, Roi Reichart, and Anna Korhonen. 2015. Simlex-999: Evaluating semantic models with (genuine) similarity estimation. *Computational Linguistics*, 41(4):665–695.

Ira Leviant and Roi Reichart. 2015. Judgment language matters: Multilingual vector space models for judgment language aware lexical semantics. *CoRR, abs/1508.00106*.

Thang Luong, Richard Socher, and Christopher Manning. 2013. Better word representations with recursive neural networks for morphology. *Proceedings of the Seventeenth Conference on Computational Natural Language Learning*, pages 104—-113.

Tomas Mikolov, Kai Chen, Greg Corrado, and Jeffrey Dean. 2013a. Efficient estimation of word representations in vector space. *arXiv preprint arXiv:1301.3781*.

Siyu Qiu, Qing Cui, Jiang Bian, Bin Gao, and Tie-Yan Liu. 2014. Co-learning of word representations and morpheme representations. In *Proceedings of COLING 2014, the 25th International Conference on Computational Linguistics: Technical Papers*, pages 141–150.

Radim Řehůřek and Petr Sojka. 2010. Software Framework for Topic Modelling with Large Corpora. In *Proceedings of the LREC 2010 Workshop on New Challenges for NLP Frameworks*, pages 45–50, Valletta, Malta. ELRA. http://is.muni.cz/publication/884893/en.

Sami Virpioja, Peter Smit, Stig-Arne Grönroos, Mikko Kurimo, et al. 2013. Morfessor 2.0: Python implementation and extensions for morfessor baseline.

Probing Biomedical Embeddings from Language Models

Qiao Jin
University of Pittsburgh
qiao.jin@pitt.edu

Bhuwan Dhingra
Carnegie Mellon University
bdhingra@cs.cmu.edu

William W. Cohen
Google, Inc.
wcohen@google.com

Xinghua Lu
University of Pittsburgh
xinghua@pitt.edu

Abstract

Contextualized word embeddings derived from pre-trained language models (LMs) show significant improvements on downstream NLP tasks. Pre-training on domain-specific corpora, such as biomedical articles, further improves their performance. In this paper, we conduct probing experiments to determine what additional information is carried *intrinsically* by the in-domain trained contextualized embeddings. For this we use the pre-trained LMs as fixed feature extractors and restrict the downstream task models to not have additional sequence modeling layers. We compare BERT (Devlin et al., 2018), ELMo (Peters et al., 2018a), BioBERT (Lee et al., 2019) and BioELMo, a biomedical version of ELMo trained on 10M PubMed abstracts. Surprisingly, while fine-tuned BioBERT is better than BioELMo in biomedical NER and NLI tasks, as a fixed feature extractor BioELMo outperforms BioBERT in our probing tasks. We use visualization and nearest neighbor analysis to show that better encoding of entity-type and relational information leads to this superiority.

1 Introduction

NLP has seen an upheaval in the last year, with contextual word embeddings, such as ELMo (Peters et al., 2018a) and BERT (Devlin et al., 2018), setting state-of-the-art performance on many tasks. These empirical successes suggest that unsupervised pre-training from large corpora could be a vital part of NLP models. In specific domains like biomedicine, NLP datasets are much smaller than their general-domain counterparts[1], which leads to a lot of ad-hoc models: some infer through knowledge bases (Chandu

et al., 2017), while others leverage large-scale general domain datasets for domain adaptation (Wiese et al., 2017). However, unlabeled biomedical texts are abundant, and their full potential has perhaps not yet been fully realized.

We train a domain-specific version of ELMo on 10M PubMed abstracts, called BioELMo[2]. Experiments on biomedical named entity recognition (NER) dataset BC2GM (Smith et al., 2008) and biomedical natural language inference (NLI) dataset MedNLI (Romanov and Shivade, 2018) clearly show the utility in training in-domain contextual word representations, but we would also like to know exactly what extra information is carried *intrinsically* in these embeddings.

To answer this question, we design two *probing tasks*, one for NER and one for NLI, where contextualized embeddings are used solely as fixed feature extractors and no sequence modeling layers are allowed above the embeddings. This setting prohibits the model from capturing task-specific contextual patterns, and instead only utilizes the information already present in the representations. In parallel to our work of BioELMo, Lee et al. (2019) introduce BioBERT, which is a biomedical version of in-domain trained BERT. We also probe BioBERT in our experiments.

Expectedly, BioELMo and BioBERT perform significantly better than their general-domain counterparts. When fine-tuned, BioBERT outperforms BioELMo, however, when used as fixed feature extractors, BioELMo is better than BioBERT in our probing tasks. Visualizations and nearest neighbor analyses suggest that it's because BioELMo more effectively encodes entity-types and information about biomedical relations, such as disease and symptom interactions, than BioBERT.

---

[1]For example, MedNLI (Romanov and Shivade, 2018) only has about 11k training instances while the general domain NLI dataset SNLI (Bowman et al., 2015) has 550k.

[2]Available at https://github.com/Andy-jqa/bioelmo.

Proceedings of the 3rd Workshop on Evaluating Vector Space Representations for NLP, pages 82–89
Minneapolis, USA, June 6, 2019. ©2019 Association for Computational Linguistics

2 Related Work

Embeddings from Language Models: ELMo (Peters et al., 2018a) is a pre-trained deep bidirectional LSTM (biLSTM) language model. ELMo word embeddings are computed by taking a weighted sum of the hidden states from each layer of the LSTM. The weights are learned along with the parameters of a task-specific downstream model, but the LSTM layers are kept fixed. Recently, Devlin et al. (2018) introduced BERT, and they showed that pre-training transformer networks on a masked language modeling objective leads to even better performance by fine-tuning the transformer weights on a broad range of NLP tasks. We study biomedical in-domain versions of these contextualized word embeddings in comparison to the general ones.

Biomedical Word Embeddings: Context-independent word embeddings, such as word2vec (w2v) (Mikolov et al., 2013) trained on biomedical corpora, are widely used in biomedical NLP models. Some recent works reported better NER performance with in-domain trained ELMo than general ELMo (Zhu et al., 2018; Sheikhshab et al., 2018). Lee et al. (2019) introduce BioBERT, which is BERT pre-trained on biomedical texts and set new state-of-the-art performance on several biomedical NLP tasks. We reaffirm these results on biomedical NER and NLI datasets with in-domain trained contextualized embeddings, and further explore *why* they are superior.

Probing Tasks: Designing tasks to probe sentence or token representations for linguistic properties has been a widespread practice in NLP. InferSent (Conneau et al., 2017) uses transfer tasks to probe for sentence embeddings pre-trained on supervised data. Many studies (Dasgupta et al., 2018; Poliak et al., 2018) design new test sets to probe for specific linguistic signals in sentence rerpesentations. Tasks to probe for token-level properties are explored by Blevins et al. (2018); Peters et al. (2018b), where they test whether token embeddings from different pre-training schemes encode part-of-speech and constituent structure.

Tenney et al. (2018) extend token-level probing to span-level probing and consider a broader range of tasks. Our work is different from them in the following ways – (1) We probe for biomedical domain-specific contextualized embeddings and compare them to the general-domain embeddings; (2) For NER, instead of classifying the tag for a given span, we adopt an end-to-end setting where the spans must also be identified. This allows us to compare the probing results to state-of-the-art numbers; (3) We also probe for relational information using the NLI task in an end-to-end style.

3 Methods

3.1 Biomedical Contextual Embeddings

BioELMo: We train BioELMo on the **PubMed** corpus. PubMed provides access to MEDLINE, a database containing more than 24M biomedical citations[3]. We used 10M recent abstracts (2.46B tokens) from PubMed to train BioELMo. The statistics of this corpus are very different from more general domains. For example, the token **patients** ranks 22 by frequency in the PubMed corpus while it ranks 824 in the 1B Word Benchmark dataset (Chelba et al., 2013). We use the Tensorflow implementation[4] of ELMo to train BioELMo. We keep the default hyperparameters and it takes about 1.7K GPU hours to train 8 epochs. BioELMo achieves an averaged forward and backward perplexity of 31.37 on test set.

BioBERT: In parallel to our work, Lee et al. (2019) developed BioBERT, which is pre-trained on English Wikipedia, BooksCorpus and fine-tuned on PubMed (7.8B tokens in total). BioBERT was initialized with BERT and further trained on PubMed for 200K steps.[5]

To get fixed features of tokens, we use the learnt downstream task-specific layer weights to calculate the average of 3 layers (1 token embedding layer and 2 biLSTM layers) for BioELMo and 13 layers (1 token embedding layer and 12 transformer layers) for BioBERT. As fixed feature extractors, BioELMo and BioBERT are not fine-tuned by downstream tasks.

3.2 Downstream Tasks

We first use BioELMo with state-of-the-art models and fine-tune BioBERT on the downstream tasks, to test their full capacity. In §3.3 we introduce our probing setup which tests BioBERT and

---

[3] https://www.ncbi.nlm.nih.gov/pubmed/
[4] https://github.com/allenai/bilm-tf
[5] We note there is a difference in the size of training corpora for BioBERT and BioELMo, but since we trained BioELMo before BioBERT was available, we could not control for this difference.

Premise: He returned to the clinic three weeks later and was prescribed with **antibiotics**. *to treat*
Hypothesis: The patient has an **infection**.
Label: Entailment

Figure 1: Relation information in a MedNLI instance.

BioELMo as fixed feature extractors.

NER: For BioELMo, following Lample et al. (2016), we use the contextualized embeddings and a character-based CNN for word representations, which are fed to a biLSTM, followed by a conditional random field (CRF) (Lafferty et al., 2001) layer for tagging. For BioBERT, we use the single sentence tagging setting described in Devlin et al. (2018), where the final hidden states of each token are trained to classify its NER label.

NLI: For BioELMo, We use the ESIM model (Chen et al., 2016), which encodes the premise and hypothesis using biLSTM. The encodings are fed to a local inference layer with attention, another biLSTM layer and a pooling layer followed by softmax for classification. For BioBERT, we use the sentence pair classification setting described in Devlin et al. (2018), where the final hidden states of the first token (special '[CLS]') are trained to classify the NLI label for the sentence pair.

3.3 Probing Tasks

We design two probing tasks where the contextualized embeddings are only used as fixed feature extractors and restrict the down-stream models to be non-contextual, to investigate the information intrinsically carried by them. One task is on NER to probe for entity-type information, and the other is on NLI to probe for relational information.

NER Probing Task: As shown in Figure 2 (left), we embed the input tokens to $\mathbf{R} = [\mathbf{E_1}; \mathbf{E_2}; ...; \mathbf{E_L}] \in \mathbb{R}^{L \times D_e}$, where L is the sequence length and D_e is embedding size. The embeddings are fed to several feed-forward layers:

$$\widetilde{\mathbf{E_i}} = \text{FFN}(\mathbf{E_i}) \in \mathbb{R}^T$$

where T is the number of tags. $[\widetilde{\mathbf{E_1}}; \widetilde{\mathbf{E_2}}; ...; \widetilde{\mathbf{E_L}}]$ is then fed to a CRF output layer. CRF doesn't model the context but ensures the global consistency across the assigned labels, so it's compatible with our probing task setting.

NLI Probing Task: Relational information between tokens of premises and hypotheses is vital to solve MedNLI task: as shown in Figure 1, the hypothesis is an entailment because **antibiotics** are used to treat an **infection**, which is a drug-disease

relation. We design the task shown in Figure 2 (right) to probe such relational information: We embed the premise and hypothesis seperately to $\mathbf{P} \in \mathbb{R}^{L_1 \times D_e}$ and $\mathbf{H} \in \mathbb{R}^{L_2 \times D_e}$, where L_1, L_2 are sequence lengths. Then we use bilinear layers[6] to get $\mathbf{S} = [\mathbf{S_1}; \mathbf{S_2}; ...; \mathbf{S_R}] \in \mathbb{R}^{R \times L_1 \times L_2}$ where

$$\mathbf{S_r} = \mathbf{P} \mathbf{W_r} \mathbf{H^T} \in \mathbb{R}^{L_1 \times L_2},$$

and $\mathbf{W_r} \in \mathbb{R}^{D_e \times D_e}$ is the weight matrix of a bilinear layer. Note that each element of $\mathbf{S_r}$ encodes the interaction between a token from the premise and a token from the hypothesis. We denote

$$\mathbf{h_{ij}} = \begin{bmatrix} \mathbf{S_1}[i,j] & ... & \mathbf{S_R}[i,j] \end{bmatrix}^T \in \mathbb{R}^R, \quad (1)$$

as the **distributed relation representation** between token i in premise and token j in hypothesis, and R is the tunable dimension of it. We then apply an element-wise maximum pooling layer:

$$\widetilde{\mathbf{h}} = \max_{i,j} \mathbf{h_{ij}} \in \mathbb{R}^R.$$

We use a linear layer to compute the softmax logits of the NLI labels, e.g. $p(\text{entailment}) \propto \exp(\widetilde{\mathbf{h}}^T \mathbf{w_{ent}})$, where $\mathbf{w_{ent}}$ is the learnt weight vector corresponding to the entailment label.

For BERT, we probe two variants. The first, denoted as BERT / BioBERT, feeds the premise and hypothesis to the model separately. The second, denoted as BERT-tog / BioBERT-tog, concatenates the two sentences by the '[SEP]' token and feeds to the model *together* to get the embeddings. This is how BERT is supposed to be used for sentence pair classification tasks, but it's not comparable to ELMo in our setting since ELMo doesn't take two sentences together as input.

4 Experiments

4.1 Experimental Setup

Data: For the NER task, we use the BC2GM dataset. BC2GM stands for BioCreative II gene mention dataset (Smith et al., 2008). The task is to detect gene names in sentences. It contains 15k training and 5k test sentences. We also test on the general-domain CoNLL 2003 NER dataset (Tjong Kim Sang and De Meulder, 2003), where the task is to detect entities such as person and location.

For the NLI task, we use the MedNLI dataset (Romanov and Shivade, 2018), where the task is, given a pair of sentences (premise and hypothesis), to predict whether the relation of entailment, contradiction, or neutral (no relation) holds between

---

[6]We also tried models without bilinear layers, which turn out to be suboptimal.

84

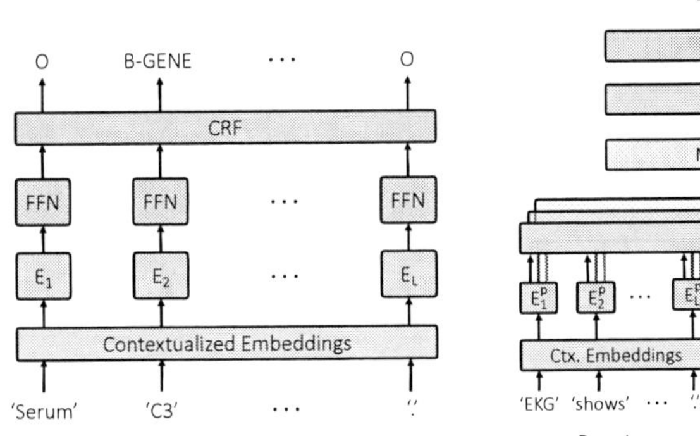

Figure 2: **Left:** NER probing task. The contextual word representations are directly used to predict the NER labels, followed by a CRF layer to ensure label consistency. **Right:** NLI probing task. Bilinear operators map pairs of word representations to relation representations which are used to predict the entailment label.

them. The premises are sampled from doctors' notes in the clinical dataset MIMIC-III (Johnson et al., 2016). The hypotheses and annotations are generated by clinicians. It contains 11,232 training, 1,395 development and 1,422 test instances. We also test on the general-domain SNLI dataset (Bowman et al., 2015), where the premises and hypotheses are drawn from image captions.

Compared Settings: For each dataset, the **Whole** setting refers to the state-of-the-art model we used (described in §3.2), including contextual modeling layers or fine-tuning of the embedding encoder. **Probing** and **Control** settings describe the probing task model introduced in §3.3. The control setting tests the representations on a general-domain dataset/task, to check whether we lose any information in domain-specific embeddings. Probing and control results are averaged over three seeds.

Compared Embeddings: We compare: (1) non-contextual biomedical w2v trained on a biomedical corpus of 5.5B tokens (Moen and Ananiadou, 2013), (2) ELMo trained on a general-domain corpus of 5.5B tokens[7], (3) BioELMo[8], (4) Cased base version of BERT trained on a general-domain corpus of 3.3B tokens[9] and (5) BioBERT[10].

4.2 Main Results

4.2.1 NER Results

In Domain v.s. General Domain: Results in Table 1 show that BioBERT and BioELMo in

Method	F1 (%)		
	Whole	Probe	Ctrl.
Ando (2007)	87.2	–	–
Rei et al. (2016)	88.0	–	–
Sheikhshab et al. (2018)	89.7	–	–
Biomed w2v	84.9	78.5	67.5
General ELMo	87.0	82.9	**84.0**
General BERT	89.2	84.9	83.6
BioELMo	90.3	**88.4**	80.9
BioBERT	**90.6**	88.2	83.4

Table 1: NER test results. **Whole**: whole model performance on BC2GM; **Probe**: Probing task performance on BC2GM; **Ctrl.**: Probing task performance on CoNLL 2003 NER. We use the official evaluation codes to calculate the F1 scores where there are multiple ground-truth tags, so the F1 scores are much higher than what were reported in Lee et al. (2019).

the Whole setting perform better than the general BERT and ELMo and biomed w2v, setting new state-of-the-art performance for this dataset.

BioBERT and BioELMo remains competitive in the Probing setting, doing much better than their general domain counterparts and even general ELMo in the Whole setting. This shows that with the right pre-training, the downstream model can be considerably simplified.

Unsurprisingly, in the Control setting BioBERT and BioELMo do worse than their general counterparts, indicating that the gains come at the cost of losing some general-domain information. However, the performance gaps (absolute differences) between ELMo and BioELMo are larger in the biomedical domain than it is in the general domain, which is also true for BERT and BioBERT. For ELMo and BioELMo, we believe it is because the PubMed corpus contains many mentions of

---

[7]https://allennlp.org/elmo

[8]Though BioELMo uses the smallest corpus to train, it performs better than BioBERT in probing setting, and general ELMo in whole and probing setting.

[9]https://github.com/google-research/bert

[10]https://github.com/dmis-lab/biobert

general-domain entities whereas the reverse is not true. Because BioBERT is initialzied with BERT and also uses general-domain corpora like Enligsh WikiPedia for pre-training, it's not surprising that BioBERT is just 0.2 worse than BERT on CoNLL 2003 NER in control setting.

BioELMo v.s. BioBERT: Fine-tuned BioBERT outperforms BioELMo with biLSTM and CRF on BC2GM. As a feature extractor, BioBERT is slightly worse than BioELMo in probing task of BC2GM, but outperforms BioELMo in probing task of CoNLL 2003, which can be explained by the fact that BioBERT is also pre-trained on general-domain corpora.

Method	Accuracy (%)		
	Whole	Probe	Ctrl.
Romanov and Shivade (2018)	76.6	–	–
Biomed w2v	74.2	71.1	59.2
General ELMo	75.8	69.6	60.8
General BERT	–	67.6	62.1
General BERT-tog	77.8	71.0	**74.1**
BioELMo	78.2	**75.5**	58.3
BioBERT	–	70.1	58.8
BioBERT-tog	**81.7**	73.8	69.9

Table 2: NLI test results. **Whole**: whole model performance on MedNLI; **Probe**: Probing task performance on MedNLI; **Ctrl.**: Probing task performance on SNLI. To make the results comparable, we only use the same number of SNLI training instances as that of MedNLI.

4.2.2 NLI Results

In Domain v.s. General Domain: Table 2 shows that BioBERT and BioELMo in the Whole setting perform better than their general domain counterparts and biomedical w2v for NLI, setting state-of-the-art performance for this dataset as well.

Once again, we observe that BioBERT and BioELMo outperform their general domain counterparts in the Probing settings, which comes at the cost of losing general domain information as indicated in the Control setting results.

Note that the Probing task *only* models relationships between tokens, but we still see competitive accuracy in that setting (75.5% vs 76.6% previous best). This suggests that, (i) many instances in MedNLI can be solved by identifying token-level relationships between the premise and the hypothesis, and (ii) BioELMo already captures this kind of information in its embeddings.

BioELMo v.s. BioBERT: Fine-tuned BioBERT does much better than BioELMo with ESIM model. However, BioELMo performs better than BioBERT by a large margin in the probing task of MedNLI. We explore this in more detail in the next section. Again, BioBERT is better than BioELMo in probing task of SNLI because it's also pre-trained on general corpora.

We notice that the *-tog* setting improves the BERT performance. Encoding two sentences separately, BioELMo still outperforms BioBERT-tog. It suggests that BioELMo is a better feature extractor than BioBERT, even though the latter has superior performance when fine-tuned on MedNLI.

4.3 Analysis

4.3.1 Entity-type Information

In biomedical literature, the acronym **ER** has multiple meanings: out of the 124 mentions we found in 20K recent PubMed abstracts, 47 refer to the gene "estrogen receptor", 70 refer to the organelle "endoplasmic reticulum" and 4 refer to the "emergency room" in hospital. We use t-SNE (Maaten and Hinton, 2008) to visualize different contextualized embeddings of these mentions in Figure 3.

In Domain v.s. General Domain: For general ELMo, by far the strongest signal separating the mentions is whether they appear inside or outside parentheses. This is not surprising given the recurrent nature of LSTM and language modeling training objective for learning these embeddings. BioELMo does a better job of grouping mentions of the same entity (ER as estrogen receptor) together, which is clearly helpful for the NER task.

ER mentions of the same entities cluster better by BioBERT than general BERT: there are two major clusters corresponding to estrogen receptor and endoplasmic reticulum by BioBERT as indicated by the dashed circles, while entities of different types are scattered almost evenly by BERT.

BioELMo v.s. BioBERT: Clearly BioELMo better clusters entities from the same types together. Unlike ELMo/BioELMo, Whether the ER mention is inside parentheses doesn't affect BERT/BioBERT representations. It can be explained by encoder difference between ELMo and BERT: For ELMo, to predict ')' in forward LM, representations of token 'ER' inside the parentheses need to encode parentheses information due to the recurrent nature of LSTM. For BERT, to predict ')' in masked LM, the masked token can attend to '(' without interacting with 'ER' representations, so BERT 'ER' embedding does't need to encode parentheses information.

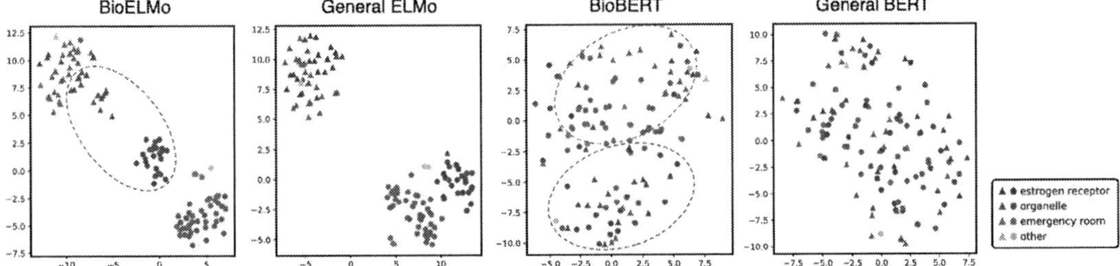

Figure 3: t-SNE visualizations of the token **ER** embeddings in different contexts by BioELMo, general ELMo, BioBERT and general BERT. ● and ▲ represent **ER** mentions within and outside of parentheses, respectively. Colors refer to different actual meanings of the **ER** mention.

Relation Type	NN w/ Representation of Same Type (%)						
	BioELMo	**ELMo**	**BioBERT-tog**	**BioBERT**	**BERT-tog**	**BERT**	**Biomed w2v**
disease-symptom	**54.2**	52.1	44.5	38.8	34.2	37.0	40.9
disease-drug	32.8	**34.4**	26.1	17.9	27.7	22.6	23.6
number-indication	70.5	63.9	47.0	45.3	48.1	49.5	**74.4**
synonyms	**63.6**	56.4	60.8	55.8	56.4	52.8	51.7
All	**57.5**	53.3	47.1	42.1	43.3	42.5	49.5
Subset Accuracy (%)	**73.9**	62.8	71.4	65.0	65.8	64.5	69.7

Table 3: Average proportion of nearest neighbor (NN) representations that belong to the same type for different embeddings, averaged over three random seeds. Biomed w2v performs best for number-indication relations, probably because it uses a vocabulary of over 5M tokens, in which about 100k are numbers. Subset accuracy denotes the probing task performance in the subset of MedNLI test set used for this analysis.

4.3.2 Relational Information

We manually examine all test instances with the "entailment" label in MedNLI, and found 78 token pairs across the premises and hypotheses which strongly suggest entailment. Among them, 22 are disease-symptom pairs, 13 are disease-drug pairs, 19 are numbers and their indications (e.g.: 150/93 and hypertension) and 24 are synonyms or closely related concepts (e.g.: Lasix® and diuretic). Figure 1 shows an example of disease-drug relationship. We hypothesize that a model is required to encode relation information to perform well in MedNLI task. We evaluate relation representations from different embeddings by nearest neighbor (NN) analysis: For each distributed relation representation (Eq. 1) of these token pairs, we calculated the proportions of its five nearest neighbors that belong to the same relation type. We report the average proportions in table 3 and use it as a metric to measure the effectiveness of representing relations by different embedding schemes. We also show model performance for this subset (78 instances for relation analysis) in table 3. The trends of subset accuracy moderately correlate with the NN proportions (Pearson correlation coefficient $r = 0.52$).

In Domain v.s. General Domain: For all relations, BioELMo is significantly[11] better than ELMo in representing same relations closer to each other, while there is no significant difference between BioBERT and BERT. This indicates that even pre-trained by in-domain corpus, as fixed feature extractor, BioBERT still cannot effectively encode biomedical relations compared to BERT.

BioELMo v.s. BioBERT: BioELMo significantly outperforms BioBERT and even BioBERT-tog for all relations. This explains why BioELMo does better than BioBERT in the probing task: BioELMo better represents vital biomedical relations between tokens in premises and hypotheses.

5 Conclusion

We have shown that BioELMo and BioBERT representations are highly effective on biomedical NER and NLI, and BioELMo works even without complicated downstream models and outperforms untuned BioBERT in our probing tasks. This effectiveness comes from its ability as a fixed feature extractor to encode entity types and especially their relations, and hence we believe they should

---

[11]Significance is defined as $p < 0.05$ in two-proportion z test.

benefit any task which requires such information.

A long-term goal of NLP is to learn universal text representations. Our probing tasks can be used to test whether learnt representations effectively encode entity-type or relational information. Moreover, comprehensive characterizations of BioELMo and BioBERT as fixed feature extractors would also be an interesting further direction to explore.

6 Acknowledgement

We are grateful for the anonymous reviewers who gave us very insightful suggestions. Bhuwan Dhingra is supported by a grant from Google.

References

Rie Kubota Ando. 2007. Biocreative ii gene mention tagging system at ibm watson. In *Proceedings of the Second BioCreative Challenge Evaluation Workshop*, volume 23, pages 101–103. Centro Nacional de Investigaciones Oncologicas (CNIO) Madrid, Spain.

Terra Blevins, Omer Levy, and Luke Zettlemoyer. 2018. Deep rnns encode soft hierarchical syntax. *arXiv preprint arXiv:1805.04218*.

Samuel R Bowman, Gabor Angeli, Christopher Potts, and Christopher D Manning. 2015. A large annotated corpus for learning natural language inference. *arXiv preprint arXiv:1508.05326*.

Khyathi Chandu, Aakanksha Naik, Aditya Chandrasekar, Zi Yang, Niloy Gupta, and Eric Nyberg. 2017. Tackling biomedical text summarization: Oaqa at bioasq 5b. *BioNLP 2017*, pages 58–66.

Ciprian Chelba, Tomas Mikolov, Mike Schuster, Qi Ge, Thorsten Brants, Phillipp Koehn, and Tony Robinson. 2013. One billion word benchmark for measuring progress in statistical language modeling. *arXiv preprint arXiv:1312.3005*.

Qian Chen, Xiaodan Zhu, Zhenhua Ling, Si Wei, Hui Jiang, and Diana Inkpen. 2016. Enhanced lstm for natural language inference. *arXiv preprint arXiv:1609.06038*.

Alexis Conneau, Douwe Kiela, Holger Schwenk, Loic Barrault, and Antoine Bordes. 2017. Supervised learning of universal sentence representations from natural language inference data. *arXiv preprint arXiv:1705.02364*.

Ishita Dasgupta, Demi Guo, Andreas Stuhlmüller, Samuel J Gershman, and Noah D Goodman. 2018. Evaluating compositionality in sentence embeddings. *arXiv preprint arXiv:1802.04302*.

Jacob Devlin, Ming-Wei Chang, Kenton Lee, and Kristina Toutanova. 2018. Bert: Pre-training of deep bidirectional transformers for language understanding. *arXiv preprint arXiv:1810.04805*.

Alistair EW Johnson, Tom J Pollard, Lu Shen, H Lehman Li-wei, Mengling Feng, Mohammad Ghassemi, Benjamin Moody, Peter Szolovits, Leo Anthony Celi, and Roger G Mark. 2016. Mimic-iii, a freely accessible critical care database. *Scientific data*, 3:160035.

John Lafferty, Andrew McCallum, and Fernando CN Pereira. 2001. Conditional random fields: Probabilistic models for segmenting and labeling sequence data.

Guillaume Lample, Miguel Ballesteros, Sandeep Subramanian, Kazuya Kawakami, and Chris Dyer. 2016. Neural architectures for named entity recognition. *arXiv preprint arXiv:1603.01360*.

Jinhyuk Lee, Wonjin Yoon, Sungdong Kim, Donghyeon Kim, Sunkyu Kim, Chan Ho So, and Jaewoo Kang. 2019. Biobert: pre-trained biomedical language representation model for biomedical text mining. *arXiv preprint arXiv:1901.08746*.

Laurens van der Maaten and Geoffrey Hinton. 2008. Visualizing data using t-sne. *Journal of machine learning research*, 9(Nov):2579–2605.

Tomas Mikolov, Ilya Sutskever, Kai Chen, Greg S Corrado, and Jeff Dean. 2013. Distributed representations of words and phrases and their compositionality. In *Advances in neural information processing systems*, pages 3111–3119.

SPFGH Moen and Tapio Salakoski2 Sophia Ananiadou. 2013. Distributional semantics resources for biomedical text processing. In *Proceedings of the 5th International Symposium on Languages in Biology and Medicine, Tokyo, Japan*, pages 39–43.

Matthew E Peters, Mark Neumann, Mohit Iyyer, Matt Gardner, Christopher Clark, Kenton Lee, and Luke Zettlemoyer. 2018a. Deep contextualized word representations. *arXiv preprint arXiv:1802.05365*.

Matthew E Peters, Mark Neumann, Luke Zettlemoyer, and Wen-tau Yih. 2018b. Dissecting contextual word embeddings: Architecture and representation. *arXiv preprint arXiv:1808.08949*.

Adam Poliak, Aparajita Haldar, Rachel Rudinger, J Edward Hu, Ellie Pavlick, Aaron Steven White, and Benjamin Van Durme. 2018. Collecting diverse natural language inference problems for sentence representation evaluation. In *Proceedings of the 2018 Conference on Empirical Methods in Natural Language Processing*, pages 67–81.

Marek Rei, Gamal KO Crichton, and Sampo Pyysalo. 2016. Attending to characters in neural sequence labeling models. *arXiv preprint arXiv:1611.04361*.

Alexey Romanov and Chaitanya Shivade. 2018. Lessons from natural language inference in the clinical domain. *arXiv preprint arXiv:1808.06752*.

Golnar Sheikhshab, Inanc Birol, and Anoop Sarkar. 2018. In-domain context-aware token embeddings improve biomedical named entity recognition. In *Proceedings of the Ninth International Workshop on Health Text Mining and Information Analysis*, pages 160–164.

Larry Smith, Lorraine K Tanabe, Rie Johnson nee Ando, Cheng-Ju Kuo, I-Fang Chung, Chun-Nan Hsu, Yu-Shi Lin, Roman Klinger, Christoph M Friedrich, Kuzman Ganchev, et al. 2008. Overview of biocreative ii gene mention recognition. *Genome biology*, 9(2):S2.

Ian Tenney, Patrick Xia, Berlin Chen, Alex Wang, Adam Poliak, R Thomas McCoy, Najoung Kim, Benjamin Van Durme, Samuel R Bowman, Dipanjan Das, et al. 2018. What do you learn from context? probing for sentence structure in contextualized word representations.

Erik F Tjong Kim Sang and Fien De Meulder. 2003. Introduction to the conll-2003 shared task: Language-independent named entity recognition. In *Proceedings of the seventh conference on Natural language learning at HLT-NAACL 2003-Volume 4*, pages 142–147. Association for Computational Linguistics.

Georg Wiese, Dirk Weissenborn, and Mariana Neves. 2017. Neural domain adaptation for biomedical question answering. *arXiv preprint arXiv:1706.03610*.

Henghui Zhu, Ioannis Ch Paschalidis, and Amir Tahmasebi. 2018. Clinical concept extraction with contextual word embedding. *arXiv preprint arXiv:1810.10566*.

Dyr Bul Shchyl[*]
Proxying Sound Symbolism With Word Embeddings

Ivan P. Yamshchikov
Max Planck Institute
for Mathematics in the Sciences
Leipzig, Germany
ivan@yamshchikov.info

Viascheslav Shibaev
Ural Federal University
Ekaterinburg, Russia
v.a.shibaev@urfu.ru

Alexey Tikhonov
Yandex, Berlin, Germany
altsoph@gmail.com

Abstract

This paper explores modern word embeddings in the context of sound symbolism. Using basic properties of the representations space one can construct semantic axes. A method is proposed to measure if the presence of individual sounds in a given word shifts its semantics of that word along a specific axis. It is shown that, in accordance with several experimental and statistical results, word embeddings capture symbolism for certain sounds.

1 Introduction

Sound symbolism is a term used to describe a hypothetical relation between sound and meaning (Hinton et al., 2006). This idea recurrently emerges in various cultures and languages dating as far back as Plato's Cratylus. Statements on sound symbolism can also be found in Japanese Buddhist monk Kukai's work *Sound, word, reality* (Kasulis, 1982). Upanishads contain a good deal of material about sound symbolism, for example, declaring that "the mute consonants represent the earth, the sibilants the sky, the vowels heaven" (Max-Muller, 1879). Early in the twentieth century, the rise of artistic symbolism and a general interest in form, as developed in (Shklovsky, 1919) and (Kruchenykh, 1923) gave rise to several artistic movements. (Sapir, 1929) made the first systematic attempt to find empirical evidence of sound symbolism.

To our knowledge, the issue of sound symbolism has still not been studied from the representation learning perspective. This submission addresses the question of whether some aspects of sound symbolism can be captured by the FastText embeddings (Bojanowski et al., 2016)[1]. We show

that the representations do seem to capture the sound symbolism of the English language to the extent that it is covered by the research literature. We also discuss the potential usage of such representations in the future, particularly for generative tasks.

2 Related work

Despite the fact, that sound symbolism is a relatively old theoretical notion, until the second half of the twentieth century there were only a few empirical results that would definitively prove it's existence in natural languages. More recently, (Whissell, 1999) has shown that certain sounds tend to be over-represented in songs or poetry to address specific emotions, but also in names (Whissell, 2006). (Shinohara and Kawahara, 2010) have demonstrated that certain sounds in the English language are associated with attributes of size. (Wrembel, 2010) has addressed the role of sound symbolism in language acquisition. (Perniss et al., 2010) provide evidence for non-arbitrary relationships at multiple levels of language, from phonology to syntax. (Adelman et al., 2018) have shown that specific sounds in English or Spanish are associated with higher levels of valence or *emotional sound symbolism*. Even more impressively, in a massive study across nearly two-thirds of the world's languages (Blasi et al., 2016) managed to demonstrate that a considerable proportion of 100 essential vocabulary items carry strong associations with specific kinds of human speech sounds, occurring persistently across continents and linguistic lineages.

More importantly for this work, (Otis and Sagi, 2008) have introduced a corpus-based method that can be used to test whether an association between sound and meaning exists within a given corpus. This result was partially reproduced in (Abramova

___
[1]https://en.wikipedia.org/wiki/Dyr_bul_shchyl
[1]We also want to explicitly state that we do not see any reason why other embeddings that to a certain extent support semantic arithmetic can not be used for this task.

90

Proceedings of the 3rd Workshop on Evaluating Vector Space Representations for NLP, pages 90–94
Minneapolis, USA, June 6, 2019. ©2019 Association for Computational Linguistics

et al., 2013), who also showed that the semantic content of at least some phonesthemes could be identified automatically using WordNet. Finally, (Auracher et al., 2010) have demonstrated the potential of sound symbolism for automatic text analysis. Their study claims that, at least in poetic language, the ratio of plosive versus nasal sounds in a text predicts its emotional tone as readers perceive. In other words, poems that have a relatively high frequency of plosive sounds are more likely to express a pleasant mood with high activation, whereas a relatively high frequency of nasal sounds indicates an unpleasant mood with low activation.

3 Sound symbolism in word representations

Semantic arithmetic is one of the key features of Word2Vec (Mikolov et al., 2013) and other modern vector representations. This property allows us to subtract a vector that corresponds to the word 'male' from the vector that represents the word 'king'. We can then add vector that represents 'female' to obtain a new vector in the proximity of representation for the word 'queen.' Using semantic arithmetic one can naturally form certain semantic axes in the space of representations. To do this, we can list a pair of antonyms, say 'good' and 'bad,' and draw a line defined by these two words. We can expect that, up to a certain level of correspondence, the projections of other word representations on this axis will correspond with their semantic relation to one of the two attributes. To make such semantic lines more robust, we defined the opposing semantic points as an average of several synonyms for each of the two words that were forming a semantic axis. The full list of the axes that were tested can be found in the Appendix. The English phonetics of the words was retrieved from a proprietary dictionary.

To test whether word embeddings capture certain elements of sound symbolism, we have carried the following experiment:

- out of pretrained FastText word embeddings 10 000 most frequent words were filtered;

- the representations of the words were projected on every semantic axis;

- the obtained distribution of the projections for the words that start with a given sound

Sound	Semantics
[ʌ]	*passive'*
[ʌ]	*awful**
[ʌ]	*ugly**
[ʌ]	*slow?**
[ɪ]	*active**
[ɪ]	*strong**
[ɪ]	*hot**
[ɪ]	*ugly!**
[ɪ]	*difficult!**
[ɪ]	*sad!**
[ɪ]	*loud?**
[ɪ]	*short?#*
[ɪ]	*powerful**
[d]	*evil**
[d]	*difficult**
[d]	*sad**
[ə]	*difficult*
[aː]	*grand***

Table 1: Associations between a sound and a semantic axis in latent space representation with Mann–Whitney U test p-value below 0.001; associations marked with ' correspond to the ones mentioned in (Wrembel, 2010), marked with * correspond with the ones, found in (Adelman et al., 2018), with ** correspond with ones found in (Shinohara and Kawahara, 2010); with # correspond with ones found in (Blasi et al., 2016); while associations with !* weakly contradict with (Adelman et al., 2018), see discussion for further details; associations marked with ? show weak correspondence with the results in the literature.

was compared to the distribution of projections for the words without it.

Table 1 and Table 2 summarize the results that were obtained with p-values below 0.001 and 0.01 respectively. Figures 1 - 3 show examples of the obtained distributions for different axes and sounds.

4 Discussion

As we can see from Table 1 and Table 2, there are several sounds which have a specific symbolic aspect that is in line with some of the previous empiric results. There are also new sound-semantic associations which have not been studied in the context of sound symbolism and could potentially be interesting for further empirical investigations. Such cases have been flagged with a question mark. The sound [ɪ] is the only sound which contradicts some of the previous findings. It might be associated with something ugly, sad or

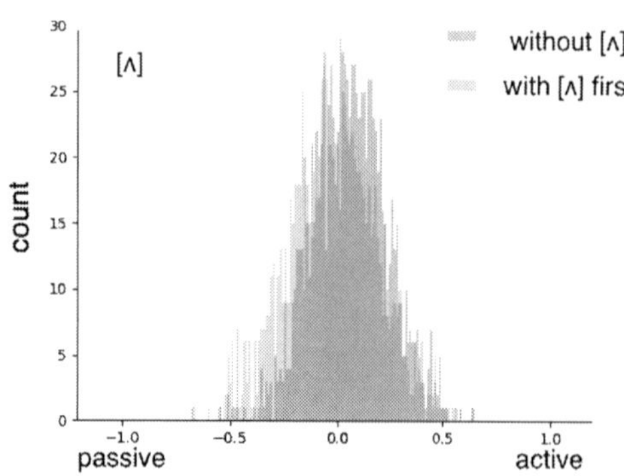

Figure 1: Distributions of representation projections on the 'passive - active' axis. Sound [ʌ] in the first position shifts the words towards the 'passive' semantic aspect.

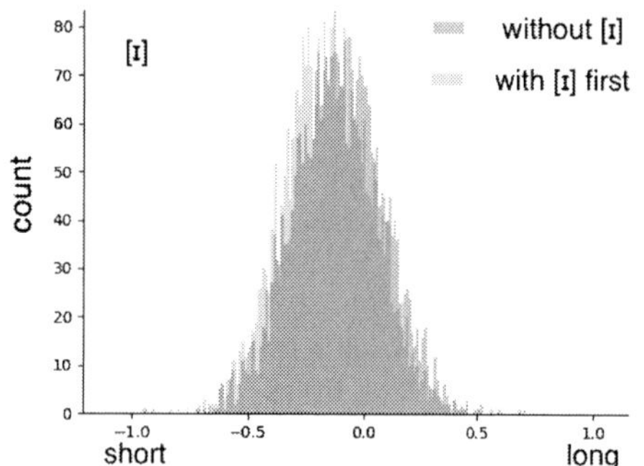

Figure 2: Distributions of representation projections on the 'short - long' axis. Sound [ɪ] in the first position shifts the words towards the 'short' semantic aspect.

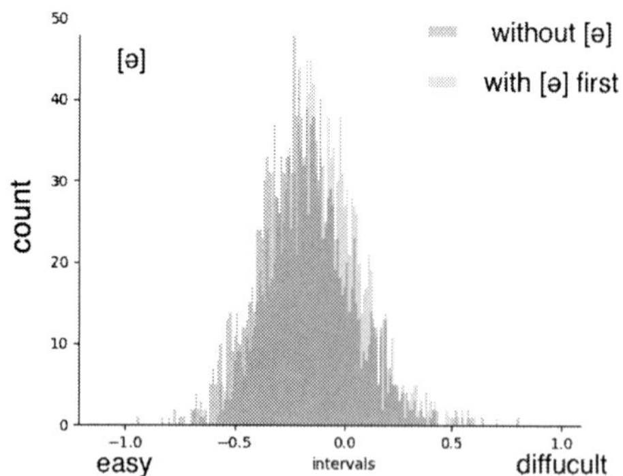

Figure 3: Distributions of representation projections on the 'easy - difficult' axis. Sound [ɔ] in the first position shifts the words towards the 'difficult' semantic aspect.

Sound	Semantics
[r]	*big*[?*]
[r]	*strong*[?*]
[r]	*sad*[*]
[m]	*feminine*
[m]	*not smooth*
[m]	*long*
[ɪ]	*dark*[!*,']
[ɪ]	*angular*
[ɔ]	*active*
[ɔ]	*fast*
[ɔ]	*sad*
[w]	*weak*
[ʌ]	*slow*[*]
[ʌ]	*evil*[*]
[ɔʊ]	*not smooth*
[k]	*safe*
[ɒ]	*benign*
[b]	*feeble*[?*]
[g]	*feeble*[?*]

Table 2: Associations between a sound and a semantic axis in the latent space representation with Mann–Whitney U test p-value below 0.01; associations marked with ' correspond to the ones mentioned in (Wrembel, 2010), marked with * correspond with the ones, found in (Adelman et al., 2018); associations with !* weakly contradict with (Adelman et al., 2018), see discussion for further details; associations marked with ? show weak correspondence with the results in the literature.

difficult according to our results, yet it is placed in the category of mildly positive valence in (Adelman et al., 2018). It could also be associated with something dark, which is in line with (Wrembel, 2010), but contradicts (Adelman et al., 2018). Further examination is needed to give a definitive answer as to the reason for this contradiction, but the most probable explanations can be summed up as follows: (Adelman et al., 2018) show that [ɪ] is associated with valence with a p-value above 0.1, and the predictive power of phonemes for valence in English is the lowest out of four languages studied in the paper. This probably means that the signal is too low to give a definitive answer about this sound. What is more interesting is that the method we used also points out several new sounds that might have a symbolic component, but have not been closely studied before. For example, [ɔ] in the context of difficulty, speed, activity and mood, [m] in the contexts of femininity, roughness and length, or [k] in context of safety.

5   Conclusion

This paper shows that word embeddings such as Fasttext can capture sound symbolism along several semantic axes. Applying the obtained sound symbolism information to generative tasks, one can expect to generate more expressive poetry in line with the results of (Auracher et al., 2010). This new approach combined with such generative methods as (Potash et al., 2016), (Tikhonov and Yamshchikov, 2018), (Vechtomova et al., 2018) or (Wołk et al., 2019). The possibility of testing specific associations between sounds and semantics computationally without any behavioral laboratory experiments or surveys might also significantly facilitate further studies of semantic symbolism. Additional research questions that naturally arise from this result include cross-lingual studies of sound symbolism captured by word embeddings and experimental research of the potential connections between sounds and semantics.

References

Ekaterina Abramova, Raquel Fernandez, and Federico Sangati. 2013. Automatic labeling of phonesthemic senses. In *Proceedings of the Annual Meeting of the Cognitive Science Society*, volume 35:35.

James S. Adelman, Zachary Estes, and Martina Cossu. 2018. Emotional sound symbolism: Languages rapidly signal valence via phonemes. *Cognition*, 175:122–130.

Jan Auracher, Sabine Albers, Yuhui Zhai, Gulnara Gareeva, and Tetyana Stavniychuk. 2010. P is for happiness, n is for sadness: universals in sound iconicity to detect emotions in poetry. *Discourse processes*, 48:1–25.

Damián E. Blasi, Søren Wichmann, Harald Hammarström, Peter F. Stadler, and Morten H. Christiansen. 2016. Sound-meaning association biases evidenced across thousands of languages. In *Proceedings of the National Academy of Sciences*, volume 113:39, pages 10818–10823.

Piotr Bojanowski, Edouard Grave, Armand Joulin, and Tomas Mikolov. 2016. Enriching word vectors with subword information. *arXiv preprint arXiv:1607.04606*.

Leanne Hinton, Johanna Nichols, and John J. (Eds.) Ohala. 2006. *Sound symbolism*. Cambridge University Press.

Thomas P. Kasulis. 1982. Reference and symbol in plato's cratylus and kukai's shojijissogi. *Philosophy East and West*, pages 393–405.

Aleksei Kruchenykh. 1923. *Phonetics of theatre.* M.:41, Moscow.

Friedrich Max-Muller. 1879. *Upanishads*. Routledge.

Tomas Mikolov, Ilya Sutskever, Kai Chen, Greg Corrado, and Jeffrey Dean. 2013. Distributed representations of words and phrases and their compositionality. In *Advances in neural information processing systems*, pages 3111–3119.

Katya Otis and Eyal Sagi. 2008. Phonaesthemes: A corpus-based analysis. In *Proceedings of the Annual Meeting of the Cognitive Science Society*, volume 30:30.

Pamela Perniss, Robin L. Thompson, and Gabriella Vigliocco. 2010. Iconicity as a general property of language: evidence from spoken and signed languages. *Frontiers in psychology*, 1:227.

Peter Potash, Alexey Romanov, and Anna Rumshisky. 2016. Evaluating creative language generation: the case of rap lyric ghostwriting. *arXiv preprint arXiv:1612.03205*.

Edward Sapir. 1929. A study in phonetic symbolism. *Journal of experimental psychology*, 12(3):225–239.

Kazuko Shinohara and Shigeto Kawahara. 2010. A cross-linguistic study of sound symbolism: The images of size. *Annual Meeting of the Berkeley Linguistics Society*, 36(1):396–410.

Victor Shklovsky. 1919. *Poetics: on the theory of poetic language*. 18 State typography, Petrograd.

Alexey Tikhonov and Ivan P. Yamshchikov. 2018. Guess who? multilingual approach for the automated generation of author-stylized poetry. In *Proceedings of IEEE Spoken Language Technology Workshop (SLT), Athens, Greece*, pages 787–794.

Olga Vechtomova, Hareesh Bahuleyan, Amirpasha Ghabussi, and Vineet John. 2018. Generating lyrics with variational autoencoder and multi-modal artist embeddings. *arXiv preprint arXiv:1812.08318*.

Cynthia Whissell. 1999. Phonosymbolism and the emotional nature of sounds: evidence of the preferential use of particular phonemes in texts of differing emotional tone. *Perceptual and Motor Skills*, 89(1):19–48.

Cynthia Whissell. 2006. Historical and socioeconomic predictors of the emotional associations of sounds in popular names. *Perceptual and Motor Skills*, 103(2):451–456.

Krzysztof Wołk, Emilia Zawadzka-Gosk, and Wojciech Czarnowski. 2019. Deep learning and subword-unit approach in written art generation. *arXiv preprint arXiv:1901.07426*.

Magdalena Wrembel. 2010. Sound symbolism in foreign language phonological acquisition. *Research in language*, 8:1–14.

6 Appendices

The list of semantic axes that were tested:

- Angular - Round; 'plump', 'lumpy', 'circular', 'round', 'rounded', 'angular', 'gnarled', 'gnarly', 'craggy', 'awkward', 'angled'

- Bad - Good; 'good', 'well', 'nice', 'pretty', 'fine', 'satisfactory', 'solid', 'fair', 'handsome', 'desirable', 'bad', 'poor', 'ill', 'amiss', 'evil', 'cheap', 'defective', 'inferior', 'low', 'mean'

- Cold - Hot; 'cold', 'chill', 'chilly', 'inclement', 'wintry', 'frozen', 'frosty', 'hot', 'ardent', 'passionate', 'violent', 'warm', 'cordial', 'thermal', 'fervent', 'heated'

- Complex - Simple; 'plain', 'simple', 'ordinary', 'elementary', 'common', 'straightforward', 'easy', 'complex', 'complicated', 'sophisticated', 'compound', 'intricate', 'composite', 'elaborate', 'tricky'

- Cowardly - Brave; 'brave', 'gallant', 'courageous', 'valiant', 'redoubtable', 'bold', 'cowardly', 'coward', 'dastardly', 'sneaky', 'sneaking'

- Dangerous - Secure; 'secure', 'sure', 'safety', 'permissible', 'foolproof', 'safe', 'wholesome', 'terrible', 'frightful', 'dreadful', 'awful', 'agonizing', 'fearful', 'formidable', 'horrible', 'desperate', 'tremendous'

- Dark - Luminous; 'light', 'clear', 'bright', 'blond', 'blonde', 'fair', 'luminous', 'lucid', 'dark', 'black', 'murky', 'shadowy', 'gloomy', 'shady'

- Difficult - Easy; 'difficult', 'hard', 'laborious', 'serious', 'severe', 'grave', 'oppressive', 'painful', 'heavy', 'weighty', 'easy', 'light', 'lucky', 'facile', 'slight', 'gentle', 'airy', 'ready', 'dolly'

- Evil - Benign; 'beneficent', 'good', 'benign', 'decent', 'gentle', 'gracious', 'kind', 'wicked', 'evil', 'vicious', 'malicious', 'spiteful', 'angry', 'fierce', 'severe', 'bad', 'mordant'

- Faded - Bright; 'bright', 'vivid', 'shining', 'cheerful', 'striking', 'glowing', 'garish', 'colorful', 'faded', 'withered', 'delicate', 'languid', 'bleak', 'flat', 'faint', 'sickly'

- Feeble - Strong; 'powerful', 'mighty', 'strong', 'vigorous', 'vibrant', 'powerfully', 'mightily', 'strongly', 'sickly', 'feeble', 'frail', 'weakly', 'puny', 'spindly'

- Masculine - Feminine; 'masculine', 'manly', 'virile', 'masculine', 'manly', 'feminine', 'womanly', 'ladylike'

- Passive - Active; 'active', 'dynamic', 'stirring', 'energetic', 'dynamical', 'favourable', 'ambitious', 'busy', 'industrious', 'passive', 'dormant', 'quiescent', 'floppy', 'unemotional', 'tame', 'effortless', 'flaccid'

- Quiet - Loud; 'loud', 'noisy', 'notorious', 'pompous', 'quiet', 'calm', 'soft', 'low', 'gentle', 'flat'

- Rough - Tender; 'tender', 'affectionate', 'gentle', 'delicate', 'soft', 'sweet', 'subtle', 'fond', 'sentimental', 'affectionate', 'rude', 'rough', 'gross', 'coarse', 'crude', 'tough', 'brute', 'barbaric', 'barbarous', 'beastly'

- Sad - Joyful; 'merry', 'gay', 'cheerful', 'airy', 'glad', 'jolly', 'joyful', 'jaunty', 'sad', 'sorrowful', 'dreary', 'deplorable', 'elegiac', 'lamentable', 'melancholy', 'sorry'

- Short - Long; 'long', 'tall', 'gaunt', 'spindly', 'lanky', 'voluminous', 'lengthy', 'short', 'brief', 'small', 'little', 'skimpy'

- Slow - Quick; 'quick', 'fast', 'swift', 'agile', 'prompt', 'speedy', 'rapid', 'ready', 'brief', 'slow', 'long', 'slack', 'sluggish', 'laggard', 'creeping', 'leisurely', 'plodding'

- Small - Big; 'large', 'great', 'big', 'greater', 'high', 'wide', 'major', 'grownup', 'hulk', 'small', 'little', 'petite', 'diminutive','short', 'trifling', 'petty'

- Smooth - rough or not smooth; 'rough', 'uneven', 'rugged', 'coarse', 'corny', 'grainy', 'harsh', 'ragged', 'shaggy', 'smooth', 'plain', 'even', 'glib', 'sleek', 'slick', 'polished', 'clean', 'fluent'

- Ugly - Beautiful; 'beautiful', 'handsome', 'fine', 'gallant', 'goodly', 'likely', 'lovely', 'personable', 'sheen','homely', 'ugly', 'mean', 'plain', 'charmless'

Multi-Context Term Embeddings:
the Use Case of Corpus-based Term Set Expansion

Jonathan Mamou,[1] **Oren Pereg,**[1] **Moshe Wasserblat,**[1] **Ido Dagan**[2]

[1]Intel AI Lab, Israel

[2]Department of Computer Science, Bar-Ilan University, Ramat Gan, Israel

[1]{jonathan.mamou,oren.pereg,moshe.wasserblat}@intel.com

[2]dagan@cs.biu.ac.il

Abstract

In this paper, we present a novel algorithm that combines multi-context term embeddings using a neural classifier and we test this approach on the use case of corpus-based term set expansion. In addition, we present a novel and unique dataset for intrinsic evaluation of corpus-based term set expansion algorithms. We show that, over this dataset, our algorithm provides up to 5 mean average precision points over the best baseline.

1   Introduction

Term set expansion is the task of expanding a given seed set of terms into a more complete set of terms that belong to the same semantic class. For example, given a seed of personal assistant application terms like 'Siri' and 'Cortana', the expanded set is expected to include additional terms such as 'Amazon Echo' and 'Google Now'.

Most prior work on corpus-based term set expansion is based on distributional similarity, where early work is primarily based on using sparse vectors while recent work is based on word embeddings. The prototypical term set expansion methods utilize corpus-based semantic similarity between seed terms and candidate expansion terms. To the best of our knowledge, each of the prior methods used a single context type for embedding generation, and there are no reported comparisons of the effectiveness of embedding different context types. Moreover, the lack of a publicly available dataset hinders the replicability of previous work and method comparison.

In this paper, we investigate the research question of whether embeddings of different context types can complement each other and enhance the performance of computational semantics tasks like term set expansion. To address this question, we propose an approach that combines term embed-dings over multiple contexts for capturing different aspects of semantic similarity. The algorithm uses 5 different context types, 3 of which were previously proposed for term set expansion and additional two context types that were borrowed from the general distributional similarity literature. We show that combining the different context types yields improved results on term set expansion. In addition to the algorithm, we developed a dataset for intrinsic evaluation of corpus-based set expansion algorithms, which we propose as a basis for future comparisons.

Code, demonstration system, dataset and term embeddings pre-trained models are distributed as part of NLP Architect by Intel AI Lab. [1]

2   Related Work

Several works have addressed the term set expansion problem. We focus on corpus-based approaches based on the distributional similarity hypothesis (Harris, 1954). State-of-the-art techniques return the k nearest neighbors around the seed terms as the expanded set, where terms are represented by their co-occurrence or embedding vectors in a training corpus according to different context types, such as linear window context (Pantel et al., 2009; Shi et al., 2010; Rong et al., 2016; Zaheer et al., 2017; Gyllensten and Sahlgren, 2018; Zhao et al., 2018), explicit lists (Roark and Charniak, 1998; Sarmento et al., 2007; He and Xin, 2011), coordinational patterns (Sarmento et al., 2007) and unary patterns (Rong et al., 2016; Shen et al., 2017). In this work, we generalize coordinational patterns, look at additional context types and combine multiple context-type embed-dings.

We did not find any suitable publicly available

---

[1]http://nlp_architect.nervanasys.com/term_set_expansion.html

Proceedings of the 3rd Workshop on Evaluating Vector Space Representations for NLP, pages 95–101
Minneapolis, USA, June 6, 2019. ©2019 Association for Computational Linguistics

dataset to train and evaluate our set expansion algorithm. The INEX Entity Ranking track (Demartini et al., 2009) released a dataset for the list completion task. However, it addresses a somewhat different task: in addition to seed terms, an explicit description of the semantic class is supplied as input to the algorithm and is used to define the ground truth expanded set. Some works like (Pantel et al., 2009) provide an evaluation dataset that does not include any training corpus, which is required for comparing corpus-based approaches. Sarmento et al. (2007) use Wikipedia as training corpus, but exploit meta-information like hyperlinks to identify terms; in our work, we opted for a dataset that matches real-life scenarios where terms have to be automatically identified.

Systems based on our approach are described by (Mamou et al., 2018a,b).

3 Term Representation

Our approach is based on representing any term in a (unlabeled) training corpus by its word embeddings in order to estimate the similarity between seed terms and candidate expansion terms. Different techniques for term extraction are described in detail by Moreno and Redondo (2016). We follow Kageura and Umino (1996) who approximate terms by noun phrases (NPs),[2] extracting them using an NP chunker. We use *term* to refer to such extracted NP chunk and *unit* to refer to either a term or a word.

As preprocessing, term variations, such as aliases, acronyms and synonyms, which refer to the same entity, are grouped together.[3] Next, we use term groups as input elements for embedding training (the remaining corpus words are left intact); this enables obtaining more contextual information compared to using individual terms, thus enhancing embedding model robustness. In the remainder of this paper, by language abuse, *term* will be used instead of term group.

While word2vec originally uses a linear window context around the *focus word*, the literature describes other possible context types. For each *focus unit*, we extract *context units* of different types, as follows (see a typical example for each

type in Table 1[4]).

3.1 Linear Context (Lin)

This context is defined by neighboring context units within a fixed length window of context units, denoted by *win*, around the focus unit. `word2vec` (Mikolov et al., 2013), `GloVe` (Pennington et al., 2014) and `fastText` (Joulin et al., 2016) are state-of-the-art implementations.

3.2 Explicit Lists

Context units consist of terms co-occurring with the focus term in textual lists such as comma separated lists and bullet lists (Roark and Charniak, 1998; Sarmento et al., 2007).

3.3 Syntactic Dependency Context (Dep)

This context is defined by the syntactic dependency relations in which the focus unit participates (Levy and Goldberg, 2014; MacAvaney and Zeldes, 2018). The context unit is concatenated with the type and the direction of the dependency relation.[5] This context type has not yet been used for set expansion. However, Levy and Goldberg (2014) showed that it yields more functional similarities of a co-hyponym nature than linear context and thus may be relevant to set expansion.

3.4 Symmetric Patterns (SP)

Context units consist of terms co-occurring with the focus term in symmetric patterns (Schwartz et al., 2015). We follow Davidov and Rappoport (2006) for automatic extraction of SPs from the textual corpus.[6] For example, the symmetric pattern 'X rather than Y' captures certain semantic relatedness between the terms X and Y. This context type generalizes coordinational patterns ('X and Y', 'X or Y'), which have been used for set expansion.

3.5 Unary Patterns (UP)

This context is defined by the unary patterns in which the focus term occurs. Context units con-

---

[2]Our algorithm can be used for terms with other part-of-speech or with other term extraction methods.

[3]For that, we use a heuristic algorithm based on text normalization, abbreviation web resources, edit distance and word2vec similarity. For example, *New York, New-York, NY, NYC* and *New York City* are grouped.

[4]We preferred showing in the example the strength of each context type with a good example, rather than providing a common example sentence across all the context types.

[5]Given a focus unit t with modifiers m_i and a head h, the context of t consists of the pairs (m_i/l_i), where l_i is the type of the dependency relation between the head h and the modifier m_i; the context stores also (h/l_i^{-1}) where l_i^{-1} marks the inverse-relation between t and h.

[6]SPs are automatically extracted using the `dr06` library available at `https://homes.cs.washington.edu/~roysch/software/dr06/dr06.html`.

Cont. type	Example sentence	Context units
Lin $win = 5$	**Siri** *uses voice queries and a natural language user interface.*	*uses, voice queries, natural language user interface*
List	*Experience in* **image processing**, *signal processing, computer vision.*	*signal processing, computer vision*
Dependency	*Turing* **studied** *as an undergraduate ... at King's College, Cambridge.*	*(Turing/nsubj), (undergraduate/prep_as), (King's College/prep_at)*
SP	**Apple** *and Orange juice drink ...*	*Orange*
UP	*In the U.S. state of* **Alaska** *...*	*U.S. state of __*

Table 1: Examples of extracted context units per context type. Focus units appear in bold.

sist of n-grams of terms and other words, where the focus term occurs; '__' denotes the placeholder of the focus term in Table 1. Following Rong et al. (2016), we extract six n-grams per focus term.[7]

We show in Section 7 that different context types complement each other by capturing different types of semantic relations. As explained in Section 2, to the best of our knowledge, several of these context types have been used for set expansion, except for syntactic dependency context and symmetric patterns. We train a separate term embedding model for each of the 5 context types and thus, for each term, we obtain 5 different vector representations. When training for a certain context type, for each focus unit in the corpus, corresponding `<focus unit, context unit>` pairs are extracted from the corpus and are then fed to the `word2vecf` toolkit that can train embeddings on arbitrary contexts, except for linear context for which we use the `word2vec` toolkit. Only terms representations are stored in the embedding models while other word representations are pruned.

4 Multi-Context Seed-Candidate Similarity

For a given context type embedding and a seed term list, we compute two similarity scores between the seed terms and each candidate term, based on cosine similarity.[8] First, we apply the *centroid* scoring method (*cent*), commonly used for set expansion (Pantel et al., 2009). The centroid of the seed is represented by the average of the term embedding vectors of the seed terms. Candidate terms become the k terms[9] that are the most similar, by cosine similarity, to the centroid of the seed. Second, the *CombSUM* scoring method (*csum*) is commonly used in Information Retrieval (Shaw et al., 1994). We first produce a candidate term set for each individual seed term: candidate terms become the k' terms[9] that are the most similar, according to the term embedding cosine similarity, to the seed term. The CombSUM method scores the similarity of a candidate term to the seed terms by averaging over all the seed terms the normalized pairwise cosine similarities[10] between the candidate term and the seed term.

To combine multi-context embeddings, we follow the general idea of Berant et al. (2012) who train an SVM to combine different similarity score features to learn textual entailment relations. Similarly, we train a Multilayer Perceptron (MLP) binary classifier that predicts whether a candidate term should be part of the expanded set based on 10 similarity scores (considered as input features), using the above 2 different scoring methods for each of the 5 context types. Note that our MLP classifier polynomially combines different semantic similarity estimations and performs better than their linear combination. We also tried to concatenate the multi-context term embeddings in order to obtain a single vector representing all the context

---

[7]Given a sentence fragment $c_{-3}\ c_{-2}\ c_{-1}\ t\ c_1\ c_2\ c_3$ where t is the focus term and c_i are the context units, the following n-grams are extracted: $(c_{-3}\ c_{-2}\ c_{-1}\ t\ c_1)$, $(c_{-2}\ c_{-1}\ t\ c_1\ c_2)$, $(c_{-2}\ c_{-1}\ t\ c_1)$, $(c_{-1}\ t\ c_1\ c_2\ c_3)$, $(c_{-1}\ t\ c_1\ c_2)$, $(c_{-1}\ t\ c_1)$.

[8]Sarmento et al. (2007) and Pantel et al. (2009) use first-order semantic similarities for explicit list and coordinational pattern context types, respectively. However, Schwartz et al. (2015) showed that for the symmetric patterns context type, word embeddings similarity (second-order) performs gener-

ally better. We opted for term embeddings similarity (second-order) for all the context types.

[9]Optimal values for k and k' are tuned on the training term list. Other terms are assigned a similarity score of 0 for normalization and combination purpose.

[10]For any seed term, cosine similarities are normalized among the candidate terms in order to combine cosine similarity values estimated on different seed terms for the same candidate term, as suggested by Wu et al. (2006).

types. We trained an MLP classifier with concatenated vectors of candidate and seed terms as input features, but it performed worst (see Section 7).

5 Dataset

Given the lack of suitable standard dataset for training and testing term set expansion models, we used Wikipedia to develop a standard dataset. Our motivation for using Wikipedia is two-fold. First, Wikipedia contains human-generated lists of terms ('List of' pages) that cover many domains; these lists can be used for supervised training (MLP training in our approach) and for evaluating set expansion algorithms. Second, it contains textual data that can be used for unsupervised training of corpus-based approaches (multi-context term embedding training in our approach). We thus extracted from an English Wikipedia dump a set of term lists and a textual corpus for term embedding training.

5.1 Term Lists

A Wikipedia 'List of' page contains terms belonging to a specific class, where a term is defined to be the title of a Wikipedia article. We selected term lists among 'List of' pages containing between fifty and eight hundred terms in order to cover both specific and more common classes (e.g., list of *chemical elements* vs. list of *countries*). Moreover, we selected term lists that define purely a semantic class, with no additional constraints (e.g., skipping list of *biblical names starting with N'*). Since there can be some problems with some Wikipedia 'List of' pages, 28 term lists have been validated manually and are used as ground truth in the evaluation. Here are some few examples of term lists: Australian cities, chemical elements, countries, diplomatic missions of the United Kingdom, English cities in the United Kingdom, English-language poets, Formula One drivers, French artists, Greek mythological figures, islands of Greece, male tennis players, Mexican singers, oil exploration and production companies.

Terms having a frequency lower than 10 in the training corpus are pruned from the lists since their embeddings cannot be learned properly; note that these terms are generally less interesting in most of real case applications. Term variations are grouped according to Wikipedia redirect information.

On average, a term list contains 328 terms, of which 3% are not recognized by the noun phrase chunker; the average frequency of the terms in the corpus is 2475.

The set of term lists is split into train, development (dev) and test sets with respectively 5, 5 and 18 lists for MLP training, hyperparameters tuning and evaluation. Each term list is randomly split into *seed* and *expanded* term sets, where we are interested in getting enough samples of seed and expanded term sets. Thus, given a term list, we randomly generate 15 seed sets (5 seed sets for each seed size of 2, 5 and 10 terms) where seed terms are sampled among the top 30 most frequent terms within the list. For the train set, the non-seed terms (expanded term set) provide the positive samples; we randomly select candidate terms that occur in the corpus but not in the list as negative samples; positive and negative classes are balanced.

5.2 Textual Corpus

The corpus contains all the textual parts of Wikipedia articles except 'List of' pages. [11] It is used for training the multi-context embedding models. 3% of the terms appearing in the term lists are not recognized by our NP chunker in the corpus. It contains 2.2 billion words, and 12 million unique terms are automatically extracted.

5.3 Public Release

We use `enwiki-20171201` English Wikipedia dump [12] to develop the dataset. Full dataset will be released upon publication and it will include train, dev and test sets including the split into seed and expanded terms, and negative samples for the train set; the textual corpus along with NP chunks and grouped term variations; term embedding model for each context type.

6 Implementation Details

Code is distributed under the Apache license as part of NLP Architect by Intel AI Lab [13], an open-source Python library for exploring state-of-the-art deep learning topologies and techniques for natural language processing and natural language understanding.

---

[11]Note that the corpus does not contain any Wikipedia meta information.

[12]`enwiki-20171201-pages-articles-multistream.xml.bz2`

[13]`http://nlp_architect.nervanasys.com`

We used the following tools for the implementation and for the development of the dataset: spaCy [14] for tokenization, noun phrase chunking and dependency parsing; textacy [15] for text normalization; word2vec [16] and fastText [17] to model term embeddings of linear context type; word2vecf [18] to model term embeddings of other context types; WikiExtractor [19] to extract textual part of Wikipedia dump; Keras [20] to implement the MLP classifier.

Similarity scores are softmax-normalized over all the candidate terms per context type and per scoring method, in order to combine them with the MLP classifier. Our MLP network consists of one hidden layer. The input and hidden layers have respectively ten and four neurons.

7 Experiments

Following previous work (Sarmento et al., 2007), we report the Mean Average Precision at several top n values (MAP@n) to evaluate ranked candidate lists returned by the algorithm. When computing MAP, a candidate term is considered as matching a gold term if they both appear in the same term variations group. We first compare the different context types; then, we report results on their combination.

7.1 Context Type Analysis

We provide a comparison of the different context types in Table 2. These context types are baselines and we compare them to the linear context that is more standard. Note that the dependency context type is affected by the performance of the dependency parser.[21] Linear context with centroid scoring yields consistently best performance of at least 19 MAP@10 points and is consistently more stable looking at standard deviation. However, other context types achieve better performance than linear context type for 55% of the term lists, suggesting that the different context types complement each other by capturing better different types of

Context	Scor.	MAP@10	stdev	best %
Lin	**cent**	**.78**	**.22**	
List	csum	.59	.30	20
Dep	cent	.53	.31	15
SP	csum	.48	.32	10
UP	csum	.47	.36	10

Table 2: Comparison of the different context types. For each context type, we report the scoring method with higher MAP@10 on dev set, MAP@10 with 5 seed terms, its standard deviation among the different test term lists, the percentage of the test term lists where the context type achieves best performance.

Method	MAP@10	MAP@20	MAP@50
Linear	.78	.71	.59
Concat.	.68	.65	.56
MLP	**.83**	**.74**	**.63**
Oracle	.89	.82	.73

Table 3: MAP@n performance evaluation of the linear context, concatenation, MLP binary classification and oracle, with 5 seed terms.

semantic relations and that their combination may improve the quality of the expanded set.

In addition, performance consistently increases with the number of seed terms e.g., MAP@10, MAP@20 and MAP@50 of the linear context are respectively .66, .58 and .51 with 2 seed terms.

7.2 Context Combination

We provide in Table 3 MAP@n for the centroid scoring of the linear context and for the MLP classification with 5 seed terms. For comparison, we report in 'Concat.' row the performance for the MLP binary classification on the concatenation of the multi-context term embeddings. In addition, we report *oracle* performance assuming we have an oracle that chooses, for each term list, the best context type with the best scoring method. Oracle performance shows that the context types are indeed complementary. The MLP classifier which combines all the context types, yields additional improvement in the MAP@n compared to the baseline linear context. Moreover, we observed that the improvement of the MLP combination over the linear context is preserved with 2 and 10 seed terms. Yet, looking at the oracle, the MLP combination still does not optimally integrate all the information captured by the term embeddings.

---

[14] https://spacy.io

[15] https://github.com/chartbeat-labs/textacy

[16] https://code.google.com/archive/p/word2vec

[17] https://github.com/facebookresearch/fastText

[18] https://bitbucket.org/yoavgo/word2vecf

[19] https://github.com/attardi/wikiextractor

[20] https://github.com/keras-team/keras

[21] We used spaCy for dependency parsing; it achieves 92.6% accuracy on the OntoNotes 5 corpus (Choi et al., 2015).

8 Conclusion

We proposed a novel approach to combine different context embedding types and we showed that it achieved improved results for the corpus-based term set expansion use case. In addition, we publish a dataset and a companion corpus that enable comparability and replicability of work in this field.

For future work, we plan to run similar experiments using recently introduced contextual embeddings, (e.g., ELMo (Peters et al., 2018), BERT (Devlin et al., 2018), OpenAI GPT-2 (Radford et al., 2019)), which are expected to implicitly capture more syntax than context-free embeddings used in the current paper. We plan also to investigate the contribution of multi-context term embeddings to other tasks in computational semantics.

References

J. Berant, I. Dagan, and J. Goldberger. 2012. Learning entailment relations by global graph structure optimization. *Computational Linguistics*, 38:73–111.

Jinho D Choi, Joel Tetreault, and Amanda Stent. 2015. It depends: Dependency parser comparison using a web-based evaluation tool. In *Proceedings of the 53rd Annual Meeting of the Association for Computational Linguistics and the 7th International Joint Conference on Natural Language Processing (Volume 1: Long Papers)*, volume 1, pages 387–396.

Dmitry Davidov and Ari Rappoport. 2006. Efficient unsupervised discovery of word categories using symmetric patterns and high frequency words. In *Proceedings of the 21st International Conference on Computational Linguistics and the 44th annual meeting of the Association for Computational Linguistics*, pages 297–304. Association for Computational Linguistics.

Gianluca Demartini, Tereza Iofciu, and Arjen P De Vries. 2009. Overview of the inex 2009 entity ranking track. In *International Workshop of the Initiative for the Evaluation of XML Retrieval*, pages 254–264. Springer.

Jacob Devlin, Ming-Wei Chang, Kenton Lee, and Kristina Toutanova. 2018. Bert: Pre-training of deep bidirectional transformers for language understanding. *arXiv preprint arXiv:1810.04805*.

Amaru Cuba Gyllensten and Magnus Sahlgren. 2018. Distributional term set expansion. *arXiv preprint arXiv:1802.05014*.

Zellig S Harris. 1954. Distributional structure. *Word*, 10(2-3):146–162.

Yeye He and Dong Xin. 2011. Seisa: set expansion by iterative similarity aggregation. In *Proceedings of the 20th international conference on World wide web*, pages 427–436. ACM.

Armand Joulin, Edouard Grave, Piotr Bojanowski, Matthijs Douze, Hérve Jégou, and Tomas Mikolov. 2016. Fasttext.zip: Compressing text classification models. *arXiv preprint arXiv:1612.03651*.

Kyo Kageura and Bin Umino. 1996. Methods of automatic term recognition: A review. *Terminology. International Journal of Theoretical and Applied Issues in Specialized Communication*, 3(2):259–289.

Omer Levy and Yoav Goldberg. 2014. Dependency-based word embeddings. In *Proceedings of the 52nd Annual Meeting of the Association for Computational Linguistics (Volume 2: Short Papers)*, volume 2, pages 302–308.

Sean MacAvaney and Amir Zeldes. 2018. A deeper look into dependency-based word embeddings. *arXiv preprint arXiv:1804.05972*.

Jonathan Mamou, Oren Pereg, Moshe Wasserblat, Ido Dagan, Yoav Goldberg, Alon Eirew, Yael Green, Shira Guskin, Peter Izsak, and Daniel Korat. 2018a. Term Set Expansion based on Multi-Context Term Embeddings: an End-to-end Workflow. In *Proceedings of the 27th International Conference on Computational Linguistics: System Demonstrations*.

Jonathan Mamou, Oren Pereg, Moshe Wasserblat, Alon Eirew, Yael Green, Shira Guskin, Peter Izsak, and Daniel Korat. 2018b. Term Set Expansion based NLP Architect by Intel AI Lab. In *Proceedings of the Conference on Empirical Methods in Natural Language Processing: System Demonstrations*.

Tomas Mikolov, Ilya Sutskever, Kai Chen, Greg S Corrado, and Jeff Dean. 2013. Distributed representations of words and phrases and their compositionality. In *Advances in neural information processing systems*, pages 3111–3119.

Antonio Moreno and Teófilo Redondo. 2016. Text analytics: the convergence of big data and artificial intelligence. *IJIMAI*, 3(6):57–64.

Patrick Pantel, Eric Crestan, Arkady Borkovsky, Ana-Maria Popescu, and Vishnu Vyas. 2009. Web-scale distributional similarity and entity set expansion. In *Proceedings of the 2009 Conference on Empirical Methods in Natural Language Processing: Volume 2-Volume 2*, pages 938–947. Association for Computational Linguistics.

Jeffrey Pennington, Richard Socher, and Christopher Manning. 2014. Glove: Global vectors for word representation. In *Proceedings of the 2014 conference on empirical methods in natural language processing (EMNLP)*, pages 1532–1543.

Matthew E Peters, Mark Neumann, Mohit Iyyer, Matt Gardner, Christopher Clark, Kenton Lee, and Luke Zettlemoyer. 2018. Deep contextualized word representations. *arXiv preprint arXiv:1802.05365*.

Alec Radford, Jeff Wu, Rewon Child, David Luan, Dario Amodei, and Ilya Sutskever. 2019. Language models are unsupervised multitask learners.

Brian Roark and Eugene Charniak. 1998. Noun-phrase co-occurrence statistics for semiautomatic semantic lexicon construction. In *Proceedings of the 36th Annual Meeting of the Association for Computational Linguistics and 17th International Conference on Computational Linguistics-Volume 2*, pages 1110–1116. Association for Computational Linguistics.

Xin Rong, Zhe Chen, Qiaozhu Mei, and Eytan Adar. 2016. Egoset: Exploiting word ego-networks and user-generated ontology for multifaceted set expansion. In *Proceedings of the Ninth ACM International Conference on Web Search and Data Mining*, pages 645–654. ACM.

Luis Sarmento, Valentin Jijkuon, Maarten de Rijke, and Eugenio Oliveira. 2007. More like these: growing entity classes from seeds. In *Proceedings of the sixteenth ACM conference on Conference on information and knowledge management*, pages 959–962. ACM.

Roy Schwartz, Roi Reichart, and Ari Rappoport. 2015. Symmetric pattern based word embeddings for improved word similarity prediction. In *Proceedings of the Nineteenth Conference on Computational Natural Language Learning*, pages 258–267.

Joseph A. Shaw, Edward A. Fox, Joseph A. Shaw, and Edward A. Fox. 1994. Combination of multiple searches. In *The Second Text REtrieval Conference (TREC-2*, pages 243–252.

Jiaming Shen, Zeqiu Wu, Dongming Lei, Jingbo Shang, Xiang Ren, and Jiawei Han. 2017. Setexpan: Corpus-based set expansion via context feature selection and rank ensemble. In *Joint European Conference on Machine Learning and Knowledge Discovery in Databases*, pages 288–304. Springer.

Shuming Shi, Huibin Zhang, Xiaojie Yuan, and Ji-Rong Wen. 2010. Corpus-based semantic class mining: distributional vs. pattern-based approaches. In *Proceedings of the 23rd International Conference on Computational Linguistics*, pages 993–1001. Association for Computational Linguistics.

Shengli Wu, Fabio Crestani, and Yaxin Bi. 2006. Evaluating score normalization methods in data fusion. In *Asia Information Retrieval Symposium*, pages 642–648. Springer.

Manzil Zaheer, Satwik Kottur, Siamak Ravanbakhsh, Barnabas Poczos, Ruslan R Salakhutdinov, and Alexander J Smola. 2017. Deep sets. In *Advances in Neural Information Processing Systems*, pages 3394–3404.

He Zhao, Chong Feng, Zhunchen Luo, and Changhai Tian. 2018. Entity set expansion from twitter. In *Proceedings of the 2018 ACM SIGIR International Conference on Theory of Information Retrieval*, ICTIR '18, pages 155–162, New York, NY, USA. ACM.

Author Index